D1237047

# MIRACLE YEAR, 1969

## AMAZING METS AND SUPER JETS

### BILL GUTMAN

www.SportsPublishingLLC.com

ISBN: 1-58261-804-6

Publisher: Peter L. Bannon
Senior managing editor: Susan M. Moyer
Acquisitions editor: Noah Adams Amstadter
Developmental editor: Regina D. Sabbia
Art director: K. Jeffrey Higgerson
Dust jacket design: Joseph Brumleve
Project manager: Kathryn R. Holleman
Imaging: Joseph Brumleve
Photo editor: Erin Linden-Levy
Vice president of sales and marketing: Kevin King
Media and promotions managers: Courtney Hainline and Nick Obradovich (regional), Randy Fouts (national), Maurey Williamson (print)

Printed in the United States of America

Sports Publishing L.L.C.
804 North Neil Street
Champaign, IL 61820

Phone: 1-877-424-2665
Fax: 217-363-2073
Web site: www.SportsPublishingLLC.com

To one of my oldest and truest friends, Joe Diamond

# CONTENTS

# ACKNOWLEDGMENTS

The author would like to thank the following people for helping with research materials and for arranging the interviews that have brought this book to life. They include Ron Colangelo and Jared Winley of the New York Jets, Lorraine Hamilton of the New York Mets, Corinne Beavers of the National Football League Players' Association and Mindy Clapp of the National Football League Alumni Association.

And a special thanks to the following players who experienced the New York Jets victory in Super Bowl III and the New York Mets triumph in the 1969 World Series. Their recollections of those great seasons of long ago were invaluable in recreating the excitement that both teams brought to the city of New York in the same calendar year. From the Jets a tip of the hat goes to Matt Snell, Dave Herman, Don Maynard, John Elliott, and Al Atkinson. And from the Mets the hat is tipped to Ron Swoboda, Jerry Koosman, Bud Harrelson, Ed Charles, and Ed Kranepool. Thank you one and all.

# INTRODUCTION

In 1968 the city of New York, like so much of the rest of the country, was beset by divided loyalties, conflicting ideas, and opposing philosophies. The state of the country wasn't good, as the Vietnam War continued to rage in Southeast Asia, claiming more American lives each week as protests mounted both worldwide and in the United States, as well. The assassination of civil rights leader Martin Luther King, Jr., at a Memphis Motel on April 4, sparked racially motivated riots in many American cities. Two months later, Robert F. Kennedy was gunned down in Los Angeles just after winning the California presidential primary, and nearly five years after his brother, president John F. Kennedy, was killed in Dallas. People began to wonder if any of their political leaders were safe or, for that matter, whether they were. Draft cards were being burned, universities shut down by protesters, and even the Democratic national convention in Chicago was beset by bloody confrontations in the streets. There was an ominous feeling in the air.

In times like these, people often look for an escape, no matter how ephemeral it might be, and one of the most popular modes of escape has always been sports. When things appear bleak, it always helps to be able to hang your hat on a favorite team, especially if it's winning, and ride with it through troubled times. Even during World War II, when some thought major league baseball should be shut down due to a depletion of players leaving to serve in the armed forces, president Franklin D. Roosevelt urged the lords of the game to keep the sport afloat. It was good for morale, Roosevelt reasoned, an American institution that had to remain up and running to give the public a feeling of stability.

So baseball endured, and that was the last time anyone thought about shutting down a major sport. By 1968, sports fans in the New York area had an extremely wide choice since the city housed the Yankees and the Mets, the Giants and the Jets, the Knicks and the Rangers, and the newly formed New York Americans of the fledgling American Basketball League. The problem wasn't the numbers; rather it was the lack of success. None of the teams were big winners, and a couple, in fact, had worn the goat horns of losers or had been bridesmaids for just too long. The city needed some excitement, but in 1968 finding it among the city's professional sports teams seemed like a lost cause. Let's take a closer look.

The logical starting point would be the New York Yankees, perennial winners since Babe Ruth joined the team in the 1920s. It seemed as if every time you turned around, another world championship flag was being hoisted at Yankee Stadium, and the endless parade of great players seemed to come from some mystical pipeline connected to a place where legends were born. Ruth, Lou Gehrig, Joe DiMaggio, Phil Rizzuto, Yogi Berra, Whitey Ford, Roger Maris, Mickey Mantle. The formula dictated that there was always a resident superstar or two in the Bronx who, combined with a strong supporting cast, spelled pennant. Only by 1968, something strange had happened. After winning five consecutive pennants between 1960 and 1964, the team had crashed. The Yanks went from still another World Series appearance in 1964 to a shocking 77-85 finish a year later, as injuries and age suddenly depleted the roster and robbed the team of its invincibility.

After an embarrassing last-place finish in 1966, the Bombers seemed to be crawling back, but at a snail's pace, not good enough for fans expecting to win. By 1968 they were a middle-of-the-pack team, struggling to stay a few games over .500. It would also turn out to be the final season for longtime star Mickey Mantle, who would finally succumb to injuries and diminishing skills, and retire before the start of the next year. Worse yet, there was no one to replace him. The Ruth to Gehrig to DiMaggio to Mantle lineage had finally been interrupted. At the outset of the 1969 season, the Yankees were no longer really the Yankees, rather imposters in pinstripes who didn't deserve the moniker of Bronx Bombers. Where then, could the New York sports fan turn next?

Toward the borough of Queens? Not if you wanted to back a winner. Sure, there was a fun team playing there, the expansion New York Mets. They had given the city a breath of fresh air in 1962, because National League fans were still suffering from a five-year-old baseball hangover caused by the sudden defection of the beloved Brooklyn Dodgers and archrival New York Giants to the west coast. Both clubs had left the Big Apple following the 1957 season, beginning baseball's great expansion into a coast-to-coast enterprise. But for so many New York fans, it was as if they had the heart taken from them by greedy owners looking for a new kind of gold rush in sunny California. As for the Mets, they entered the league as part of baseball's first expansion. The new team even came with a built-in superstar. Unfortunately, he wasn't a player.

Casey Stengel, the venerable old manager who had his greatest success with the 1950s Yankees, had come out of retirement to pilot the Mets. The state of the team could be gauged by the now famous Stengel lament, "Can't anyone here play this game?" After losing a record 120 games in 1962, the Mets earned the tag of "loveable losers" and their record of futility continued, even after they deserted the antiquated Polo Grounds for spanking new Shea Stadium in 1964.

By 1968 there was a glimmer of hope. The Mets actually finished ninth in a 10-team league. By then they had a manager who was a New York icon, Gil Hodges, a mainstay of those great Brooklyn Dodgers teams of the late 1940s and early to mid-1950s. Not only was Hodges a beloved figure, especially to former Dodgers fans, but he soon showed he could manage. In addition, the team also had a pair of young pitchers who looked like winners. Tom Seaver was 16-12 in his second season after going 16-13 as a rookie in 1967, while lefty Jerry Koosman surprised everyone with a 19-12 record.

What did it all mean? Maybe, just maybe, the Mets would become a .500 team in 1969. The fans had continued to come to Shea, but the mindset was slowly beginning to change. They no longer simply reveled in the trials and tribulations of their lovable losers. They wanted more. Give them a winning team and things would change in a hurry. Only it didn't seem that 1969 would be the year. At best, the Mets appeared to be a few years away.

On the football front, things weren't much better. The National Football League Giants were the people's choice in the Big Apple, a venerable old franchise that had crested in the late 1950s and early 1960s. There was an NFL championship in 1956, and appearances in title games in 1958 and 1959, then again from 1961-63. Though the team won just one title, it had nevertheless appeared in a half-dozen championship games in an eight-year span. The New Yorkers had a dominant team and chants of "Defense! Defense! Defense!" became a regular Sunday ritual at Yankee Stadium. But like the other inhabitants of the House that Ruth Built, the football Giants' fortunes had faded. After the 1963 title run, which ended in a 14-10 loss to the Chicago Bears, the team crashed. The Giants were 2-10-2 in 1964 and 1-12-1 two years later. In 1967, the club crawled back to .500, but there was no real prospect of another title run in 1968.

Out at Shea Stadium, however, football fans had some hope. The New York Jets seemed to be an improving American Football League team, having gone 6-6-2 in 1966 and then 8-5-1 a year later. The AFL had begun play in 1960, and after the usual gloom-and-doom predictions that always greet the creation of a new sports league, this one now appeared as if it was going to make it. There were more fine players coming in, and its teams played wide-open, fan-friendly football. The problem in New York was the usual one. The Jets had never won a title, but the team had arguably the most glamorous player in either league in quarterback Joe Namath. "Broadway" Joe was not only a prodigious passer with a rifle arm, but a flamboyant personality who seemed to thrive in the pressure-cooker of New York, reveling in its nightlife, being part owner of a restaurant/bar called Bachelor's Three, and producing on the football field. He brought excitement to the Jets and to the city. The only thing lacking was a championship.

As for the Knicks and Rangers, well, futility had been the name of the game for a long time. Even though they had some good teams in the 1960s, the Rangers had not won a Stanley Cup championship since 1940, a non-title run that was approaching 30 years. As for the Knicks, they had yet to win a single NBA championship, dating back to when the league officially began in the 1946-47 season. While the Knicks were slowly building a winning team with some fine players, basketball fans were used to watching the Boston Celtics beat everyone. Led by Bill Russell, the team had won its 10th NBA title in 12 years in 1967-68, and though the Celtics were an aging dynasty, there seemed to be several other teams ahead of the Knicks in the rush to dethrone them. The New York Americans were almost a non-entity. Playing in the newly formed American Basketball League, and exiled to Commack on Long Island, there wasn't a real fan base as yet for the red, white, and blue basketball of the ABL and the teams that went with it.

By the time the New York Jets began training camp in July of 1968, it was apparent to the city's sports fans that neither the Yankees nor the Mets would be contending for a championship. The problems in the country continued, and sports fans in the city began to look toward their two professional football teams. The real war in Vietnam was brought home on television every night, its horrors streamed into living rooms around the country. The gridiron wars, however, were different, a welcome diversion and a place where warlike terms such as "throw the bomb" and "blitz," had more friendly connotations. This was entertainment. Only the Giants didn't appear much better than a .500 team again. The fans would come out, all right, but would it be enough? What New York City really needed in the later summer and fall of 1968 was a winner. That would have been the perfect antidote to the troubled times. And once the training camps opened, Joe Namath and the New York Jets seemed to have the best chance to make a serious run. What nobody knew then, and what no one could have predicted, was that lightning was about to strike New York City not once, but twice over the ensuing 15 months. The stage was set for a couple of unforgettable sports miracles that would leave a lasting effect on the city of New York and on the sports world as a whole, miracles that are remembered even today with a combination of fascination, nostalgia, and awe.

# PART ONE
# THE 1968
# NEW YORK JETS

# 1

# THE AFL,
# BROADWAY JOE, AND A
# COACH NAMED LOMBARDI

Though it may be difficult to fathom today, professional football in the mid-1950s wasn't looked upon as a major sport. Though the National Football League had been in existence in one form or another since 1920, stability didn't come quickly or easily. The structure of the league often changed, and early franchises came and went, sometimes in the course of a single season. In those bygone days, the league was mostly located in the Midwest, often in small towns, and without real stadiums in which to play. Some of the pioneer teams are now not only a distant memory, but their names don't always seem suited for the game they played. Only those with a real sense of NFL history would remember the Canton Bulldogs, Columbus Panhandles, Duluth Eskimos, Pottsville Maroons, Providence Steamrollers, and Oorang Indians.

The league didn't organize into two divisions until 1933, so before that, there wasn't even a real championship game. The years of the Great Depression saw some stability and more modern teams arrive. In those days, the game was still played mainly in the trenches, with teams just trying to push and muscle their way downfield with tight running plays. The forward pass didn't come into play as a major weapon until late in the 1930s when a thin quarterback from Texas Christian University joined the Washington Redskins. "Slingin'" Sammy Baugh threw for 1,127 yards as a rookie in 1937 and joined Green Bay's Arnie Herber as two NFL quarterbacks who could light it up through the air.

That still didn't mean the big time for the league. By the mid-1950s, when Willie Mays, Mickey Mantle, and Duke Snider were sparking a who's-the-best-center fielder debate among the baseball fans of New York, the National Football League was still struggling for an identity, for fans, and for more television coverage. Then, in 1958, there was a game that changed it all. Fortunately, it was the biggest game of the year, the championship contest between the New York Giants and the Baltimore Colts. The Giants had a number of glamour players such as Frank Gifford and Sam Huff, a handsome halfback and a rugged linebacker. In fact, Huff was one of the first defensive specialists to attract a huge following. He led a spirited defensive unit that was the heart of the team.

Baltimore had a young, crew-cutted quarterback named John Unitas, who played with the nerve of a riverboat gambler and threw with the precision of a delicate artist. The game was played on the big-city stage of Yankee Stadium with more than 64,000 fans in attendance, augmented by a national television audience. It was a rugged, hard-fought contest from the beginning with the Giants holding a slim, 17-14 lead in the final minutes. With 1:56 left in the game, the Giants had the Colts pinned back to their 14-yard line. That's when Unitas took over and showed the football world just what a great quarterback could do. He drove the Colts up field, often going to his favorite receiver, Raymond Berry, and the Giants couldn't stop them. With just seven seconds left, Steve Myhra kicked a 23-yard field goal and the game was tied. When the clock ran down, it became the first NFL title game to go into sudden-death overtime.

The Giants got the ball first but couldn't move it. A punt then pinned the Colts back at their own 20, and Unitas went to work again with his aerial magic, keeping the Giants honest with a couple of running plays as he drove the Colts toward the New

York goal line. A final pass play to tight end Jim Mutscheller brought the ball to the one, and on the next play, fullback Alan Ameche plunged into the end zone and into history. The Colts had won it, 23-17. The game drew huge attention in the media and was given a euphemistic nickname that still exists today. It was called "The greatest game ever played."

The Giants-Colts championship game put the sport on the map once and for all. The NFL was comprised of 12 teams in 1958, broken into Eastern and Western Divisions. It wasn't long before there was talk of expansion, adding more teams, and allowing the league to grow. Among the cities desiring an NFL franchise were the Texas towns of Houston and Dallas. A pair of young Texans, Kenneth S. "Bud" Adams and Lamar Hunt wanted to head these new franchises. However, while there were plans to put a team in Dallas, the franchise was not awarded to Hunt, and the NFL bigwigs also decided it wasn't time for a team in Houston. Hunt, with help from Adams and a few others, decided to take the bull by the Longhorns. They would still have their franchises, all right, and if they couldn't have them in the NFL they would simply start their own league. Their initial efforts were met with skepticism and doubt, but in the true entrepreneurial spirit of America, they did it.

In the fall of 1960, the eight-team American Football League began play in direct competition with the established NFL. Soon, the real pro football wars would begin, a ten-year period in which the new league worked to grow against sometimes overwhelming odds, then the creation of a special championship game to prove once and for all which league was best, and finally a merger creating one, huge National Football League. It would, however, be a decade of change and controversy in which the new league would surprise a lot of people and one of its players would become one of the most publicized and well-known athletes in the land. His name: Joe Namath. His team: the American Football League New York Jets.

The AFL began play with franchises in New York, Boston, Buffalo, Houston, Los Angeles, Oakland, Dallas, and Denver. The

Los Angeles Chargers would move to San Diego in 1961, and the Dallas Texans would become the Kansas City Chiefs two years later. The only other change was the name of the New York franchise. The team was originally called the Titans, and after a change in ownership prior to the 1963 season, they morphed into the Jets. Other than those changes, the league remained amazingly stable in its growth years.

At first, however, the NFL wasn't worried. They had dealt with renegade leagues before. The All-America Football Conference was formed in 1946 and competed for players with the NFL. One team, the Cleveland Browns coached by Paul Brown, won all four AAFC titles. The AAFC, however, folded in 1950, though three of its teams—the San Francisco 49ers, Baltimore Colts, and Cleveland Browns—were absorbed into the NFL. The Browns showed immediately they were no fluke. Led by quarterback Otto Graham, they took the NFL by storm and won the 1950 championship by defeating the Los Angeles Rams, 30-28, in one of football's classic games. As good as the Browns were, the AAFC as a league lasted only four years. Now, ten years later, the NFL was facing another upstart group.

For the AFL, players were tough to come by at first. The league began with a hodgepodge of castoffs, over-the-hill veterans, guys looking for a second chance, and some NFL retreads. But the league didn't settle for just that. They went after some marquee names, as well, and signed a plum in Heisman Trophy winner Billy Cannon of LSU. Cannon, in fact, had signed contracts with both the NFL Rams and the Houston Oilers of the AFL. Both teams claimed him, and when the dispute went to court the decision went in favor of Houston. Add to that the AFL's landing a five-year, nearly $9 million television contract from ABC, and the new league was quickly on the map. The NFL knew it would have a battle on its hands.

That didn't mean the early years were easy. Some of the teams lacked modern stadiums in which to play, a few had money problems, the quality of football wasn't always top notch, though it was entertaining. The league felt that the fans would love a wide-open, pass-happy game, and that was the product they put on the field. The Houston Oilers, led by the aforementioned Cannon and former NFL quarterback, the veteran George Blanda, won the league's first championship, defeating the LA Chargers, 24-16, the big play fittingly an 88-yard pass play, Blanda to Cannon. The league survived its first year, now it was time to grow.

One of the big worries for the AFL then was the New York franchise. The Titans were forced to play their first two seasons in the antiquated Polo Grounds, former home of the New York baseball Giants, who had migrated to San Francisco in 1958. Not only didn't the team have a good product on the field, but fans also seemed reluctant to buy tickets, and attendance was terrible.

In 1961, owner Harry Wismer was feuding with the rest of the league, and a year later he went broke to the point where he wasn't even making payroll, and that included the players. Many thought a floundering New York franchise could sound the death knell for the league. Little did they know that help was just around the corner. It began when the league's 1962 champion, the Dallas Texans, moved the franchise to Kansas City and immediately sold 15,000 season tickets for 1963. But the big news came out of New York.

The old Titans were gone, at least in name and ownership. Sonny Werblin, a man with a strong show business background and a penchant for promotion, had purchased the team and almost immediately changed the name to the Jets. Werblin then hired Weeb Ewbank to be his coach. Ewbank had an easy identification in the sports world. He was the man behind the bench when the Baltimore Colts defeated the New York Giants in that landmark NFL title game back in 1958. With Johnny Unitas at the helm, Ewbank's Colts won a second consecutive championship the next year, again topping the Giants. Unitas was already carving his place in signal-calling history, and Ewbank had made his mark as a coach. But when the Colts fired the diminutive Weeb following the 1962 season, Werblin was quick to grab him for his renamed Jets. Also in the offing for the team was a brand-new stadium in Queens. Shea Stadium would be ready for the 1964 season and the team would be sharing it with the new National League baseball team, the Mets.

While the Jets were just 5-8-1 their first season under Ewbank, there were plans in place for both the team's and the league's future. In 1964, the AFL received a number of solid shots in the arm, beginning with a brand-new television deal. NBC picked up the AFL for five years, signing a $36 million contract with the league with the provision that it would pay each franchise $900,000 a year. And when the Jets opened the 1964 season at Shea Stadium, there was an AFL-record crowd of 46,665 fans in attendance. The team would break that mark twice more before the season ended. Suddenly, it was beginning to look as if the AFL was here to stay.

By that time, the two leagues found themselves in an increasingly hostile bidding war for talent, and the AFL was starting to "raid" NFL teams, inducing some players to jump leagues. It was a bidding war that would soon become very costly, though there was still evidence that some NFL teams didn't take the new league seriously. In addition, some top players were choosing the AFL because they felt they would get a chance to play. Fullback Matt Snell, coming out of Ohio State, was one of those players. Both the Giants and the Jets drafted him, and like so many others back then, he had a big decision to make.

"Part of it was money," Snell said, "but there were other factors, as well. Once I knew I was drafted by both teams I went to my college coach, Woody Hayes, for advice. Agents were just beginning to be a factor then, but Woody wouldn't allow them on campus, so he kind of represented all of us. When I sat down with Woody he advised me to look at the AFL. 'If you go to the AFL you can play right away,' he told me. Woody didn't believe in sitting on the bench to get experience. He knew with the Giants I'd be sitting behind veterans like Alex Webster and Kyle Rote, and wouldn't play until they retired. He said if the money is close to equal, he would go to the place where he could play.

"Running backs never know how long their careers will last. You can get hurt in practice and you can take a pounding in practice, even if you aren't playing in games. I figured that by sitting on the bench for three or four years I'd be shortening my career. So I took Woody's advice and signed with the Jets."

It turned out to be the right move. In 1964, Snell won the starting fullback job and led the team in rushing with 948 yards on 215 carries, and also caught 56 passes (second on the team) for another 393 yards. So by going to the AFL he had not only established himself immediately, but had given his team an outstanding fullback around whom to build a running attack.

Lineman Dave Herman was another player who was drafted by both the Giants and Jets prior to the 1964 season. Herman had played under Duffy Daugherty at Michigan State and was a guy who simply loved to play and usually didn't worry about the other things going on around him. He didn't make any comparisons between the AFL and NFL. He just figured wherever he went it would be a matter of his showing he was good enough to play.

"I decided to sign with the Jets," Herman recalls, "and my decision was based strictly on money. You won't believe how much. I think the difference was probably around $600. The last time I saw [longtime Giants owner] Wellington Mara, I reminded him of it. But I had no hidden ambitions. I just wanted to play some football and then take advantage of some other opportunities in New York. Many players couldn't survive on their salaries in those days, and I not only worked in the off season, but finally got a job on the business side of broadcasting with a company called Blair Television. I would go to my job in the morning, then out to practice in the afternoon. Weeb once told me I was the only guy who came to practice wearing a suit and tie."

That's how the team was building players. Besides Snell and Herman, the Jets already had a group of core players who would be instrumental in the club's greatest season just four years later. They included wide receivers Don Maynard and Bake Turner, kicker Jim Turner, linebackers Larry Grantham and Ralph Baker, offensive tackle Winston Hill, center John Schmitt, defensive end Gerry Philbin and tackle Paul Rochester, and defensive back Billy Baird. Maynard was an especially interesting case. He had been with the Jets since their first year of 1960, when they were the Titans, and since that time had been one of the most explosive players in the league.

"I started with the Giants before the AFL came into existence," he said. "I had a great year with them as a punt and kickoff returner in 1958, and played as a backup to Frank Gifford. I was devastated when I was cut before 1959 because I could easily outrun the guy they kept. [Vince] Lombardi wanted to pick up my option to come to Green Bay, but I had already gone up to Canada to play with Hamilton. When the Jets called, I decided to return to New York."

Maynard proved his worth in a hurry. In 1960 he caught 72 passes for 1,265 yards and six touchdowns, and would become, arguably, the AFL's most dangerous deep receiver for the next decade. So he saw the league build from the beginning.

"We started having guys come over from the NFL early on who still had a lot of football left in them," Maynard explained. "Within just a few years I began to get the feeling that the first 11 guys on offense and defense on our best teams were equal to those in the NFL. The difference then was depth, the 23rd to 35th player. But with each passing year we were getting closer."

For the Jets, the gap began to close in 1965. That's when the team made a move that would not only change the face of the team and the American Football League, but the entire professional football world, as well. One of the most intriguing players coming out of college in 1964 was Joe Namath, a quarterback from the little town of Beaver Falls, Pennsylvania, who took his talented right arm south to play for the legendary Paul "Bear" Bryant at the University of Alabama. Namath spent three seasons at the helm for the Crimson Tide, setting school records for pass attempts (428), completions (230), yards (3,055) and touchdowns (29).

Though limited by a knee injury his senior year in 1964, the 6'2", 190-pound Namath was still good enough to lead his team to a national title. He showed his stuff to the nation in the 1965 Orange Bowl, coming off the bench with his knee heavily taped and braced to complete 18 passes for 255 yards and two touchdowns. Even though Texas beat Alabama that day, 21-17, Namath was chosen the game's Most Valuable Player, and pro football scouts from both leagues began to salivate when they pictured him quarterbacking for their teams. That spring, Namath learned he had been the top pick of the St. Louis Cardinals of the NFL and the New York Jets of the AFL. This one, followers of the game felt, would be interesting. Namath was a valuable commodity. The Cards wanted him as their quarterback, all right, but the Jets' Sonny Werblin saw him as more than just a prolific passer who could help his team win. With his show business background, Werblin knew that star power sold tickets. That's what he saw in Joe Namath, and he wasn't about to let him get away.

Let the bidding begin. Remember, this was 1965, long before the day of million-dollar players. Dave Herman joined the Jets a year earlier and had to find a second job ... during the season. Namath supposedly told Bear Bryant that he hoped to get in the area of $100,000 a year. The word was that Bryant said why not throw caution to the wind and ask for twice as much, $200,000? That's what Joe did, throwing in a request that a Lincoln Continental be added to the pot. Imagine his surprise when the Cards agreed without so much as a blink of the eye. The Jets, however, weren't done. They countered with a larger offer and when it finally ended, Namath cast his star with Sonny Werblin and the Jets for an unheard of signing bonus of around $427,000. The amount was not only staggering, it sent a message to both leagues that the bidding wars were getting out of hand.

"Sonny Werblin knew how to promote and sell," said Don Maynard, who had seen Werblin in action ever since he bought the team. "That's what he did when he took over ownership and why he signed Joe to that huge contract. As soon as he signed, Joe's picture was on all the magazines, even women's publications, and everyone was curious about him. The publicity he got was great for everyone, as well as for the team. Mr. Werblin would also have a press party every week with all kinds of people coming out to the Diamond Club at Shea. He made the writers and media people feel more at home and because of that they went out of their way to promote the team."

Namath, of course, could have easily taken the St. Louis offer. Word had it that the Cards were also in a similar price range, but the free-spirited quarterback undoubtedly heeded Werblin's message, that his star power could best be served in New York where he would not only quarterback an up-and-coming team, but would have access to Madison Avenue and everything else the Big Apple had to offer.

Matt Snell, who was entering his second year with the Jets in 1965, remembers the day Namath arrived at camp … in a chauffeured limousine. "To be honest about it, there was a lot of jealousy on the team at that point," Snell admits, looking back nearly 40 years. "There were still a lot of older guys on the team, some of them rejects from the NFL who were getting a last chance and not making much money. I think they resented the way Joe came to camp in a chauffeured limo. But that was Sonny's work, a way to get PR and hype the team.

"The younger players like myself and Jim Hudson saw Joe's coming as giving us a better way to compete. Dick Wood had been the team's quarterback the year before and he was playing on two terrible knees, a guy at the end of the line. I could see the difference as soon as Namath started throwing. When he cut it loose it was like the ball was on a rope."

Dave Herman was another who saw Namath's coming as an opportunity for everyone. "For a guy drafted number one, Joe had a great attitude," Herman said. "He knew the game, had great instincts and abilities. He did the right thing without having to think about it. Beyond that, he was a great teammate, probably the best teammate I ever had."

Don Maynard sensed Namath's arrival as something more, something he felt could not only turn the Jets into winners, but turn him into a more dangerous pass receiver, because he now had a guy with a rocket arm throwing to him.

"Up to the time Joe arrived, I must have played with some 25 quarterbacks in my career," Maynard said. "I had watched Joe in that Orange Bowl game against Texas and saw what he could do. So when he came to camp I made it a point to talk to him as soon as I could. I said, 'Joseph, I'm a communicator. You and I are going to talk and make a success of our passing game. I told him I had learned from Sammy Baugh, and that we were going to talk in practice and always set things up. I'll make you a better quarterback,' I told him, 'and you'll make me a great receiver.'"

As one of the real veterans of the pro football wars, a guy who had watched many of the good ones, Maynard saw immediately the kind of technical proficiency Namath brought to the position. "He was so strong throwing the ball, and his accuracy was unbelievable," Maynard said. "He had enough strength in his arm that he could throw with a short, quick motion. That's the 'quick release' you're always hearing about. But I always said the greatest ability he had was his anticipation. He was always one step ahead."

The Jets of 1965 had some other new faces besides Namath. Defensive end Verlon Biggs and linebacker Al Atkinson also joined the team, as did defensive back Jim Hudson, cornerback Cornell Gordon, and wide receiver George Sauer. The core group was growing, but the team still wasn't ready to win. In fact, Coach Ewbank, not wanting to throw his prize rookie to the wolves, started the season with veteran Mike Taliaferro at quarterback. Even with Namath on the bench, the effect of No. 12 was felt immediately. The Jets opened before 52,680 fans in Houston, many of whom undoubtedly wanted a glimpse of the 400-grand bonus baby. A week later, 53,658 fans crowded into Shea to officially welcome Namath to New York. He didn't play again, but the crowds that were following him showed all over again that the AFL was certainly no Mickey Mouse league. Now, it had real star power.

The problem was that the Jets weren't winning. They dropped five of their first six games that year, the other ending in a tie. Rookie linebacker Al Atkinson remembers very clearly the low point of that season.

"We were leaving Shea one Sunday with our 0-5-1 record and not feeling very good," Atkinson said. "I got in my car and turned on the Howard Cossell radio show. I always had the feeling Howard was a Giants rooter. Anyway, there was a garbage strike going on in the city then and I'll never forget what Howard said next, in that inimitable, halting fashion he had. He was breaking for a commercial and he said, 'I'll be back in 60 seconds to talk about the real garbage in New York City, the New ...York ... Jets.' Hearing that really irked us and we wanted to get that guy back. I guess the best kind of payback is to win. Weeb finally started Joe the next week against Denver and we won. Better than that, we all knew right away that Joe had a gifted arm and a gifted feel for the game.

"All he did that day was to throw five touchdown passes and we won going away. Joe had quick feet and a young body, and we saw right away that he wasn't afraid to throw into a crowd, with two guys on the receiver. He threw when other quarterbacks would shy away. Even as a rookie he dared the defense and while he would look for the receiver who was open, he wasn't fearful of challenging the defense and threading it in there."

With Namath taking over, the Jets finished the 1965 season at 5-8-1, second behind Buffalo's division-winning 10-3-1 mark. They weren't one of the AFL's elite teams yet, but had a made a start with a quarterback who was attracting more attention than any other player in the game.

As for the game itself, the Namath signing proved to be the tip of the iceberg that would soon sink the bidding wars. When the 1966 draft was held, three players—running backs Donnie Anderson and Jim Grabowski, and super linebacker Tommy Nobis—all signed contracts larger than Namath's, and all went to the NFL. Then the New York Giants raided the AFL and signed the game's first soccer-style place kicker, Pete Gogolak, away from the Buffalo Bills. The men who ran the game had seen enough. They felt they had better declare a truce before the players began breaking the bank. That truce came in the form of a merger.

Before the 1966 season had even started, the entire pro football world had been reorganized. The two leagues agreed to a full merger that would be completed in the 1970 season. That year, all the AFL teams would become part of a larger National Football League under the guidance of NFL commissioner Pete Rozelle. Until then, there would be some other changes that would start soon. For example, beginning the following year there would be a common draft. No more bidding wars for the top players. There would also be some preseason games between the two leagues, which should attract some major fan interest. It was the final piece of news, however, that had many professional football fans, as well as the players, the most excited.

Following the 1966 season, the two league champions would meet in a special championship game. It wasn't yet called the Super Bowl but would be known simply as the AFL-NFL World Championship Game. It would, however, in the minds of many, settle the question once and for all which league was better. The pressure, of course, would be on the NFL representative, because NFL purists had derided the wide-open style of the AFL for so long. Now they would have a chance to prove it. For the AFL, they felt they had four years to get a victory over the NFL in the title game. Because until the full merger went into effect at the outset of the 1970 season, the two leagues would retain their individual identities.

The Jets continued to build their team in 1966 and 1967. The club was just 6-6-2 in 1966 and then 8-5-1 the next year. That year, the team seemed to be headed for its first division title by starting the year at 7-2-1. Only this time they fell victim to injuries as much as anything else. By the end of the season some 15 players had undergone knee surgery, including their starting backfield of Snell and halfback Emerson Boozer, who had joined the team the year before. Namath had shown flashes of brilliance, but he also had a number of multi-interception games; usually when the club tried to come from behind and everyone knew Joe would throw. So the Jets players could only sit and watch as the two AFL champs from 1966 and 1967 went to the first ever AFL-NFL championship games. Both times, the Kansas City Chiefs and then the Oakland Raiders had to meet a legendary team, Vince Lombardi's Green Bay Packers.

The NFL couldn't ask for a better representative. Lombardi's Packers might have been aging, but the club had stars everywhere on both offense and defense, all driven by a coach who strove for perfection and wouldn't accept anything else. "Winning isn't everything," Lombardi was purported to have once said, "It's the *only* thing."

The Kansas City Chiefs were 11-2-1 in the 1966 season, and then defeated the Buffalo Bills, 31-7, in the AFL title game. Coached by Hank Stram and led by quarterback Len Dawson, the Chiefs had a huge team, and great skill players such as Dawson, running back Mike Garrett, and wide receiver Otis Taylor. They had stars on both offense and defense, and ran multiple formations that often dazzled AFL opponents. The Packers, of course, were known for their famed sweep, with Jim Taylor and Paul Hornung carrying the football behind two great pulling guards. But they also had a precision passer in Bart Starr and an outstanding defense. Matt Snell remembers watching the Packers run their sweep, relating to it from his own experience as a back.

"The Packers were so basically sound," Snell said. "They would tell the world they were going to run the sweep, then dare them to stop it, but they ran it so perfectly that no one could. I can picture Hornung running behind those guards, just running patiently, watching, and waiting for the hole to develop as he knew it would. They had the blocking down to a science and it was a thing of beauty."

Though Hornung was aging and injured, Green Bay had other backs to run the sweep. Yet there were some who felt the Chiefs had a chance, and when the first half ended with the Packers holding a slim, 14-10 lead, it looked like anybody's ball game. But a Willie Wood interception on the Chiefs' first drive of the second half took the air out of the pretenders. Wood returned the ball to the Kansas City five and Green Bay scored easily. From there, the Packers coasted to a 35-10 victory, firmly cementing the NFL's superiority in everyone's minds.

A year later Green Bay was back, only this time they were facing the Oakland Raiders. Oakland had been 13-1 in the regular season and had beaten Houston soundly, 40-7, in the AFL title game. The Raiders were a deep passing team with quarterback Daryle Lamonica known as the "Mad Bomber" for his long throws. As for the Packers, they were just 9-4-1 in the regular season, and some thought they were over the hill. In the NFL title game they met the young, strong, Dallas Cowboys in subfreezing weather at Green Bay. In an epic battle, known today as the "Ice Bowl," the Packers pulled out a last-second, 21-17 victory on a Bart Starr quarterback sneak with time running out. Many felt that the Packers were now ripe for the picking.

With more than 75,500 fans jammed into the Orange Bowl in Miami, the two teams met in the second NFL-AFL title game. This one wasn't as close as the first. Though the statistics were fairly even, the Packers capitalized on Raider mistakes, led 16-7 at the half, and cruised to a 33-14 victory. Now, everyone said the NFL had proven it was still the best ... by far. But a few looked at it another way. They said all it proved was that Lombardi and the Packers were the best, an enduring dynasty that was coming to the end of the line, but had summoned up enough pride and talent with the driving force that was their coach, to crush two highly talented, but mistake-prone young teams.

For the AFL, however, many felt there were now just two years left to win a title for a league that would soon be a memory. Oakland and Kansas City were still considered the class of the league. Then after the 1967 season, Vince Lombardi retired. The Packers would be a year older and have a new coach. Chances are they wouldn't win again. So at the outset of the 1968 season, the NFL title was up for grabs. Most figured the AFL champion would come from the west where the Raiders and Chiefs were expected to run neck and neck during the regular season. Maybe it was the veteran Don Maynard, however, who sounded a prophetic warning. Speaking of his team, the Jets, Maynard said, "In 1967 we had 15 key players go down to knee surgery and we only missed winning the division by a single game."

# 2
# THE JETS AND NAMATH GET READY FOR BATTLE

Before the 1968 season even started, the Jets had to deal with some controversy. Sonny Werblin, the man who had brought Joe Namath to New York sold his share of the team for two million dollars to his four partners, Donald Lillis, Leon Hess, Townsend Martin, and Philip Iselin. The flamboyant Werblin apparently wasn't happy with the upcoming merger and was a guy who liked to run the whole show. So he opted out. Any change in ownership always worries everyone below because it usually means other changes are in order. Donald Lillis became the new team president, but he died unexpectedly just two months later while the team was already at training camp. Phil Iselin then assumed the top job.

By this time, Joe Namath's celebrity status had grown to almost legendary proportions, as did the worry about his gimpy knees. A player who never shied away from contact, many thought that Namath was just a single hard hit away from seeing his career go down the drain. Still, he had never missed a regular-season game, but his dedication to the sport didn't prevent him from making off-field news. Namath loved to be seen at many of Manhattan's best nightspots, usually squiring a different woman and hanging out with the so-called beautiful people. He was one of the first athletes to grow a Fu Manchu mustache, and in the winter showed up at various events wearing a white mink coat. In an era when there were still many crew-cutted, 1950s-type athletes, Joe Namath was the hippie, a guy the new generation of young fans could identify with, a man who went his own way and didn't conform to stereotypes. The reporters loved talking to and writing about him, broadcast journalists sought him out, and the paparazzi had a field day following him around New York City.

Dave Herman got a taste of Namath's popularity first-hand during training camp. "Joe asked me to go with him to get something to eat," Herman recalls. "We went to a sandwich shop and before we could sit down to eat there was a whole line of people waiting for his autograph. I just looked at him and said, 'Joe, don't invite me to lunch again.' He looked back at me and laughed."

Namath also had his share of critics. Some criticized his long hair, his wardrobe, the publicity he got for his fancy apartment and the way it was decorated with a llama rug, Siberian snow leopard and zebra pillows, and a cheetah bench. Namath just laughed when he heard these things, saying he left it up to a professional decorator to choose the motif for his apartment. During the era of the Vietnam War he heard some of the same cries that Mickey Mantle had listened to years earlier when the Korean conflict was raging. There were cries of "draft dodger" sometimes coming from the stands.

"The army doesn't want me," Namath would say. "I'm 4-F. My knees are just in too bad a shape."

That part was true. Joe had some off-season surgery to clean out one of knees before training camp even began in 1968. Love him or hate him, he was obviously the focal point of the Jets, the guy most people hung their hopes on to bring the team a title. But football is a team game, and what the average fan may not have realized, the Jets had gone about building a very solid and deep team prior to the 1968 season. If this club could do something the previous team could not—remain healthy—they had the talent to surprise a lot of people.

"I felt good about our team at the beginning of the 1968 season," Matt Snell said. "Up to that point I always felt our offense was ahead of the defense. Now, we had depth at a number of positions, and the defense was getting stronger. For example, we finally had a defensive backfield with guys like Jim Hudson, Randy Beverly, Cornell Gordon, and Johnny Sample. George Sauer was a great complement to Maynard at wide receiver. Bill Mathis could play both halfback and fullback in place of me or Emerson Boozer. And the move to get [offensive guard] Bob Talamini was one of the greatest trades ever made. I just felt that we were now a balanced team with enough talented veterans to compete."

John Elliott remembers getting a feeling of unity as soon as the team reported to training camp in 1968. "We were all real close," he said. "That was the first year we trained at Hofstra [University]. Up to then we always trained at Peekskill, New York. Everything at Hofstra was much better—the dorms, the training facilities, the fields, the food. We just had a feeling that the front office was doing everything it could to make us a winner. They were spending the money and we all had pride in the facilities that were made available to us. It brought us even closer together as a team."

Al Atkinson feels there was a special kind of motivation going into the 1968 season, and it could be traced back to the end of the previous year, when the team finished a game behind Houston at 8-5-1.

"I think a lot of guys were ticked off at the beginning of 1968," Atkinson said. "The season before we knew we had faded at the end. Part of it was playing the tough teams then—Kansas City, Oakland, and San Diego. I remember we played our last game New Year's Eve at San Diego. We hadn't been playing well for a month and were officially eliminated that afternoon when Houston won their game. So we went into that game knowing we had blown it, and we already wanted to make amends in

1968. When we came into camp in 1968 we wanted our shot at the playoffs, and wanted it badly."

So the motivation and the camaraderie were certainly there as the New York Jets began preparing for the new season. The strength of the AFL still seemed situated out west, where Oakland, Kansas City, and San Diego were all fast-striking, offensive teams. The Raiders and Chiefs were probably favored because of their defensive capabilities, but all three had a pretty good history of beating the Jets, especially when the New Yorkers traveled west. Despite Namath's presence, the Jets still didn't have the reputation of winners, and despite what the players felt going in, there still had to be some doubts.

Let's take a quick look at the team that Coach Ewbank would be putting on the field at the start of the 1968 season. It started, of course, with Namath. Broadway Joe, as the media now dubbed him, had shown himself to be a dynamic and dangerous passer with quick feet, a lightning release, and strong arm. The one thing he had yet to prove was that he could lead a team to a championship. But, like every great quarterback, he needed a surrounding cast to excel. Most felt that a healthy Namath could get the job done given the offensive weapons with which to work and a defense that would get him the ball and not give up a ton of points.

The team even had a solid backup. Babe Parilli had been the longtime quarterback of the Boston Patriots, joining them in 1961. He was no Namath but would provide a steady leadership hand and a good passing arm if called upon. Having him was better insurance than a young, untried signalcaller.

The offensive backfield also seemed well manned. Fullback Snell, a 6'2", 220-pounder, had proved himself by gaining over 900 yards as a rookie in 1965. A knee injury limited his output in 1967, but at full strength he was a tough, off-tackle runner and more than adequate pass receiver. Halfback Emerson Boozer, at 5'11" and 207 pounds, was an elusive runner and a good pass receiver. He joined the Jets in 1966 and was coming into his own in 1967 when he, too, was sidelined by a knee injury. A healthy

Snell and Boozer would give the Jets a very good, if not out-standing pair of running backs. Veteran Bill Mathis was a 220-pounder who could play both backfield positions and was the team's primary backup. He knew his role and filled it well.

Namath couldn't have been happier with his wide receivers. The aforementioned Don Maynard was one of the league's best deep threats who worked extremely well with his quarterback. The two could strike from anywhere on the field, witnessed by Maynard's 71 catches for 1,434 yards and 10 touchdowns in 1967. Maynard routinely averaged more than 20 yards a catch. Young George Sauer was a great complement to Maynard, a receiver who ran precise routes and had a great pair of hands. Sauer grabbed 75 passes in 1967, for 1,189 yards and six touch-downs. Tight end Pete Lammons was a tough blocker and good enough receiver to grab 45 tosses in 1967. Veteran Bake Turner was an A-1 backup and a guy who could play in three-wide out situations.

What would make this group go would be the offensive line, and the Jets seemed to be forming a good one. Rookie Sam Walton, a 6'5", 270-pounder, would join veteran Winston Hill, 6'4" and 280 pounds, to give the club a pair of huge offensive tackles. Guards Dave Herman and Randy Rasmussen were both young and en route to becoming outstanding players, and center John Schmitt did a fine job in the middle. Bob Talamini, anoth-er veteran guard, came over from Houston. Talamini would be a backup for most of the year until a daring move at playoff time would make a huge difference to the team's ultimate success. The guards and centers all weighed between 245 and 255 pounds, not big by today's standards, but average for the day.

"Back when we played, the guards weighed in the 250-pound range," Dave Herman said. "It was every coach's rule, whether the coach was Ewbank or Lombardi. I remember coming to camp some years at about 257 or 258 pounds and the first thing the coaches would tell me was to get my weight down. None of us lifted weights back then, either. We weren't allowed. The feeling was that if you lifted your muscles would get overly tight, making you more susceptible to injuries."

This was a solid group that had been forming for several years. Schmitt, Herman, and Hill were the veterans, Rasmussen and Walton the youngsters. There was a lot of pride when they took the field, and they were well aware of their primary job. According to Dave Herman, they also had an excellent teacher.

"Our first goal was pass blocking," Herman said. "That isn't to say we didn't work on our run blocking as much as anyone else, but we knew how important pass blocking was because of Joe. We had to give him time and try to keep him healthy. What most people didn't know is that we had a great pass-blocking coach in Weeb Ewbank. He didn't coach on an everyday basis, but he knew more about pass blocking than any coach I ever had. His thoughts and techniques for playing the offensive line were terrific, and we all benefited from having him there."

Herman also remembers what each member of the line contributed in terms of skills and temperament.

"Winston Hill was the best athlete we had on the line," he explained. "He was a natural, and while he weighed more than 275 pounds, he had all the quickness and skills needed to excel. Randy [Rasmussen] was like me. His accomplishment came from hard work. He came out of a small school in Nebraska, a farmer like I was. He always looked to me to give him security because I had the experience. John Schmitt at center was a guy who played his heart out, a player who kept getting better. He came in the same year as I did, only from a small school [Hofstra] and had to learn the pro game while on the job. Sam Walton at right tackle was a rookie, and everything was a bit overwhelming for him. Though he had talent, he sometimes lost concentration in games and even on the practice field.

"I think the talent of our line can be explained by the fact that Bob Talamini couldn't crack the starting lineup. Bob was a great player and an established veteran, but he stayed at backup until the playoffs, when we made a very bold move that wound up paying dividends."

It was on defense where the Jets had begun to make major strides. It started with the guys up front. The Jets had a fine pair of defensive ends, the talented Verlon Biggs, who was 6'4" and 270 pounds, and the quick and determined Gerry Philbin, 6'2" and 245. Both were plenty rugged and loved to go after the opposing quarterback. And, like the rest of the Jets defense, they were fast. The starting tackles were veteran Paul Rochester, a 6'2", 255-pounder, and young John Elliott, who stood 6'4" and weighed 245. Again, this wasn't an overly large group. But they were quick, determined, and sure tacklers. Backing up the starters were youngsters Steve Thompson and Carl McAdams. McAdams had been a ferocious college linebacker, every bit the equal of Tommy Nobis, but he tore up an ankle badly his rookie year, costing him some speed and mobility. But he was still an effective sub at both end and tackle.

John Elliott, who was just starting his second season in 1968, remembers with pride how well the defensive line performed together.

"Paul Rochester was the old man," Elliott said. "He told me when I joined the team that he would show me the ropes, that he wouldn't be around that much longer but would teach me everything he knew, and he did. Rocky was great against the run but wasn't a real good pass rusher, so in some passing situations Carl McAdams would come in. He and I were both young and full of piss and vinegar. I always felt Gerry Philbin never got the credit he fully deserved with his quickness and the things he could do for a man his size. I know he always had a lot of sacks, a statistic they didn't keep in those days. Today, if you have a lot of sacks, you're all everything. Verlon Biggs wasn't as fast, but he was the most intimidating guy on the line because of his size. He did have good quickness for a guy that big. Looking back, I think our strong suit was the fact that we simply played so well together."

The linebackers were small and quick. The veteran was Larry Grantham, who was just six feet tall and weighed 210 pounds. But he always used his quickness to make a ton of tackles. The other outside backer was Ralph Baker, at 6'3", 225 pounds. Like Grantham, he could move very well and had a nose for the football. In the middle was the unit's hardest hitter, 6'1", 230-pound Al Atkinson. Mike Stromberg and Paul Crane were the backups. While the starting trio didn't scare teams when they took the field, they always made their presence felt by the time the final gun sounded.

"Yeah, we were small," Al Atkinson says today. "But when you looked at the AFL on the whole, there weren't too many 250 or 255 pounders. We were the linebackers of the mid-1960s. Even some of the top guys in the NFL, like Sam Huff and Joe Schmidt, were in the 230- to 235-pound range. The exception, of course, was Dick Butkus. I graduated the same year he did and played in a couple of college all-star games with him. He would get on the scale after practice and tip it at 262. I was a defensive end in college at 230. Dick was a mauler. We were all about speed."

The defensive backs were an improved group. Texan Jim Hudson was the free safety, who had the size of a linebacker at 6'2", 210 pounds. He could run and he could hit, not a guy running backs wanted to mess with. Veteran Billy Baird was the free safety and, according to Don Maynard, the second fastest player on the team. Cornell Gordon and Johnny Sample were slated to start at the corners, but when Gordon was hurt, Randy Beverly stepped in. The leader of the secondary was Sample, who had played with the Baltimore Colts' 1958 and 1959 championship teams. He was outspoken and brash, and angry. Cut unceremoniously by the Colts several years earlier, Sample was out to prove the AFL was the equal of the older league, and wanted nothing more than to get back at his former team. He would have that chance sooner than anyone thought.

"We had a lot of pride in the defensive unit," says John Elliott. "The kind of pride that made us want to be the best in the league. In fact, we used to compete within the team each week, the offense and the defense, to see which would play better. And that's a healthy competition because everyone benefits."

That was the essential cast of characters that would be taking to the gridiron for the 1968 season. But what about leadership? This wasn't present-day professional football when it sometimes seems as if there are more assistant coaches than players. Though there were certainly coaching legends, like Lombardi and George "Papa Bear" Halas, among others, these were still the *old days* to some extent. There was a head coach, a few handpicked assistants, and that was it. With the Jets, Weeb Ewbank was a well-respected head coach with a track record. His assistants weren't that well known. The defensive assistants were Walt Michaels and Buddy Ryan (in his first year), and working with the offense were Clive Rush and Chuck Knox. All would become head coaches in the future.

The diminutive Ewbank was the leader. Born in Ohio in 1907, Weeb played the game early and then trained with a master, becoming an assistant coach under Paul Brown in 1949. That's when the Cleveland Browns were in the old All-America Football Conference. Weeb came along quickly, becoming a head coach five years later when the Colts named him in 1954. Four years later he became known nationwide when the led the Colts to that great victory over the Giants in 1958, then coached his team to a repeat championship the next season. He was also the coach under whom Johnny Unitas matured as a great quarterback. But in the what-have-you-done-for-me-recently world of professional sports, Ewbank found himself out of a job just three years later when the Colts finished the 1962 season at 7-7. It wasn't much of a thank you for a successful coach who certainly didn't lose his touch in three years. When offered the Jets job just a year later, Weeb jumped at it.

What kind of a coach was Weeb Ewbank in 1968? Dave Herman has already said what a great pass-blocking coach he was, yet he didn't actually coach every day. He seems to have totally trusted his handpicked assistants, but he was still the boss. Don Maynard recalls the way he put the teams' offensive plays into the book.

"Weeb had a rather unique way of doing things," Maynard said. "He wanted you to memorize each play so that every single player on the offense would know just what he had to do. Nothing wrong with that, obviously. But he did it his own way. Every morning during practice at training camp he would put in one running play, and in the afternoon one passing play. The next day he did the same thing—a running play in the morning and a pass play in the afternoon. When you run that same play 30 times in 30 minutes, you sure as hell have it memorized."

According to John Elliott, Weeb left it up to Walt Michaels to draw up the defensive game plan. During practice, Michaels worked with the linebackers and defensive backs, while Buddy Ryan handed the defensive line and special teams. Weeb didn't become too involved with the defense. Apparently, he preferred to work with his quarterback and on the offensive game plan.

Matt Snell remembers Weeb as something akin to a politician as much as for being a head coach. "Weeb always had to deal with the press, the owners, the front office, and double as general manager," Snell explained. "I never felt that he was a total, hands-on type of coach. But he was always able to get great coaches to work with him and would turn the daily operations of the team over to them. His assistants always ran practices and worked with the individual players. Of course, Weeb was the boss on the sideline during games.

"You could always see that he had a brilliant football mind. He would make suggestions during meetings and helped build the offensive playbook. I think he enjoyed wearing all the hats but because of that didn't always have time to work with us on a daily basis. Yet on game day, you always knew he was in control and that his mind was totally on the game."

Al Atkinson liked his coach's style because he felt Weeb knew how to put together winning teams. He also respected the way the coach handled players. "He never embarrassed a ballplayer in public," Atkinson said, "but he never forgot a major mistake a player made. I also liked the way he brought Namath along as a rookie. A lot of the guys felt Joe should be starting as early as the second game, but Weeb waited until he felt Joe has seen enough plays, watched enough films, and had a feel for the offense. He finally started him in the seventh game and he was right to wait that long."

Weeb was both a realist and a motivator. When the Jets embarked on their 1968 odyssey, the AFL Western Division teams were still looked upon as the league's elite. Before it all started, Matt Snell remembers his coach talking about the Chiefs, Raiders, and Chargers, then adding, "We're not yet in that group."

Was it Weeb's way of motivating? Maybe. The face of the AFL had also changed somewhat in 1968. A year earlier, the Miami Dolphins had become the league's ninth team, and now the Cincinnati Bengals joined the league. All this was in anticipation of the merger that was to be completed in 1970. Yet a strong AFL feeling still existed. Most veterans felt their league had played a more exciting, wide-open game. It was the AFL that instituted the option of the two-point conversion, something that would later be adopted by the NFL. They also used the scoreboard clock as the official game clock. In the NFL, the referee kept the official clock on the field and it often differed from the scoreboard, sometimes confusing fans and players alike. That, too, would eventually become an NFL trademark. So would the player's names on the backs of their uniforms, another innovation started by the AFL.

How did some of the Jets feel about their NFL counterparts at the beginning of that 1968 season? In the eyes of most, the gaps between the two leagues were closing, maybe closing faster than most fans thought.

"The NFL was definitely the superior league when I joined the Jets in 1965," Al Atkinson said. "But oddly enough, I always liked the AFL brand of ball better. I remember coming home from a high school game in 1960 and watching George Blanda bring the Oilers back from a 42-14 deficit to win it, 52-49. It was really exciting. Shortly after I watched an NFL game and the

Eagles beat someone by a 10-6 score. The AFL was simply more electrifying to watch.

"Maybe the NFL still proved it was the better league when Green Bay won the first two championship games, but you also have to remember they didn't blow out the Chiefs or Raiders in the first half. Mistakes and the pressure got to the AFL teams in the second half each time. By 1968 there were many fine athletes in the AFL, and a lot of real good quarterbacks. The Jets, for instance, weren't a good football team in 1965, but with the addition of young players and good draft choices, we were very good by 1968."

Dave Herman recalls players from the cross-town Giants pretty much treating the Jets with disdain prior to 1968. "Maybe they didn't show overt disrespect," Herman said, "but they pretty much treated us as if we were in the inferior league. It was apparent they still looked down upon the AFL."

Don Maynard, who said that depth had always been the difference between the two leagues, acknowledged that the gap was closing by 1968. "Our league was growing and maturing, getting better players, and that meant more depth," he offered.

Dave Herman began to sense hostility when the Jets met NFL teams in the preseason. He remembers a couple of incidents that were directed at him.

"We were playing against Pittsburgh one year and I'm up against Mean Joe Greene," Herman said. "My blocking style was working perfectly against him, especially the pass-blocking. Late in the third quarter Joe got off another pass with no problem, and Mean Joe hadn't even come across the line of scrimmage. I turned and said, 'Way to go, Joe,' to Namath when I felt something whizzing past my head. Mean Joe tried to hit me. I screamed at the ref about it, but he just told me to calm down. If Joe had connected, my head would have been back in Ohio.

"Another time I was playing opposite Alex Karras in Detroit. He had bragged before the game that he was going to hurt Joe and put him out of action, so I vowed he'd have to go through me to do it. Then Joe called a draw play. I faked that I was going to pass block, then blocked for a run. I hit Karras and he went flat on his back as Matt Snell ran past him for about a ten-yard gain. Karras got up and stuck his fist in my stomach. It felt as if it went right up to his elbow and I woke up on the sideline ... furious. Weeb told me to calm down. 'You can still play,' he said. So I said to him, 'Why don't you let him hit you and see how you like it?' By then, though, I think the NFL guys were getting a little frustrated because they were finding out we were good."

In the preseason games in 1968, the Jets began showing just how far they had come. Among their opponents were two NFL teams, the Detroit Lions and Atlanta Falcons. New York beat them both. They took the Lions by a 9-6 score, then made it easy against the Falcons, winning 27-12. Neither NFL team was able to score a touchdown against the Jets' quick defense, all points coming on field goals. If NFL teams, players, coaches, writers, and fans were still running around telling people the NFL was much better than the AFL, you couldn't prove it by the Jets. They had just handled a pair of NFL teams, and other AFL teams won their share of preseason games, as well.

With their team seemingly more talented and deeper than ever before, the Jets were ready for the season. It appeared they would rely on quickness on both sides of the ball. Namath's quick release and Maynard's ability to go deep gave the team the potential to strike from anywhere on the field. But the passing game was based on more than just Namath dropping back and throwing the ball as far as he could.

"On long passes, I always ran what we called the fade," Maynard explained. "Not all receivers could run it, and not many quarterbacks, if any, could throw it like Joe. What that means is that when I'd run a deep fly pattern, straight down the field as if I was running on a railroad track with the defender running with me, Joe just wouldn't throw it straight over my head. He would throw the ball about four yards to the outside and I would have to fade, or drift, out to where the ball was going to fall. Joe and I really had it down pat, and when he threw like that, I was the only one who could catch it. There was no way the defender to get it or even knock it down because he was running on the inside."

Maynard also explained how he and the other Jets receivers always ran what he calls two-part patterns. "Say I'm running an out pattern," he said. "If the out is there, Joe will throw and I'll catch it on the out. But if it isn't there, I'll convert it into a go and head downfield. So the out is really an out and go. If I run a hook pattern, it becomes a hook and go. A post pattern becomes a post and up, where you come back to the ball. Joe knew all our moves and always knew where to look for us.

"We had it all set up beforehand and often used hand signals if we wanted to change the play. Suppose Joe calls an out pattern for me in the huddle. If I didn't like the defensive lineup, I'd give him a hand signal. It might be one or two fingers, or a hand on the hip, a tap on the helmet, a hand on my knee. It was almost like signals in baseball, and doing it that way, the crowd noise didn't affect us. So if Joe looked at me and I didn't want the out, I'd give him a signal for another rout. Bake Turner and I did it at first, then [George] Sauer and [Pete] Lammons picked up on it. By 1968 I really think we had fine tuned our passing game."

The team's running attack wasn't fancy, but it was effective because there was such an emphasis on pass blocking. The linemen weren't built to run sweeps like Lombardi's Packers, a fact that Matt Snell confirmed.

"Our guards and center were relatively short and stocky," the fullback said. "We had a couple of big tackles [Hill and Walton], but the line was built to protect Namath. We didn't run power sweeps, because our linemen didn't have the ability to pull and lead runs like that. We were much more effective running trap plays that required straight-ahead blocking. With good power blocking we were much more effective running traps inside between the tackles."

The only question was that Snell and Boozer were both coming off knee injuries. Boozer was having his best season in 1967 before going down and wound up leading the team with just 442 yards on 119 carries. Snell was limited to 61 carries for 207 yards.

While the Jets might have lived and died with Namath's right arm, they still needed that solid running game to keep the defense honest. Because of the injuries to Snell and Boozer, Namath was forced to throw early and often, and wound up the season with 258 completions in 491 attempts for a whopping 4,007 yards, a pro record at the time. No one wanted him to throw that much again because it pointed up a lack of balance on the offense. So the running game was something of a question mark as the team prepared to start the new season.

As for the defense, it appeared to be better than ever with speed, quickness, sure-handed tackling, and opportunistic ball-hawking the key ingredients. Al Atkinson confirmed that the New York defense was pretty simple and uncomplicated.

"Our defense was definitely based on the speed of the team," he said. "That, and a whole lot of unity. John Elliott was our youngest starter, but a lot of the others had at least several years' experience, so we knew each other very well. We had two basic defenses—the 5-1 and the 5-under—with the only thing changing being the coverage. With the 5-1, I had to cover the halfback. If he went 50 yards downfield I had better be sure to stick with him. With the 5-under I'd have the fullback if he came down the field. But basically, we just challenged teams to beat us. We watched films, knew the tendencies of our opponents, and went about neutralizing them. If you have the better athletes, you win most of the time."

John Elliott echoed what Atkinson said, giving his description a self-effacing, humorous bent. "The defense was kept simple because some of us weren't the sharpest knives in the drawer," he said. "But we had a tremendous game plan each week and always worked on our strengths against our opponent's weaknesses. We used our speed and quickness, had guys who wanted to play and who had the desire to do what it took to win. There were no prima donnas on defense. If one guy made a mistake, we did our best to cover up. Everyone played together, and we took a great deal of pride in our defensive unit."

Now the moment of truth was close at hand. It was time for the 1968 season to begin. Oakland and Kansas City were still considered the class of the AFL, with the Jets becoming the favorites to win a weaker Eastern Division. In the NFL, it was pretty much a given that the Green Bay Packers' dynasty was over. Phil Bengston was the new coach, and the team was aging rapidly. Among the teams expected to emerge from the pack and challenge for the title were the Dallas Cowboys, Cleveland Browns, Los Angeles Rams, and Baltimore Colts. And, of course, whichever team emerged as the NFL champion would have the added burden of trying to defend the honor and assumed superiority of the older league in the third AFL–NFL World Championship Game, a game that would finally be given its famous and lasting name a year later and would eventually become one of sport's greatest spectacles. Following the 1969 season, the title game would be forever known as The Super Bowl.

# 3
# SETTING THE TONE FOR THE SEASON

The Jets' 1968 season would open with what could easily be called a "barometer" game. They would be facing one of the league's best, the Kansas City Chiefs, and would have to play them on the road. Though one game certainly does not a season make, how the team opened against this powerful football team might tell a lot about their ultimate success for the entire year. Hank Stram's Chiefs were loaded with individual stars. Quarterback Len Dawson was perhaps the most accurate passer in the league, having completed some 58 percent of his passes the season before. Mike Garrett was still a star at running back, while wide receiver Otis Taylor was considered one of the very best in all of football.

There was a huge offensive and defensive line. In fact, the defensive tackles, 6'7", 287-pound Buck Buchanan, and 6'9", 290-pound Ernie "Cat" Ladd, were the biggest and maybe the baddest in the game. The linebacking trio of Bobby Bell, Willie Lanier, and Ed Lynch, were also considered the equal of any trio in either league, while defensive backs Johnny Robinson and Emmitt Thomas were both all-stars in a solid defensive backfield. This was truly a star-studded team and one still smarting from its loss to the Packers in the first ever AFL-NFL title game. They wanted another shot at the NFL before the full merger. It was no surprise when the Chiefs were installed as six-and-a-half-point favorites.

In addition, the Jets' recent history against the Chiefs wasn't good. The team had lost three straight to Kansas City, including games of 42-18 and 21-7 the season before. In the 42-18 game, the Chiefs had really beat the Jets up physically and some wondered if the New Yorkers might be somewhat intimidated by the size and physical prowess Hank Stram's ball club. Even Coach Ewbank admitted he was concerned with the Chiefs' size and already talked about a lineup change.

"When Buchanan plays tackle, I'll probably use Bob Talamini at guard," the Jets coach told the media. "Talamini has the experience to handle Buchanan [because] he's played him ever since he came into the league. But if Buchanan goes to end and Ladd moves over to the right side, I'll probably use Rasmussen more. Ladd is a more straight-ahead guy, and Randy is big enough and strong enough to play him."

So there was concern on opening day. Usually it's play your regulars and see what you've got, but Coach Ewbank was already contemplating tinkering with the lineup. Once the game began, however, there was no need to change anything. The Jets came out playing with confidence and verve. Namath was throwing well, and the defense was putting the clamps on Len Dawson and company. Namath and Maynard worked their magic, using all the tools and tricks they had worked on since Joe joined the team in 1965. Catching one of Namath's long "fades," Maynard scored on the receiving end of a 57-yard aerial and soon after grabbed a 30-yard touchdown pass. Jim Turner and Jan Stenerud of K.C. traded field goals, and the Jets came off the field at halftime with a 17-3 lead.

Up to now, the Jets couldn't have written a better script. But no one was getting overconfident. For one thing, they knew the Chiefs could strike quickly and decidedly, and secondly, many of those on the ball club remembered blowing a 17-0 lead in the opener a year earlier. Then, when the Chiefs' Noland Smith returned a Curley Johnson punt 80 yards for a score, the momentum began to turn. The Chiefs closed the gap to 17-10. Two more Stenerud field goals made it 17-16, the last one coming only 45 seconds into the fourth quarter. Kansas City had scored 13 unanswered points. Worse yet, both field goals came as the result of New York turnovers, a Boozer fumble and an interception of a Namath pass. Many New York fans watching the came on television began a popular refrain. *Same old Jets.*

Only this was now a veteran team, a tougher team than in the past, a close-knit team with a lot of character. As fast as Kansas City was coming on, these Jets weren't about to roll over and play dead. Once again the two kickers matched field goals, Turner hitting from the 42 and his K.C. counterpart connecting from the 28, his fourth three-pointer of the game. With 5:56 left, the Jets had a slim, 20-19 lead. Up to that point, all of Stenerud's kickoffs had gone through the end zone for touchbacks, the ball coming out to the 20. Only this time he shanked the kick and it drifted toward the sideline near the goal line. If the ball had bounced out of bounds, Stenerud would have had to kick it again, only from five yards deeper in his own territory. Unfortunately, Jets return man Earl Christy didn't let it bounce out of bounds. Instead, he grabbed the ball and then stepped out of bounds at about the five.

Now the Jets were in trouble. If they went three-and-out and had to punt, Kansas City could well get the ball inside the 50 with plenty of time to get into position for a winning field goal. So when Namath came out on the field with the offense, there was a lot at stake. On first down, Joe gave the ball to Boozer, who promptly lost a yard to the four. The drama was building. Second down. This time Namath dropped back and threw a slant in the direction of Maynard, but cornerback Emmitt Thomas got there on time and jarred the ball loose. Now came the biggest play of the game, third and 11. If they didn't get a first down, the Jets would be forced to punt.

With that magical communication they had been building, Namath decided to throw the same pass to Maynard, the one that had just missed on the play before. Once again he stepped back as Maynard ran the identical play he had on the prior down. This time he grabbed Joe's quick toss for a 17-yard gain and a first down. From there, the Jets began a sustained march, mixing running plays with short passes and eating up the clock. Twice Namath completed first-down passes on second-down plays and then, just after the two-minute warning, he hit Maynard again for a 19-yard gain and another clutch first down, this time on a third-and-eight play.

All told, the Jets held the ball for 14 plays, including one delay-of-game penalty. Finally, with the ball at the Kansas City 33, Namath handed the ball to Snell who just ran half-speed into the line. The reason he didn't have to go harder was that the gun had sounded. The Jets had won the game, 20-19, holding the ball for nearly six minutes in their final drive and denying the Chiefs a chance to win it. Matt Snell saw it as a turning point, a very early one.

"That game did more for our confidence than any other," he said. "We had marched nearly 70 yards and eaten up a huge chunk of time. This was the one game that told me we had finally arrived as a team. Now, we felt we could beat anyone."

Even Kansas City coach Hank Stram was impressed. "There was no way in the world I thought they could go from the four-yard line and maintain possession until the end of the game," he said. "I thought we could hold them and get into position for a field goal to win it."

It was a tremendous victory over an elite team. Namath had completed 17 of 29 passes for 302 yards and a pair of touchdowns. Maynard, who had played only one preseason game because of a heel injury caught eight passes for 203 yards and both scores. It was the first 200-yard receiving game of his career. And Emerson Boozer showed everyone he was well on the way to full recovery from his knee injury the previous year. He ran for 75 yards on 18 carries and, along with Snell, helped sustain the final drive that sealed the Chiefs' fate. The team emerged from the game with no serious injuries. All things considered, you couldn't have scripted a better start to the new season.

Game two had a strange twist to it. The Jets were supposed to visit the Boston Patriots (before they were dubbed the New England Patriots and moved to Foxboro), but the Red Sox were playing at Fenway Park, the Pats' home at the time, so the game was moved to Legion Field in Birmingham, Alabama. The Jets had played some preseason games there, but Birmingham was lobbying for a possible pro franchise, and there was some talk about possibly moving the Patriots south. Playing in the south wasn't always easy then, especially for African-American players at a racially charged time in history. Matt Snell remembers.

"We had played some games there before, mainly because of Namath's popularity and what he had done as a collegian at Alabama," Snell said. "Many of the hotels were still segregated then, and we made it plain to Weeb that we wouldn't stand for segregated hotels and wouldn't play in front of segregated crowds. We were assured that things would be all right in Birmingham, but you always had to watch yourself in the smaller towns at the time.

"I remember one funny story from a game we played in Atlanta in 1966. Again, we had the problem of segregated hotels, but Weeb was always understanding and got things together. I remember going into a bookstore with a teammate at the time, Bill Perkins. He began thumbing through one of the books when the owner of the store began asking, in a southern drawl, why Bill was looking at a Russian book. Without warning, Bill starts speaking in Russian. He was fluent in it, and this guy was shocked. Oddly enough, he spoke some Russian as well and the two talked for a few minutes. He couldn't believe that a black man was fluent in Russian, and I was surprised that a guy with a southern drawl like he had could also speak Russian. Small world, huh."

John Elliott, who was a white man from Texas, said that the Jets were so close as a team, united in a common goal, that the racial issue never came up.

"Sure, we read the papers and knew what was happening, but we couldn't allow it to affect us," Elliott said. "I had a brother in Vietnam and we paid attention to everything that was going on, but we drew our paychecks from the Jets and gave them everything we had every game. We had a lot of guys from the south on the team, both black and white, and the racial issue never came up. You couldn't ask for better relationships between blacks and whites on the team. I had gone to a segregated high school in Texas, and many of the colleges were still segregated then, but I loved the black guys on the team as much as anyone else. I think that was one of the unusual things about our team and one of the great things about it. We had southern guys on the team, but we all got along so well. We were men and we acted like men, and we were a team and knew we couldn't do it without each other. I can honestly say there wasn't one problem on our team related to race."

The problem in Birmingham belonged to the Patriots. For openers, only slightly more than 29,000 fans showed up at the game, roughly half the number that had attended the Alabama-VPI game in the same stadium the night before. This, of course, was a situation that would never exist in today's pro game and shows that both leagues were still experiencing growing pains, having to take one team's home game and play it some 1,500 miles away. But all things considered, there were still 60 minutes of football to be contested.

This one was the proverbial laugher. The Jets moved out to a 14-3 first-quarter lead, extended it to 20-10 at the half and cruised to an easy 47-31 victory. It was the second highest point total in club history and everyone had a hand in the victory. Namath was 13 of 25 for 196 yards and a pair of touchdowns, one to Maynard and the other to tight end Pete Lammons. Emerson Boozer scored for the first time since his knee injury the season before, and Randy Beverly returned an intercepted pass 68 yards for a score. Add four field goals from Jim Turner and another relatively injury-free game, and the Jets were a very solid,

2-0, already in first place in the AFL East. The pessimists were beginning to fade away. But they would soon be back.

That's because the Jets next traveled to Buffalo to meet a Bills team that had been Eastern Division champions just two years earlier. Since then, the Bills had been in a crash dive and had already lost their first three games of the season. This one seemed like a slam-dunk, the Jets were installed at 17-point favorites against a team going nowhere fast. But as someone once said when describing the possibilities of upsets in the NFL, "On any given Sunday ... "

In other words, the upset was always possible, but no one figured it would happen to the Jets, not after their fast start and opening victory over the Chiefs. But when your quarterback throws seven touchdown passes, only three of them to the opposing team, the recipe for disaster has been written. All told, Broadway Joe was intercepted five times, with three of the passes taken into the zone, including a 100-yard return by Tommy Janik. The final score was 37-35, with the wrong team on top. It was one of those erratic games Namath seemed to have every so often and, as usual, the stand-up quarterback never pointed any fingers.

"Of course I blame myself," he said to the members of the media gathered round after the game. "I was the one who threw the damn ball. It's all the dumb guy sitting right here ... I just wasn't throwing good. What was it? Five interceptions, three for touchdowns. That's the whole story."

Coach Ewbank said he considered replacing Joe with veteran Babe Parilli, but then decided to stick with his starter. "[He's] the guy who gets you there, and he did come back for two touchdowns."

The biggest plus to come out of the game was the running of Matt Snell. Having signed a new, multiyear contract earlier in the week, Snell celebrated by carrying the ball 12 times for 124 yards, breaking away for runs of 60 and 36 yards, both of which set up New York touchdowns. The problem was the loss. Ironically, it would be the only game the Bills would win all year, so they definitely were a team in eclipse. Losing to them would be a test of the Jets' character. Would they bounce back or would they become a mistake-prone team, as they had sometimes been in the past? Maybe the early-season loss was a good thing. The bad game was now out of their system. Don Maynard remembers the team still being loose when they met on Tuesday and watched the films of the Buffalo disaster.

"We were such a close-knit ball club, and we always found a way to have fun," Maynard said. "When we flew to Buffalo, I remember the plane going over Niagara Falls, giving us a little sightseeing tour. Then Buffalo came out and kicked our ass. After we watched the films and began to break up to go into offense and defense meetings, Gerry Philbin shouted at Joe. 'Hey, Namath,' he said, 'Remember, we're wearing green this week.' He was referring to Joe's five interceptions. Joe just laughed. Because we were so close, we could kid each other like that, and still be dead serious about what we were doing. I talked to Joe just recently and that incident came up. Joe said he remembered it like yesterday. Some quarterbacks might have gotten teed off about being reminded of five interceptions, but Joe was always a stand-up guy. He knew what he had done and didn't mind a little ribbing."

Next came the San Diego Chargers, another west coast team with a history of beating the Jets. But the Chargers weren't quite the powerhouse they had been in the early days of the AFL, and this time they would be coming into New York to play the Jets at Shea. New York was the favorite, but Coach Ewbank rode the team pretty hard during the week. He was especially on the case of rookie tackle Sam Walton, who had difficulty handling Buffalo's veteran defensive end, Ron McDole. He did what any head coach would do, let Walton know that if he couldn't do the job, someone else would.

"I know I didn't have a good game," the rookie told reporters, "but I consider it an education, not a shock. That guy [McDole] was a lot smarter than I was, and I got rattled when I realized I was being outsmarted."

That's the nature of professional sports. Even on a winning team all the parts have to function smoothly or a replacement will be found. Healthy competition within the team also serves as a motivating tool, each player trying to do as well as the other. No one wants to be singled out. Coach Ewbank may not have embarrassed his players, but he let them know when they weren't doing the job. Winston Hill, the veteran tackle who played opposite Walton, was quick to defend the rookie, whom he had taken under his wing.

"[Sam] has progressed faster as a rookie than any [I've seen] since I've been here ... He's been playing good ball, but he came up against a good man."

San Diego still had a quick-strike offense led by veteran quarterback John Hadl and wide receivers Lance Alworth and Gary Garrison. Needless to say, they loved to throw the ball downfield. At 2-1, the Jets wanted a victory to keep them from falling back to .500. In addition, any time they beat one of the west coast teams it was looked upon as another step up the ladder. With an AFL-record crowd of 63,786 fans jamming into Shea Stadium, the game turned out to be a thriller. It was close and hard fought from the beginning, the lead changing hands several times. The Chargers had a 20-16 lead with time running down in the fourth quarter and the Jets driving. Finally, with 1:43 left, Emerson Boozer bulled into the end zone from a yard out, giving the Jets the lead. Jim Turner's extra point made it a 23-20 game, but the Chargers would have one more chance.

Now it was time for the New York defenders to step up. The Jets went into a prevent defense, with three linemen and five deep backs. The purpose of the "prevent" is to keep the opposing team from breaking off a long play. Many football purists don't like it, because it opens the middle of the field for short to medium passes, and good passing teams, like the Chargers, can eat up real estate quickly enough to get themselves in position for a last-second field goal try.

At first, the Chargers stalled. An incomplete pass and holding penalty pinned San Diego back at their own eight-yard line. But suddenly quarterback Hadl began finding his mark. He hit Garrison for 23 yards and then rookie Ken Dyer for 22 more. Now the ball was at the Jets' 47. When Garrison caught yet another pass in between the Jets' defenders, he gained 15 and advanced the ball down to the 32. Now they were in field goal range for their kicker, Dennis Partee. Partee was anxious to make amends for missing an extra point earlier. Had he converted after the middle touchdown, the Chargers would only trail by two with a chance to win it. Still, if they could tie, they'd salvage something.

With 55 seconds left, San Diego wanted to get even closer. Hadl's next pass for Garrison was incomplete, but there was a flag. San Diego was offsides. The Jets took the penalty, moving the ball back five yards. Hadl then faded to pass again, and this time he was looking deep. Just as he got set to release the ball, Gerry Philbin came barreling in and hit the quarterback as he threw. The ball was headed toward Dyer at the goal line, but Philbin had disrupted Hadl just enough. John Sample raced over and picked the pass off at the four-yard line. He then returned it all the way to the 44. The final seconds elapsed and the Jets had won. The defense had come up big, and the veteran Sample made the final key play.

Whenever a team wins a close one, no matter how well or how poorly they may have played, it becomes important. The more close games you win, the more you begin to believe you'll win. And when you start beating good teams in the close ones, then you begin believing you can beat anyone. Conversely, when you lose to bad teams, it can be a confidence breaker. The loss to the Bills two weeks earlier was looked upon as an aberration, something that wouldn't happen again, and the victory against the Chargers seemed to confirm it. So when the Jets hosted the 1-3 Denver Broncos at Shea and were installed as 19-point favorites, no one expected a repetition of the Buffalo game.

But that's exactly what they got. The week before they had run the ball 40 times, 24 of the carries by Boozer, so Namath wasn't under pressure to pass. Against Denver, Joe went back up top and with disastrous results. Once again he was intercepted five times as the Broncos shocked the Jets and their fans, 21–13. For a second time, the Jets' offensive line had trouble with an opposing defensive end as Rich Jackson, one of the AFL's best, seemed to be in the Jets' backfield all afternoon. It was a shocking loss to a mediocre team. As usual, Namath made no excuses, acknowledging that the fans had a right to boo.

"I just stink," was all he said. Joe had already thrown 13 interceptions in five games, not a good statistic. However, 10 of them came in just two contests, and Broadway Joe had always shown a proclivity to throw picks in numbers every now and then. The team could only hope he had it out of his system now.

Coach Ewbank defended his quarterback, who almost brought the team back in the final minutes. "The interceptions were not Joe's fault," the coach said. "They were really rushing in there and we couldn't stop that Jackson all day."

Once again the culprit was rookie tackle Walton. He seemed to be having problems with the better defensive ends in the league. It had been just two weeks earlier when Ron McDole of Buffalo had beaten him badly.

"It's tough for a rookie playing the offensive line," Dave Herman said. "We all knew that Sam had talent and Winston [Hill] was always working with him. As the season wore on he began making more mental mistakes. Remember, a pro season is a lot tougher and a lot longer than a college season, and facing so many good defensive ends isn't easy."

Statistically, the Jets' passing game still ranked among the league's best. George Sauer had grabbed nine passes for 191 yards in the loss to Denver, while Don Maynard had seven catches for 140 yards. Sauer was now tied with Lance Alworth of the Chargers with 30 catches on the year, while Maynard's 555 yards on 23 catches gave him a league-best 24.1 yards per catch. Despite the interceptions, Namath was the league's third leading passer behind Len Dawson of the Chiefs and John Hadl of the Chargers, while Matt Snell was the league's fifth best rusher with 264 yards on 54 carries for an impressive 4.9 yards a carry.

At 3-2, the Jets were already at a pivotal spot in their season. A couple of weeks earlier it seemed they would walk away with the AFL Eastern title. A loss to Houston the next week would mean they were back at .500. History was not on their side since the team had never won a single game in Houston during the previous eight years of the AFL's existence. The Oilers weren't the powerhouse of old, coming in at 2-4, but they were still a competent team, considered much superior to Buffalo and Denver, the two clubs that had beaten the Jets. So while the New Yorkers were favorites, this game, too, would not be easy.

There was one difference in Houston this time. All the previous Jets defeats had been outdoors. Now, the Oilers were playing in the Astrodome, on turf, a place the Jets had never visited before. Prior to the game the team worked out at Hofstra University's brand-new Astroturf surface, giving them a feel for playing in a stadium dubbed The Eighth Wonder of the World. The Oilers were defending divisional champions, and combined with their record of futility in Houston, the Jets still considered them a difficult opponent. Before the game, the Jets already knew that Boston had beaten Buffalo, so the Patriots were now even at 3-3. A loss to Houston would drop the Jets into a first-place tie with the Pats.

What looked at first like it would be an easy game suddenly turned into another barnburner, the kind the Jets had been playing lately. In the first half, the Jets defense dominated, keeping the Oilers off the scoreboard. In the meantime, the New Yorkers scored on a safety, when Paul Crane blocked a Houston punt out of the end zone, and then Namath scored on a quarterback sneak. The Jets then made a two-point conversion when Babe Parilli passed to Billy Mathis following a fake kick. That made it a 10-0 game at intermission. Neither team scored in the third quarter, then Turner kicked a short field goal just a few seconds into the final period, giving the Jets a 13-0 lead. It looked as if they were going to breeze home.

That's when things changed. Bob Davis, playing quarterback in place of starter Pete Beathard, who was ill, was injured on a hit by Verlon Biggs and helped off the field. Because Beathard was unable to play, the Oilers sent veteran Don Trull into the game. Houston had traded Trull to the Patriots a year earlier, but when the Pats cut him the Oilers brought him back for insurance. Now they needed some and they got it. Trull caught fire and drove the Oilers downfield twice in the next eight minutes, first hitting Alvin Reed with a nine-yard touchdown pass and then Jim Bierne with a 19-yard scoring aerial. The extra points gave the Oilers the lead at 14-13. Two key Jets penalties, holding on Dave Herman and a roughing-the-passer call on Carl McAdams helped Houston to their second score. Now the Jets had just 4:19 left to try to pull the game out.

The Jets began at their own 20 with just over four minutes left. Undaunted by his poor performance of a week earlier, Namath immediately went to the air. He completed three straight passes to the elusive Sauer, good for 14, nine, and 13 yards, giving the Jets a first down at the Houston 44. Now Joe broke the rhythm. Instead of throwing again, he gave the ball to Boozer, and Emerson cut back over the middle behind some great blocking and ran 17 yards to the Houston 27. At this point, Joe wanted to play it close to the vest, kill the clock, and not risk an interception. He gave the ball to Boozer again, who ran for about two yards. Two-minute warning.

On the next play it was Boozer again, this time running left behind a Dave Herman block and rambling down to the 10-yard line. With his running game in gear, Namath stuck with it. He gave the ball to fullback Snell, who cut off a John Schmitt block and ran it all the way to the two. Knocking on the door, Namath gave it to Snell again, who this time ran over the left side between Hill and Randy Rasmussen, and bulled into the end zone for the score. Turner's kick gave the Jets a 20-14 lead with just 46 seconds left. On the ensuing kickoff, Houston's Zeke Moore was leveled by Gerry Philbin, and the ball squirted loose. Bill Rademacher recovered for the Jets to seal the deal. The victory gave the Jets a 4-2 record, kept them in first place, and also brought them their first win ever in Houston. Once again, things were looking up.

Next the Jets returned to Shea to play the Patriots in what would mark the halfway point in the season. With another big crowd on hand, including seven-year-old John F. Kennedy, Jr., the team finally had themselves a laugher. It must have been a relief after all of the close games. The New Yorkers eased out to a 10-0 halftime lead, extended it to 20-0 after three and cruised home a 48-14 winner. Not only did they take the measure of the team that was a game behind them in the standings, they buried them, bringing their record to 5-2 at the halfway point and giving them a nice two-game lead in the Eastern Division race.

It was the defense that really excelled in this one. The Jets intercepted five Patriots passes and limited Boston's outstanding fullback, Jim Nance, to just 14 yards on six carries. They also dumped the Patriots quarterbacks seven times for 50 yards' worth of lost turf. Gerry Philbin led the parade by slamming the Pats quarterback to the ground three times, causing fumbles on each, two of which were recovered by the Jets for easy scores. They didn't call them sacks in those days, but the cat-quick Philbin was a terror. Who knows how many he might have had during the year had records been kept?

Namath had a quiet game. He didn't throw for a touchdown but was picked off once. In addition, he gave the team a couple of scares. In the first quarter he was thrown hard to the ground by the Pats' Larry Eisenhauer and bruised his coccyx, his tailbone, but stayed in the game. Then on the first play of the final quarter he jammed his thumb as his pass was partially blocked and intercepted. He left the game holding his right thumb as Babe Parilli finished up by leading the Jets to four, fourth-period touchdowns. Namath said later that he had been nursing the hurt thumb since the second game of the season and could have stayed in, or returned, if he was needed. It was a game in which everyone played. Reserve fullback Billy Joe ended up the team's leading rusher with 80 yards on 11 carries, doing most of his damage in the final period.

With the season now at the halfway point, the team seemed to be putting it together. Obviously, there were still no chickens to count. The veterans remembered very well how a 7-2-1 start the year before had deteriorated to a 7-5-1 final mark. They didn't want that to happen again. But these Jets were a close-knit team who were able to concentrate on football, even with the turmoil of the times swirling all around them.

"In a sense, we couldn't let the politics of the world concern us," Don Maynard said, looking back. "Sure, it mattered, but we had to concentrate on the game. I've learned more about politics in recent years, but back in 1968, we were so dedicated and focused. We knew we had something going that year and didn't want to let it slip away."

Matt Snell said that the state of the world rarely was a topic of conversation when the press met with the athletes. "We were certainly aware of everything," he explained, "but back then sports wasn't as out front as it is today, and sports stars weren't expected to have opinions about everything. So the media concentrated on asking us about football, not about politics."

"The intensity of the season didn't allow us time to worry about politics," was the way Dave Herman put it. "There was a special group of personalities in our 1968 team, guys who liked each other and really had a common goal. Winning was always number one."

Now the Jets were about to move into the second half of the season. Though the team had built up a degree of confidence, they still knew it wouldn't be easy. Even if they won the Eastern Division, chances are they would have to meet either Oakland or Kansas City in the AFL title game. They had already beaten the Chiefs, but the game was very close. As for the Raiders, those were always wild and woolly affairs. Just how wild the team would soon find out.

# 4
# A WILD FINISH AND A LITTLE GIRL NAMED HEIDI

T he second half of the season didn't start with a real bang. In fact, if the Jets were looking for a sign that they had turned things around, they didn't get it. Game eight was with the Buffalo Bills, the team that had upset the New Yorkers early in the season. That was still the only game the Bills had won all year, making it pretty obvious that they were not a good football team. It seemed logical that they wouldn't beat the Jets again. In fact, most experts figured the New Yorkers should pretty much treat them the same way they had manhandled the Patriots. The oddsmakers agreed, installing the New Yorkers as 19-point favorites. In the week before the game, much of the attention focused on Namath and the thumb injury that he now admitted had been bothering him most of the year.

Now in his fourth season, Namath had still never missed a game because of injury. While many saw him as a bon vivant, a glorified playboy who spent his nights prowling Manhattan's trendiest nightspots, earning and re-earning his nickname, Broadway Joe, Namath was nevertheless all football player. If he hadn't been, serious types like Dave Herman wouldn't have called him "the best teammate I ever had." And like many of the great ones, Namath had the ability to play with pain. He admitted that his knee always pained him. Now it was the thumb on his throwing hand, which certainly might explain some of the things that had happened with the team's passing game.

"You can called it jammed," he said of the thumb, adding that he had a similar injury the season before and even during a point in the off season, "They were afraid it was broken. Then I hurt it again in the second game of the season and hurt it once more against the Patriots on the play when I was intercepted."

Looking back, it was obvious that the thumb had been bothering him. Joe had played an outstanding game in the opening win over Kansas City, passing with assurance and accuracy. The next week he injured the thumb and the week after that threw for five interceptions in the upset loss to Buffalo. He also had not thrown a touchdown pass in four games and had a second five-interception day in the team's only other loss, to Denver. Critics also pointed out that many of his long passes intended for Don Maynard had been underthrown. Maynard had spoken about how well Joe threw long, how he had the knack of "fading" the ball to the outside so only he could get it. All the evidence, it would seem, pointed to the fact that the thumb injury was affecting his ability to throw, especially the long ball. It was also pointed out that the team had been running the ball more, staying on the ground as long as they could.

The logical question was would the thumb would get worse, stay the same, or get better? The answer might well determine just how far the team could go in the second half of the season. But that answer didn't come against Buffalo. The point spread might have read 19, but the game score certainly didn't. The Jets needed Jim Turner's talented right leg to pull the game out as the veteran tied an AFL record by booting six three-pointers, including two in the final three and a half minutes as the New Yorkers came from behind for a 25-21 victory after the Bills had taken a 21-19 lead. The Jets' only touchdown came in the second quarter when Johnny Sample intercepted a Kay Stephenson pass and took it in from the 36. Needless to say, Namath again failed to throw a touchdown pass.

In fact, this one pretty much belonged to the defense. Even after the Bills had taken their fourth-quarter lead, it was the defense that rose to the occasion. After the Jets had taken a 22-19 lead on Turner's fifth field goal, the Bills began to drive again. It was middle linebacker Al Atkinson who intercepted a Stephenson pass at the 20 that set up Turner's final three-pointer, with 52 seconds left. But Buffalo came at the Jets again, moving quickly to the Jets 20. The Bills still had a chance to win it on the last play of the game, but this time defensive tackle John Elliott deflected Stephenson's pass, and it was over. When someone reminded Namath afterwards that he hadn't throw a touchdown pass in five games, Joe said, simply, "This will be a win in the standings, no matter how we did it."

The good part was that the Jets were finding ways to win. Everyone was contributing, as Turner and the defense came up big. The bad part was the continuing questions about Namath's thumb and how it might be affecting his throwing. There were, obviously, no ready answers. Only Joe knew, and he wasn't saying much. He was healthy enough to play and didn't plan on sitting out, not with Houston and then a huge game with Oakland coming up. The fans just hoped that their quarterback would regain his magic touch ... and soon.

In typical Namath fashion, he made some news off the field before he made any more on it. During the week Broadway Joe's personal manager, George Scheck, announced that there were several show business projects involving the quarterback in the works. According to Scheck, Joe would soon be singing, along with a combo, in nightclubs, as well as making personal appearance tours. There were also plans in the works for films, recordings, and TV commercials all, of course, to be pursued vigorously after the season ended. Some people might find these kinds of ambitious plans for an athlete distracting. Had his teammates not known the kind of players Joe was, the kind of character he had, they might have been annoyed by all the extra attention. But because they knew he was a gamer, and he was Joe, it didn't cause any problems.

A more pressing question was whether the Oilers would cause problems. Houston was in second place with a 4-5 record, two and a half games behind the Jets. So the game was important for more than one reason. In fact, someone put a newspaper clipping on the team bulletin board that read, "Will The Jets Blow It Again?" It was a reference to the Houston game of a year earlier, when Namath threw six interceptions and the Oilers managed a 28-28 tie. It was the start of the Houston resurgence and the Jets' late-season collapse. But most of the Jets didn't need the extra motivation provided by a piece of print journalism.

"We know what this game means with that," guard Randy Rasmussen said. And kicker Jim Turner added, "We were ready. We still remembered last year's game, and we were ready."

There were more than 60,000 tickets sold for the game, which had become the norm. But on a chilly, rainy November day, only some 36,500 fans braved the elements to watch the action. If nothing else, this game proved that the Jets' defense was for real. The defenders had another banner day, putting the clamps on the Houston passing game. Quarterbacks Pete Beathard and Don Trull threw for just 41 yards. Unless your ground game is running rampant, you can't win like that. Houston generated little offense on the muddy field, the Jets winning, 26-7, with Jim Turner booting four more field goals, to break his team record of 20 that he had set the week before.

Namath came out throwing and did well on a day when it wasn't easy to grip the football. The team used a three wide receiver set, and Broadway Joe went up top early. He didn't throw for a touchdown for the sixth game in a row, but his passes had zip and accuracy. Four of his completions went to George Sauer for 128 yards and the wide receiver talked about the less-than-ideal conditions.

"The receiver always has an advantage on a field like this," Sauer said. "[These were] the worst conditions I ever played under. I was wishing it was over from the first play."

Billy Baird and Ralph Baker both had interceptions that led to scores, while Johnny Sample grabbed his seventh pick of the year. With a 7-2 record, the Jets now had a commanding lead in the AFL East race. The West was still up for grabs. It was round up the usual suspects with Kansas City at 8-2, and Oakland and San Diego right behind with 7-2 records. Now the stage was set for perhaps the biggest game of the year. The Jets would be traveling west to meet the Oakland Raiders. Not only would this be a memorable contest, setting the stage for much of what would follow, but it would also change the face of television's coverage of professional football from that point on. This would be a game cemented in the memories of all pro football fans. It would become known as the infamous *Heidi* game.

To begin with, Jets–Raiders was always something special. Though the Raiders had been the superior team over the years, this was already a major rivalry. Al Davis, a transplanted New Yorker, was the team owner and had even coached the club between 1963 and 1965. Johnny Rauch was the coach now, but everyone felt that Davis still called most of the shots and was the architect of the franchise. He was an intense competitor and would do anything to win. Matt Snell remembers how it had always been between the two teams, especially since he joined the Jets in 1965.

"The Raiders had some great teams and they seemed to make a habit of beating us in the closing seconds," Snell said. "It happened a number of times after I got to New York. One year we were beating them at Shea and their only chance was a Hail Mary pass in the final seconds. [Quarterback Daryle] Lamonica goes back and throws one high and deep into the end zone. Cornell Gordon was right there. He started to go up to grab the ball or bat it away, but he slipped and fell. Warren Wells just stood there and caught the ball for the winning touchdown.

"I always liked Al Davis, liked him very much. You would always see him standing there at the games, as if he was just waiting for something to happen. I think he sort of had Weeb and Walt Michaels psyched out. I remember one year we went out there to play them in Oakland. They were playing at a college stadium then and we went over to the field on a Saturday. It was a nice field, with bleachers, and thick, short, green grass. When we came back on Sunday for the game, the field was nothing but mud. Weeb and Walt went nuts because Davis told them the watering system had gone out of whack and soaked the field. I think it was Al's way of slowing down Don Maynard because his cornerbacks didn't have Don's speed.

"The mud hole he created was the equalizer. It deflated us to see the field like that and gave them a psychological advantage. Al could have cared less about that kind of mess, but we did, and they won the game. For a while, it seemed as if everything he did worked."

Don Maynard feels the team was real loose before the Oakland game, their confidence high. "I remember the day before the game," he said. "We were at our hotel and I jumped in the swimming pool, clothes and all. Someone challenged me to do it. I told them to put some money in my boots and said I'd do a gainer off the high board. Before the game Weeb said he was gonna fine me for jumping in the pool. But I know we went out there feeling we were going to play well and keep winning."

Surprisingly, the Jets were seven-and-a-half-point underdogs, but linebacker Larry Grantham felt the team was now poised to win. "I don't see any team in pro football that's in as good a position in their race as we are," he said. He also felt that defense had become the main ingredient to the New Yorkers' success. "The key to our loss in Oakland last year was when [strong safety] Jim Hudson got hurt. Now we have some depth in the secondary and we've got a defense, which is how great teams of the past, like the Giants and Bears, won championships."

That was true. Only when the Jets and Raiders played, the games rarely followed the script. The game would certainly be a test for quarterback Namath, who was beaten up pretty badly in the Jets' loss a year earlier. The Raiders often came at Namath hard, especially their two huge defensive ends, Ben Davidson and Ike Lassiter. Some felt the Raider defenders were cheap-shot artists, but Namath discounted that as a factor.

"Every team has a couple of guys who might give you a cheap shot," he said. "Heck, they even say it about a couple of our guys. Just say I think I like Oakland less than any other team in the league. Maybe it's because I've always been frustrated against them because we haven't been able to beat them much."

In the odd ways in which the public looks at professional athletes, especially those who defy convention, there was more interest in the drooping "Fu Manchu" mustache that Namath had been growing the past couple of weeks. It was still an era of the All-American, crew-cut sports hero, a few years before the Oakland A's baseball team decided to grow mustaches, and the unshaven hair sprouting on the quarterback's upper lip got more attention in some circles than the upcoming football game. "How dare he?," was the implication. "Now he's like the rest of the hippies." But Joe didn't look at it that way. It was just something he wanted to do and he did it. No way it would affect his passing arm or the way he would perform against the Raiders.

At game time there were 53,318 fans at the Oakland Coliseum to witness what would be another epic battle between the heated rivals. As usual, it was a brutal game, featuring vicious blocks, hard tackles, and a lot of penalties. There was no love lost between the two ball clubs. It was a tight battle all the way. At halftime, the Raiders held a scant, 14-12 lead. By the end of three it was 22-19, Oakland ahead, but still anyone's ball game. Namath was throwing well, beginning to look like his old self. Then early in the fourth period he proved it.

With the ball at midfield, Joe dropped back and looked for the fleet Maynard. He released long and Maynard caught it in full flight for a 50-yard touchdown strike, Joe's first touchdown pass in six games. Turner's kick gave the Jets a 26-22 lead, and when Turner booted a short, 12-yard field goal minutes later, the lead was up to 29-22. Now the game was about to get interesting. Oakland quarterback Daryle Lamonica, who had missed the previous game with knee and back problems, was showing no ill effects from his injuries. After Turner's field goal he quickly brought the Raiders back, and with 11:10 left on the clock, he passed 22 yards to Fred Biletnikoff for a score. The extra point tied it at 29. This was certainly not turning into a defensive struggle. It was beginning to look like a case of last one to score wins.

But the defenses tightened for the next several minutes. Finally, with time beginning to run down, the Jets began driving again. This was quickly turning into the most exciting game of the year. Once again Broadway Joe looked to Maynard, who had been his prime target the entire game. This time the redoubtable pair connected on a 42-yarder. After Namath released, he was blistered by Ben Davidson, and a roughing-the-passer penalty was tagged onto the play, bringing the ball down to the Oakland 18. But the Raiders didn't earn their reputation by giving in. Their defense tightened, and Jim Turner came on once again to boot his fourth field goal of the game, this one a 26-yarder that gave the Jets a 32-29 lead with just 65 seconds to play.

That's when the game took a strange turn. Not on the field, but for the millions of people watching it on an NBC national hookup. After Turner's field goal, the network broke for a commercial. When they returned, viewers on the east coast had to look twice. The picture was not of the Oakland Coliseum. Rather, it was the credits rolling for a new production of the classic story, *Heidi*. Fans looked twice, then checked to make sure their sets were on the right channel. Sure enough, the Jets-Raiders game was nowhere to be found. NBC had switched off from the game to the planned production of the classic children's story without a word of explanation. Suddenly, thousands of fans began deluging the NBC switchboard, demanding to see the end of the game. Of course, there were just 65 seconds left and the Jets had taken the lead. Chances were pretty good they simply held on to win it.

But hold the phone. What so many fans were missing was one of the most exciting and surprising finishes in AFL history. After the Jets' kickoff, Oakland brought the ball out to its own 22. Lamonica came on and promptly passed to halfback Charley Smith for a 20-yard gain. Tack on a facemask penalty and the ball was moved to the Jets' 43. On the very next play Lamonica again threw to the speedy Smith who beat rookie Mike D'Amato to the end zone for the go-ahead score. It had taken the Raiders just two plays and they had the lead. The kick made it 36-32, with 42 seconds left. D'Amato, by the way, was in the game because strong safety Jim Hudson had been tossed late in the third quarter for protesting several officials' calls that went against the Jets. Had Hudson been in the game, who knows what might have happened?

But it wasn't over yet. With Namath's arm and Maynard's speed, maybe the Jets could pull off a miracle of their own. The Raiders kicked off, Mike Eischied booting a squibbler in an effort to avoid a possible long runback. The bouncing kick did its job, bouncing in and out of Earl Christy's hands at the 15. Maybe Christy should just have fallen on the ball and let Namath take a few shots. Instead, he picked it up and tried to run as a horde of Raiders zeroed in on him. He tried to spin away from one tackler, bumped into one of his own blockers, then was hurled down, the ball coming loose as he fell. As it bounced around toward the goal line, special team player Preston Ridlehuber of the Raiders picked it up and ran it into the end zone. Just like that. The Raiders had scored twice in a span of 32 seconds to turn a 32-29 Jets lead into a 43-32 Oakland advantage. In another 33 seconds the game was over. The Raiders had done it again, beaten the Jets in the final seconds. And this one hurt.

"That was definitely the toughest loss of the year," Don Maynard said. "We had them down, and I had one of the best games of my career. It would have been a great win. Only it didn't happen. All we could hope for was to get another shot at them, and to do that it would have to be in the AFL title game."

Maynard did have a great game, catching 10 of Namath's passes for a club record 228 yards. In all, Namath had thrown for 381 yards, including his touchdown toss to Maynard, and had even run one in on a bootleg play. So Joe was back, but the team had lost.

And what about all those fans who suddenly found themselves watching *Heidi* instead of the exciting final 65 seconds of the football game? They screamed bloody murder, and the explanation from NBC didn't hold much water. NBC broadcast operations supervisor Dick Cline explained what happened this way.

"[Prior to the game being played] it was determined that *Heidi* would air at 7p.m.," he said. "If football wasn't over, we would still go to *Heidi* at seven. So I waited and I waited and I heard nothing. We came up to that last magic hour and I thought, 'Well, I haven't been given any counter order, so I've got to do what we agreed to do.'"

NBC continued to receive a slew of protests. Fans were outraged, especially when they found out what they had missed in those final seconds. A professional football game would never be pre-empted again, save for a national disaster. As *CBS Sports* executive producer Terry Ewert said in 1998, "[That game] put the AFL on the map. And it was an indicator of the importance of pro football."

One newspaper headline the next day gave the score as "Jets 32, Oakland 29, Heidi 14." And from that point on, the Jets-Raiders game from November 1968, has always been referred to in three simple words. *The Heidi game.*

Unfortunately, for the Jets, the *Heidi* game left the team with more serious questions. Larry Grantham had to leave with a concussion and missed the entire second half. Reserve fullback Billy Joe tore up a knee and was out for the season. Otherwise, only the team's pride was hurt. The game certainly didn't dash the Jets' title hopes. At 7-3, the team's remaining games were against San Diego, Miami twice, and Cincinnati. What the *Heidi* game did confirm was that the Raiders still seemed to have the Jets' number. And if the Jets continued on to the divisional title, there was a chance they would have to meet the Raiders once more. The good part was that the AFL title came this year would be played in the East Division city. No matter who they played, the Jets would have home-field advantage.

As for *Heidi*, the ramifications continued. It was noted that in addition to cutting away, NBC never returned to the game or gave the score until much later. About an hour and a half after the game ended, NBC rolled a graphic across the bottom of the screen that read, "Final score of the Jets-Raiders game was 43-32, Oakland. The Raiders scored two TDs in the last minute to overcome a three-point deficit. Further details on the 11 o'clock news." Needless to say, that didn't make too many fans happy, and NBC immediately promised the AFL it would never happen again.

There was still more fallout. During the game the Jets were penalized 13 times for 145 yards, a club record. In addition, they had several players tossed out. Safety Jim Hudson was tossed for protesting too many of the calls against the Jets, and defensive tackle John Elliott was banished after decking Oakland's center, Jim Otto. Elliott protested, saying he was goaded by Otto. And after the game, Hudson, Coach Ewbank and defensive coach Walt Michaels all criticized the officiating. That got NFL Commissioner Pete Roselle into the act. With the merger pending, Roselle already had taken over as boss of the AFL, as well. After reviewing all the complaints, he fined the Jets $2,000 (mild, by today's standards), for criticizing game officials. That wasn't all. Walt Michaels and Hudson were fined $150 each for berating game officials near the locker room, and both Hudson and Elliott received automatic $50 fines for being ejected.

One thing the Jets had to do was put the Oakland game behind them and quickly. The team would remain on the west coast for another meeting with the San Diego Chargers. San Diego was 8-2 and tied with the Raiders, just half a game behind Kansas City at 9-2. West coast trips had often proved disastrous for the Jets in the past and the crushing, last-minute loss to Oakland didn't help. Though another defeat probably wouldn't cost them the Eastern title, it would affect them psychologically if they advanced to the title game. So, in a sense, this one was a must.

The team would not quite be at full strength. Grantham was out. Verlon Biggs, who hurt a leg against Oakland, saw just limited duty, and Johnny Sample didn't start because he had the flu. Paul Crane, Carl McAdams, and Cornell Gordon started in their place. Even Namath had a light practice schedule because he was nursing a sore foot. These injuries are all part and parcel of a football season. At this point in the year, no one ever feels 100 percent. Teams only hope to avoid the major hurts that put players out for good or greatly limit their effectiveness. Namath would have to be throwing well against the Chargers because they would be countering with that quick-strike offense of their own, John Hadl throwing to Lance Alworth and Gary Garrison.

Before the game it was noted that the quick defensive line of the Jets had dumped opposing quarterbacks 33 times, second best in the AFL. The 317 yards in losses were a league best. Meanwhile, the offensive line had done a good job of protecting Namath and Babe Parilli, the Jets' quarterbacks having been dumped just 14 times, second lowest in the league. As it turned out, this was a game in which Joe Namath would begin to assert himself even more. It started early, in the first quarter.

With the ball at their own 13 early in the first quarter, Joe dropped back quickly, looking for Maynard. The Chargers blitzed, but Pete Lammons and Emerson Boozer both threw key blocks, giving Joe those extra precious seconds. Then he let fly, and the fleet Maynard ran under the perfectly thrown ball, taking it all the way to the end zone for an 87-yard touchdown. It set a Jets record and gave the New Yorkers the early lead. They were never challenged after that, leading by 27-7 at the half and cruising to an easy, 37-15 victory over a very good Chargers team. Maybe the real New York Jets had finally stood up.

Namath had a brilliant day, completing 17 of 31 passes for 337 yards and two scores before being relieved by Parilli in the final quarter. Maynard had his second straight huge day, grabbing six passes for a big 166 yards, Snell ran for more than 90, and the New York defense held the mighty Chargers to just 46 yards from scrimmage, while intercepting Hadl four times. San Diego didn't get inside the Jets' 40 until midway through the third period, and their first-half touchdown was the result of a 96-yard punt return by Leslie "Speedy" Duncan. Jim Turner kicked three more field goals, and with his three conversions now had 124 points for the season, breaking George Blanda's AFL kicking-only record of 118. His 31 field goals broke the pro record for three-pointers in a single season. It was an exciting win, the significance of which was stated by linebacker Al Atkinson.

"We made a west coast trip every years, playing Oakland and San Diego," Atkinson said. "In 1967 it ended badly in our final game New Year's Eve. Then we went to Oakland and lost the *Heidi* game, which was a very difficult defeat. I really thought we should have won it, but we didn't. It really would have been easy to lay down the following week against San Diego. But we were a bunch of ticked-off guys after the Oakland game, and we didn't want things to end up as they had in 1967, so we knew we had to bounce back. Remember, the Chargers were still the third or fourth best team in the league, and we beat them soundly. Take away that 90-yard punt return, and they scored just once. Before that, we had only beaten them in close games, but this time we went out and smashed them.

"That's when I began to think we could go even further than maybe we thought we could. Smashing them like that was a tonic for us. We were still a young team getting the thrill of winning game after game. Remember, *Heidi* was our only loss in six games. Many of the guys remember when we lost game after game, and we liked it this way much better. So I really think it was the San Diego game when a lot of us realized we could be something special."

Now the countdown began. The win over the Chargers put the Jets in direct line for an AFL East title. One more victory or another loss by the second-place Oilers would do it. Though a professional athlete should never be satisfied, and a division title is just step one, there had to be some excitement in that the Jets had never won one before, not since the team and the AFL came into existence in 1960. But this Jets team, while not looking ahead, was well aware of that progression, that winning the AFL East had to lead to more for the season to be a total success. And in the pro football world of 1968, a league title still left some unfinished business. Despite the pending merger, there was still that other league out there, and that final game that would soon be known as the Super Bowl.

As for the fans, their excitement was building, as well. The Jets had always played second fiddle to the Giants in New York, and fans of the older team often looked down their collective noses at the new kids on the block. Matt Snell remembers how it took time for the fans of the Jets to begin believing.

"I could sense that our fans were craving for a winner," Snell said. "I didn't have that feeling before, in earlier years, when we were up and down. Even as we edged closer to the title, I think many of our fans were still apprehensive, that they weren't convinced that we were for real. They kept wondering if there would be another letdown. Early in the season I didn't get the feeling that our fans anticipated that it would be our year. But you could feel the excitement building as the season wore on. You could feel it at Shea. The fans began honing in on us, starting to believe that we were the real deal."

On Thanksgiving Day, the Jets and their fans had more to celebrate than the usual holiday meal. The players and their families gathered at Shea Stadium for the annual team dinner only this year there was a Turkey Day game on television that occupied everyone's attention. The Chiefs were playing the Oilers, and if Kansas City won, that would clinch the division for the Jets. One of the veterans said that in a way, he'd almost like to see Houston win, and that a number of players agreed with him.

"The feeling on the club is that we'd almost like to see Houston win so we can wrap it up on our own Sunday," he said. "We'd rather do it that way than slip in through the side door."

Maybe. But a title is a title, and if it comes just a little bit easier, no harm done. The Chiefs, still fighting with Oakland for the AFL West, didn't let up and whipped Houston, 24-10. The Jets were in, and suddenly it didn't matter how it happened.

Everyone at Shea toasted the team's first ever crown. The coaching staff breathed a sigh of relief because with the division in tow they could now give a number of banged-up players some additional rest. The so-called walking wounded included Namath, Boozer, Biggs, and Grantham. But again, none of the injuries were serious.

Though the game that Sunday against the Miami Dolphins at Shea didn't have quite the same significance, the Jets nevertheless played well. At this point in a season, a team heading to the playoffs doesn't want to let down or lose momentum. Coach Ewbank, however, stayed true to his word and rested the players who were hurt. Namath started and played the first half. He fired a 54-yard touchdown strike to Maynard and a short, five-yarder to tight end Pete Lammons, leaving the field with the Jets leading, 14-10. Babe Parilli came in for the second half and, after the Dolphins took a 17-14 lead at the start of the final session, the veteran quarterback showed he still had some life in his 38-year-old arm.

Parilli threw two scoring passes to Maynard, of 47 and 25 yards, and then fired a 40-yarder to another vet, Bake Turner, to lead the Jets to a 35-17 victory. The defense had another stellar game, chasing Dolphins quarterback Bob Griese all over the place and dumping him five times. Jim Turner's five extra points gave him 129 points for the season, the ninth highest one-year total in pro football history. But the big story of the game was the veteran, Don Maynard. The 31-year-old veteran caught seven passes for 160 yards and three scores. That gave him a total of 9,332 total yards receiving, enabling him to pass Raymond Berry and become football all-time yardage receiving king. All of the yardage, except for 84 yards with the Giants in 1958, came with the Jets. And when someone said inferior league, Maynard took exception.

"I've played in both leagues, and I know the players hit just as hard here," he said. "I learned a long time ago that you don't measure success by achievements. You measure it by how many times a guy gets knocked down and gets backed up. I've been knocked down two or three times."

The Jets, too, had been knocked down several times, early in the season to weaker teams, and then in the heartbreaking defeat of the *Heidi* game. But like their redoubtable wide receiver, they had gotten back up. Now they had a 9–3 record and a division title. There were still two regular-season games remaining, but the next important date was December 29. That's when the team was scheduled to host the AFL title game. The only question that remained was would it be Oakland or Kansas City? At this point, the Jets felt they would be ready for anyone.

# 5

# THE AFL CHAMPIONSHIP GAME ... AND MORE

With two games yet remaining in the regular season, the end-of-the-year wrap-ups were already beginning. On December 8, it was announced that six Jets—three from the offensive unit and three from the defense—had been named to the AFL All-Pro Team as a result of balloting by a panel of sportswriters and sportscasters representing the ten cities in the league. Those named were Joe Namath at quarterback, wide receiver Don Maynard, center John Schmitt, defensive end Gerry Philbin, tackle John Elliott, and strong safety Jim Hudson. Not surprisingly, Weeb Ewbank was selected as Coach of the Year. While not everyone puts too much stock in all-pro teams, the voting showed the high level at which the Jets were playing, and the fact that three were from the offense and three were from the defensive side of the ball indicated balance.

But those six couldn't have done it alone. The Jets had obviously become a fine all-around team on both sides of the football. They went out to Shea the day after the voting was announced and easily defeated the Cincinnati Bengals, 27-14, with Coach Ewbank finding time for everyone to play. He couldn't completely rest the regulars because he wanted to keep the team sharp. Namath played the first half once again and left with a 17-7 lead, throwing touchdown strikes to Maynard and Sauer. Broadway Joe had definitely sharpened up his game since the early-season flurry of interceptions and subsequent touchdown drought. Veteran Babe Parilli finished up and played well once more, leading the club to its final 10 points. Snell and Boozer showed they were at full speed, and the defense made a dramatic four-play, goal-line stand at the end of the third quarter.

On the downside, five players emerged from the game with injuries. Maynard pulled his left hamstring on the second play of the final quarter. Then George Sauer left the game with a strained right elbow. Guard Dave Herman sprained an ankle, while Bob Talamini hurt his neck, and backup running back Bill Mathis aggravated a bruised shoulder. Injuries are always the x-factor, and no team can predict the health of its players from game to game. Any one play in a football game can end the season of any player. That's one of the risks of a high-contact sport. You can play a regular for just one play and lose him, so there's no way to shelter your stars. You've got to keep them sharp for the playoffs and let the chips fall where they may. Hopefully, none of the injuries were serious.

Now there was one game left, and the only mystery was who would be the Jets' opponent in the AFL title game. Both the Raiders and Chiefs were still in the running for the Western Division crown. Some news reports at the time said the Jets' players didn't care which team they faced. Bring on either one. But looking back, some of the players acknowledged there was a very heated rivalry that, in their hearts and minds, they felt they had to settle.

"We wanted to play the team that beat us, and that was Oakland in the *Heidi* game," linebacker Al Atkinson said. "Ever since I joined the Jets it seemed we always had close games with them, great games with them. The rivalry was very intense with all the games seeming to go down to the final minute. So that was our rivalry game. Even though the teams were based 3,000 miles apart, that was the one we wanted."

Defensive tackle John Elliott said pretty much the same thing. "Kansas City had a great team, but our rivalry with Oakland was more intense," he said. "From my standpoint, they had a pretty decent offensive line, one that got away with holding better than any team in the league. And there was a lot of animosity between Raiders owner and president Al Davis, and our defensive coach, Walt Michaels. I think the players picked up on it. We didn't like Oakland, and even today I still don't like Oakland."

It was still wait and see. There was one non-football diversion prior to the final regular-season game, and looking back now, it seems pretty ridiculous. Naturally, it involved Joe Namath. Some weeks earlier, the AFL had ordered all players to shave their facial hair and shorten long sideburns. Looking at today's athletes, a simple mustache or beard seems pretty tame. But the late 1960s were still not too far removed from the 1950s, when the image of the professional athlete was that of a clean-cut, smooth-shaven All-American boy. Most of the athletes complied, but Joe held out. Asked when he would comply with the league directive, he would smile and say, "Soon."

Finally, it was announced that Joe would shave the famous Fu Manchu, but would do it as a commercial for a razor company. Several other Jets had shaved with a specific razor, supposedly receiving a $250 fee for the endorsement. It was reported, however, that Joe's agent has been asking up to $10,000 for his famous client to shave using a specific product. Though terms for the unveiling of Namath's clean upper lip were not revealed, it was apparent that Joe had received a considerable fee from an electric razor company. Joe also spoke up about the league policy. Naturally, he wasn't for it.

"I didn't think it was any of their business," he said. "And I don't think it's the personal business of any other player. I don't understand why hair, all of a sudden, became bad. Things come in and they go. After all, the most perfect guy in the world had long hair and a beard."

Leave it to Joe to tell it like it is. But, then again, he had the platform and enough celebrity status to do it. In the eyes of most, his shaving of the mustache was done in a fun, lighthearted way, though he was certainly paid well for it. And he also managed to get his point across. It wouldn't be too many years down the road before athletes would have long hair, Afros, beards and mustaches. Like Joe said, things come and go. He was just a few years before his time.

The final game with Miami was a mere formality. The Dolphins put up little resistance, and the Jets won easily, 31-7. It was the New Yorkers' eighth win in their last nine games and gave them a fine 11-3 record for the year. As soon as it ended, the Jets defense learned it had finished number one in total defense and rushing defense in the AFL, and second in pass defense. The offensive unit was third in total offense. So the "D" had come up big as the tremendous pride the players had in themselves and in the unit as a whole paid off. In addition, eight Jets were chosen to start for the East in the postseason AFL annual East-West All-Star game. They were Namath, Maynard, Philbin, Sauer, Biggs, Herman, Hill, and Jim Turner.

There were also some fine individual performances. Matt Snell ran for 747 yards on 179 carries, an average of 4.2 yards a pop. Emerson Boozer followed with 441 yards of 143 carries. The two wide receivers had big years. George Sauer finished with 66 catches for 1,141 yards and three touchdowns. He averaged 17.3 yards a catch. As for Don Maynard, he grabbed 57 tosses for 1,297 yards and 10 scores. His per-catch average was 22.7, once again making him the premier deep threat in the league. Namath completed 187 of 380 passes for 3,147 yards. He threw for 15 touchdowns and had 17 passes picked off.

Joe's numbers were a bit misleading. Remember, 11 of his interceptions came in just two games, while he also had a six-game dirge with no touchdown tosses. In a number of late-season games he was absolutely brilliant with his A-game strongly in evidence. A healthy Namath would be a major asset in the playoffs. But there was still one thing left unsettled. Though the regular season had ended, the Jets still didn't know which team they would play in the AFL title game. Both Oakland and Kansas

City had finished with identical 12-2 records and had to meet in a playoff for the AFL title.

So on Sunday, December 22, the Jets were the only playoff team in both leagues with a day off. Oakland and Kansas City were meeting for the AFL Western Division title, and in the National Football League the four division winners had to meet to determine the conference champions. It would be Cleveland against Dallas and Baltimore against Minnesota in the older league. The Jets could sit back and watch the other teams bang each other around, while giving their own bumps and bruises an additional week to heal. It was a good situation for them.

What was expected to be a close, hard-fought game between the two reigning AFL powers turned into something quite different. Playing at home before more than 53,000 fans, the Raiders totally humiliated the proud Chiefs, 41-6, behind five touchdown passes by "Mad Bomber" Daryle Lamonica. As if they needed proof, the Jets knew they would not have a walk in the park. They felt they had an advantage in that the game would be held at Shea, where the weather was likely to be cold. Traditionally, warm-weather teams have had difficulty adjusting to late-season games when weather conditions were harsh. But the Raiders weren't just any warm-weather team. They always had a reputation for toughness, and it was unlikely that they would let sub-freezing temperatures deter them.

Most of the Jets had watched the Chiefs-Raiders game at John Schmitt's house in Merrick, New York, on Long Island. Admit it or not, they had to be impressed with the way the Raiders played.

"They were ready, really up for the game," Schmitt said. "Kansas City could not do anything against them, and I guess we were disappointed that the Chiefs didn't make a better game of it."

Al Atkinson was impressed by quarterback Lamonica. "When a guy is as hot as he was, he's tough to beat. [I think] Oakland was a little better prepared than Kansas City."

But the consensus seemed to be that Oakland was really the team they wanted. No matter how you cut the pie, the *Heidi* game was stuck in their collective craws. As John Schmitt said, "We owe them something from the game in Oakland." Al Atkinson saw nothing new in what the Raiders were doing, but acknowledged they would be tough to stop.

"They just stick to their usual game plan," he said. "They figure they're as good as you are, and they dare you to try and stop them. Kansas City couldn't. We have to figure we'll see the same Oakland team the Chiefs saw, and it's up to us to stop them. They're going to be ready for us ... but you can bet we'll be ready for them."

Don Maynard put it this way. "As soon as Oakland beat Kansas City, that became our biggest game. Not only did we have to beat them to win the AFL title, but that was also the game we had to win to get a chance to play the NFL champion. Even before we knew the outcome, I always felt Oakland would be our toughest game. They were always tough, an unbelievable team, and if we beat them, I couldn't imagine any other team being tougher."

With Oakland looming on the horizon, Coach Ewbank and his staff made a strategic move that would pay dividends, not only in the Oakland game, but also in what was to follow. Dave Herman remembers, because he was one of the players directly involved in a shakeup on the offensive line.

"Sam Walton, our rookie right tackle, had been making mistakes, and they were increasing by the end of the season," Herman said. "You've got to remember that one pro season is almost like two college seasons, and rookies sometimes wear out mentally, especially someone playing the offensive line. The week before we played Oakland, Weeb came up to me and said he wanted to make a change. He wanted me to move from guard to right tackle. 'I know you can do the job and won't make mistakes,' he assured me. It was a move he could make because we had the extra guard when we got Bob Talamini from Houston before the season started. With Bob and Randy Rasmussen at guard, we still had a great tandem. It would be up to me to hold up my end at tackle. If you remember, Oakland had a huge defensive end in Ike Lassiter. Weeb must have feared that Walton wouldn't be able to handle him. He felt, if nothing else, I could keep Lassiter from getting to Joe.

"I always felt we had a great line. I'm not necessarily talking strength, but quickness and intelligence. We didn't get the notoriety with Joe behind us and playing in the AFL, but if you look at what happened from start to finish in 1968, it was a great year for us up front."

That was the only major adjustment the Jets made. Fortunately, everyone was healthy and ready. This was expected to be an epic battle, and there would be no excuses. The two teams were obviously very evenly matched—two great passing attacks, two great defensive units, and big play capability everywhere. The Jets hoped one of the factors would be the weather at Shea. When they practiced several days before the game, there was a brutally cold wind swirling about. Had it been game day, that would have made it difficult for everyone.

"The wind factor is the biggest thing," Namath explained. "The rain and cold doesn't bother you nearly as much as the wind." Namath explained that the best way to counter the wind was to throw tight spirals. "If you throw it the least bit wobbly, the wind takes the ball and you can forget about it."

Finally, it was game time, the biggest game in the Jets' brief history. The weather wasn't too bad for the end of December, cold but no rain or snow, and tolerable winds. Dave Herman, who was playing tackle for the first time, remembers what happened the first time the Jets had the football.

"I told Joe in the huddle to run the first play right over me," Herman explained. "He looked at me and said, 'What?' I told him I would set the tone for the game, and I wanted to do it right away. Joe agreed and called 18-straight, a run, right over the top of me. I got down in my position and then hit big Ike Lassiter harder than I had ever hit anyone in my life. Just as I expected, he got mad, real mad. The hit had served its purpose.

It took Ike's mind off Joe, as well as Snell and Boozer's running, because all he wanted to do after that was annihilate the obnoxious little tackle in front of him. Me. That's what I wanted, for him to get so mad that he just wanted to go through me."

It also set the usual physical tone for the game, but in the first quarter it was the Jets showing more finesse. The New Yorkers drove early and with less than four minutes gone, Joe dropped back and whipped a 14-yard touchdown pass to Don Maynard to give the Jets the early lead. Turner's kick made it 7-0. Midway through the quarter Turner added a 33-yard field goal to make the score 10-0, and it remained that way the rest of the period. But no one, not the players nor the fans, thought this one was in the bag. They all knew the Raiders too well. Sure enough, Oakland came back early in the second when Lamonica hit Fred Biletnikoff for a score from 29 yards out. George Blanda's kick made it 10-7. Then Turner and Blanda exchanged field goals before the half, the Jets leaving the field for intermission with a slim, 13-10 lead. That set the stage for what was to follow.

Midway through the third quarter, the Raiders began driving. A touchdown would give them the lead, but this time the Jets' defense came up big. Living up to his reputation, Lamonica threw 37 yards to Biletnikoff and then completed a 40-yarder to Warren Wells, giving the Raiders a first down at the Jets' six. Two tries by Charlie Smith brought the ball to the three. Then, on third down, fullback Hewritt Dixon went over the middle, but Al Atkinson and Jim Hudson combined to stop him at the one. The Raiders didn't want to risk it on fourth down and settled for a game-tying field goal by Blanda.

Namath and the Jets responded immediately. Starting from their own 20, the New Yorkers drove 80 yards in 14 time-consuming plays, the final 20 coming on a Namath-to-Lammons pass for the go-ahead score. Turner's kick made it 20-13, and that's the way the third quarter ended. The ebb and flow of the game was beginning to take a familiar turn. There probably wasn't a single person watching who A) could predict who the eventual winner would be and, B) didn't think that they were in store for a very dramatic ending, perhaps a la the *Heidi* game. With 15 minutes to play, the excitement was building.

Early in the fourth quarter, the Raiders showed again why they had such a resilient and great team. Lamonica completed a long, 57-yarder to Biletnikoff, bringing the ball to the Jets' 11-yard line. Oakland was now poised to tie the game, but once again the Jets defense showed why it was ranked number one in the AFL. On first down, the Raiders tried to run with Charley Smith, but linebacker Ralph Baker used his speed to throw Smith for a one-yard loss. When Lamonica went back to the air on the next two plays, Randy Beverly and Jim Hudson were there to knock the ball away. Once again, the Jets had held the Raiders in close and Oakland had to settle for a 20-yard Blanda field goal, bringing the score to 20-16.

It was at this point when Namath made his only mistake of the game. After the ensuing kickoff, the Jets had the ball at their own 22 and Joe tried to throw a sideline pass to Maynard on his left. Only this time he underthrew, and Raider cornerback George Atkinson dashed in front of Maynard, got the ball at the 37 and ran it all the way down to the Jets' 5-yard line. It was Namath himself who drove Atkinson out of bounds. But this time the Raiders wouldn't be denied. On the first play, halfback Pete Banazak ran it into the end zone for the score. Blanda's kick gave the Raiders their first lead of the day, 23-20, with just 8:20 left in the game. Was the Jets' dream about to disappear under the *Pride and Poise* that was the Raider's banner?

As the Raiders got set to kick off, the crowd of more than 62,000 fans at Shea had fallen strangely silent. The interception, return, and resultant touchdown appeared to have taken the heart out of them. It was as if they felt the *Heidi* game was happening all over again, that somehow the Raiders always seemed to find a way to win. Earl Christy took the kickoff three yards deep in the end zone and made a gutsy, battling run out to the 32. Out came Namath and the offensive unit, the entire season perhaps riding on this next drive. A three-and-out, and the

Raiders would surely be in the driver's seat. Only Joe Namath wasn't about to let that happen.

On the first play he immediately dropped back and hit Sauer for a ten-yard gain to the 42. Next came a play that Jets fans will remember to this day and, according to Don Maynard was set up early in the game.

"I went up to Namath some time after the game started and said to him, 'Joseph, I got a long one when you need it.' After they took the lead Joe leaned down in the huddle and said, 'Okay, we're gonna go for it. No one hold.'"

Maynard lined up wide and at the snap took off. He ran straight down the left side of the field, George Atkinson to his inside. He figured Joe would throw the *fade* over his outside shoulder. Joe backpedaled, saw Maynard and let the ball go deep. Maynard describes what happened next.

"I'm running straight down that railroad track with the defender inside me. I saw the ball and began reaching up to catch it to the outside, at about 10 o'clock. At the last second, the wind caught the ball and pulled it back inside. Somehow, I adjusted quickly, stayed with it, and caught it at about 2 o'clock. I was pushed out at the six-yard line and always said it was the greatest catch I ever made. Years later, I saw Steve Sabol's film of great catches and it was ranked number two."

Maynard's great catch brought the crowd and the Jets back to life. Now the ball was at the six and Namath wasted no time. He didn't want to risk a fumble on a running play or give the Raiders the advantage of a goal-line stand. He dropped back immediately, looked the field over, then fired into the end zone. Maynard again. Touchdown!

"When Joe called the play in the huddle, I was the number-one receiver," Maynard said. "But just as the ball was snapped, the Raiders defense changed. Suddenly, I'm number four. That's how quickly things can change. Joe looked at Sauer, then Lammons, then Billy Mathis, and finally to me on a delayed route, a post, go in, curl around and come back. Joe released quickly. The pass was low, but I managed to reach down and get it."

Turner's kick made it 27-23, the Jets regaining the lead, and Shea Stadium erupted once more. But with the Raiders, it's never over until it's over, and the defense came on the field knowing they still had to hold up their end. With 7:47 left, there was still plenty of time. With its back against the wall, Oakland was an even more dangerous team. Led by Lamonica, they drove downfield, finally getting a first down at the Jets' 26. But then the Jets defense, which had come up so big all year, stiffened again, and three plays produced no yardage. A field goal wouldn't help at this point, so the Raiders decided to go for it on their fourth down. Again Lamonica dropped back looking to put the ball in the end zone. Only this time Verlon Biggs beat Raider tackle Bob Svihus to the outside and nailed Lamonica for a six-yard loss.

The Jets got the ball but couldn't kill the clock. They had to punt, and the Raiders then had yet another chance. Again Lamonica proved tough to stop. Starting at the 15, the quarterback threw 24 yards to Biletnikoff, bringing the ball to the 39. Then he hit the fleet Warren Wells for 37 more, and when Jim Hudson was called for piling on, the ball was advanced all the way to the Jets' 12. First down. Now Lamonica and the Raiders could taste victory. On first down, Lamonica tried to throw a little swing pass to halfback Smith toward the sideline. However, the ball went behind Smith and started rolling toward the sideline.

"Once the ball bounced away, most of the Raiders just stood there. They all thought it was an incomplete forward pass," said Matt Snell. "I remember seeing Lamonica just standing there looking at it. But you've got to play until the whistle blows. Only Ralph Baker had the sense to pick it up."

Baker picked it up, all right, and took off, running 70 yards, all the way to the end zone. The fans roared, the Raiders were protesting, and for a minute or so, confusion reigned. Then it was sorted out. Because the ball was thrown backwards, behind Smith, it was ruled a lateral, not an incomplete forward pass as the Raiders argued and hoped. That meant it was a free ball and, as it turned out, the pivotal play of the game. But it wasn't a touchdown. The rules said that a recovered lateral could not be advanced. Strange rule, maybe, but the ball was brought back to the Jets' 30. The good news was that it had changed hands.

Back in the driver's seat, the Jets stayed on the ground, but again couldn't run out the clock. When Oakland got it back, however, there were just 45 seconds left. This time they couldn't move it and the clock ran out with the ball still on the Raiders' side of the 50-yard line. The Jets had won it, 27-23. They were AFL champions. At last!

The game had really been an offensive explosion. Lamonica, for example, completed 20 of 47 passes for 401 yards, while Namath hit on 19 of 49 for 266 yards. Both passers were well under a 50-percent completion percentage showing how often they had thrown downfield, typical of the wide-open game of the AFL. Biletnikoff caught seven for 190 yards, while Don Maynard grabbed six for 118 yards. The Jets, however, dominated on the ground. Snell had 71 rushing yards, while Boozer had 51, part of a 144-yard rushing attack. By contrast, Raiders runners gained just 50 yards. The quickness of the Jets defensive line and linebackers was too much for them. But in the end all the stats could be thrown out the window. The bottom line was the "W", and that belonged to the Jets.

The victory had the city of New York delirious. Fans (and when a team wins there are five times as many of them) had a sports champion during a troubled year for both the city and the entire country. The Jets were literally the toast of the town. Not only had their team taken the AFL championship, it would now have a chance to represent the city and the league in the biggest game of all, the Super Bowl. Though the game was still officially called the AFL-NFL World Championship Game, it had been referred to as the Super Bowl by increasing numbers of people ever since Kansas City Chiefs owner Lamar Hunt suggested it. Hunt got the idea from his young daughter who told him one day that she was playing with a "super ball." In another year, the name would be official.

But the Jets players still weren't thinking about that. They were still reveling in winning the AFL title and coming to the realization that they had bonded together as an outstanding football team and had beaten the archrival Raiders.

"I'll tell you the biggest thing we have going for us," said Gerry Philbin. "We have so much confidence in Joe and in our offense. We make mistakes on defense. We made a lot of them today. But Namath is unbelievable. He comes right back. He came to the sideline after the interception and he said, 'We'll get it back ... We'll get it back.' And he did."

Larry Grantham, one of three original Jets (Don Maynard and Bill Mathis were the other two), was ecstatic over the victory. He had waited a long time. "Today is probably the greatest day I've ever lived," he said, after the game. "Even though we gave up points on defense, when we got behind, our offense came back and picked us up."

One of the reporters in the locker room asked Namath if he felt the team would come back after they fell behind. The quarterback answered without hesitation.

"If you don't feel you can come back, you don't belong on that field," he said.

For Matt Snell, the game meant something a little extra because of their opponent they had just vanquished. "We felt extra good because we exorcized the demons that were the Raiders."

John Elliott remembers being exhausted after the game. "It was a cold and nasty day," he said, " and we all left everything we had out on that field."

But perhaps it was Namath who was the first, during the locker room celebration, to throw up a word of caution. Asked if the victory over the Raiders was the biggest thrill of his life, Joe answered, "Yeah ... yeah, I guess so." Then he paused for a second, as if thinking about something, and quickly added, "Not yet, baby, not yet."

There was another event happening on that December 29 afternoon. This one took place at Municipal Stadium in

Cleveland, where more than 80,000 fans gathered at the huge old stadium to watch their team, the Cleveland Browns, play a football game. That afternoon, the Browns looked totally over-matched, boys playing against men. For in the National Football League championship game, they were totally beaten by the Baltimore Colts, 34-0. For the Colts it was the culmination of a year that saw them win 13 games and lose only one. Baltimore had taken the mantle from the Green Bay Packers. They would be representing the NFL in the biggest game of the year, now called Super Bowl III, where they would meet the upstart Jets. The stage was set.

# 6
# A GUARANTEE
# FOR THE AGES

The balance of power had not really changed in the National Football League. Just one super team was gone. The great Green Bay Packer dynasty had given way to age and the retirement of coach Vince Lombardi. It had been pretty much a foregone conclusion right from the beginning of the season that the Packers would not emerge as champions in 1968 and thus would not be back to defend their first two Super Bowl titles. With Lombardi and the Packers as the NFL representative in such a huge game, a game that was being played for league pride and bragging rights, everyone was pretty confident the old guard would prevail. No way, football pundits reasoned, would Lombardi let one of his teams be humbled by these upstarts from the American Football League. They were right. The Pack played flawless football and pulled away from both Kansas City and Oakland in the second half of their games to win both easily.

Now, another team would have to take the NFL flag into battle. Among the candidates expected to battle for the crown the Packers had abdicated were the Dallas Cowboys, Cleveland Browns, Minnesota Vikings, Los Angeles Rams, and the Baltimore Colts. When the Cowboys finished the regular season with a 12-2 record, many thought they would become the heir apparent. After all, they had come within a whisker of defeating the Packers in the NFL title game the year before, the infamous Ice Bowl. Tom Landry's club was stacked on both offense and defense, but then they were upset by the Cleveland Browns (10-4), 31-20, in the Eastern Conference title game. In the West, Baltimore (13-1) beat out the Rams (10-3-1) in the regular season, then toppled Minnesota (8-6), 24-14, to take their conference title. Then the Jets, after winning the biggest game in franchise history, watched Baltimore finish off Cleveland in devastating fashion, 34-0. So it would be the Colts that would be coming to Miami to meet the Jets in Super Bowl III.

When fans saw the early line on the game, the point spread, they couldn't believe it. The Colts were being installed as 17-point favorites, a prohibitive number. Even the Packers hadn't been that kind of favorite. Green Bay was given a 13 1/2-point advantage over the Chiefs in the first Super Bowl and a year later was looked upon as 13 points better than the Raiders. Did the so-called experts really think the Colts were that good ... or was it that they considered the Jets that bad? It was one of the biggest point spreads in championship game history.

Just what kind of team were the 1968 Baltimore Colts? The team was still coached by Don Shula, who had taken Weeb Ewbank's job back in 1963. Shula was considered a boy wonder then but had matured quickly into a fine coach. That was irony number one. Shula would be coaching against Ewbank, the man he replaced. Other than that, the Colts were a veteran team whose symbolic leader was quarterback John Unitas, the man who had helped put Baltimore and pro football on the map back in 1958 when he led the Colts to that great sudden-death title game against the Giants. Since that time, Unitas's stature continued to grow, to the point where he was already being called the best ever at his position.

In addition, Unitas was considered the anti-Namath, a quarterback and athlete a generation removed, a laconic, crew-cutted throwback to an earlier time. Unlike Namath, Unitas wasn't talkative and shunned the spotlight. He was a quiet leader who commanded respect among his teammates and inspired fear with his opponents. Before big games, various Colts players used to say a few words to inspire the team. Whenever someone looked to Unitas to say something, the reply was said to always be the same.

"Talk is cheap," Unitas would say. "Let's play."

There was one problem. Unitas had been injured for much of the 1968 season. A bad elbow had relegated him to the bench, then to part-time duty. The word was that he would be ready to play in Super Bowl III, but only if needed. Instead, the Colts had turned to veteran Earl Morrall, who had spent the 1967 season backing up Fran Tarkenton with the Giants. Coming over to the Colts, Morrall was expected to play the same role behind Unitas. Pressed into duty after Johnny U. was hurt, all he did was become the NFL Player of the Year. Morrall had completed 182 of 317 passes for 2.909 yards, 26 touchdowns against just 17 interceptions. In addition, he completed some 57 percent of his passes, compared to just 49 percent for Namath. Looking strictly at the numbers, Morrall appeared to have had a better year.

Veteran Tom Matte was the Colts' leading rusher, having amassed 662 yards on 183 carries, an average of just 3.6 a tote. The team didn't have a breakaway threat as they did with Lenny Moore some years earlier. Huge tight end John Mackey was the leading receiver with 45 catches for 644 yards and five scores. Wide receiver Willie Richardson caught 37 for 698 yards and eight touchdowns, while veteran Jimmy Orr grabbed 29 for 743 yards and six scores. Orr averaged 25.6 yards a catch and was the team's primary deep threat.

The team had a solid, though not huge offensive line, but in the eyes of many, the heart and soul of the Colts was their defense. There were a number of stars, beginning with huge defensive end Bubba Smith, who was 6'8" tall and weighed 320 pounds. Bubba was also fast for his size and could be a one-man wrecking crew. Middle linebacker Mike Curtis played like a wild man, leading the defense with his emotion and hitting like a Mac truck. Lenny Lyles, Bobby Boyd, and Rick Volk led a very savvy defensive backfield and the team had a number of hard-nosed roughnecks like defensive tackle Billy Ray Smith. Most experts felt this Baltimore defense would chew up and spit out the Jets' offense, while Baltimore's well-oiled offense wouldn't make mistakes and would score enough points to win easily. But a 17-point spread? That seemed almost inconceivable. Yet Las Vegas oddsmaker Jimmy "The Greek" Snyder said that each unit (running backs, wide receivers, offensive line, defensive line, linebackers, defensive backs) on the Colts was superior to that of the Jets. The only position there was a standoff, according to The Greek, was at quarterback, where Namath and Morrall were even.

Explaining the inordinately high point spread to reporters, The Greek put it this way, "Four points because the Colts' offensive line was better than the Jets'; four points because the Colts' linebackers were better, four points because their cornerbacks were better, two points for better running backs, and three points for the NFL mystique and Don Shula's coaching." So many people accepted this as gospel that by kickoff time, betters has pushed the odds to 19 1/2 points.

Looking back over some 35 years, it really seems as if nearly the entire pro football world, including a whole phalanx of "experts," had been seduced by the myth of NFL superiority. Sure, Green Bay had won the first two Super Bowls rather easily, but both games were close in the first half until Kansas City and Oakland began making mistakes. Yet very few people seemed to consider the fact that maybe the elite teams in the AFL were getting very close to the NFL's best. The AFL still played a more wide-open brand of football. Many of its quarterbacks, like Namath and Lamonica, threw downfield and deep, accounting for completion percentages of less than 50 percent. A quarterback like Kansas City's Len Dawson didn't, so his percentage was higher, closer to that of NFL passers.

The Jets, however, never considered themselves underdogs at all, let alone 17 points under. During the locker room celebration after their title game victory over Oakland, cornerback Johnny Sample was the first to say it. Remember, Sample had been in the NFL and had played for the Colts. So maybe he wasn't talking completely out of his hat when he said, "The way this ball club is playing now, we *will* win the Super Bowl."

There would be a much more public "guarantee" of the Jets' success a short time later, but before detailing the way Joe Namath acted when the team arrived in Miami to prepare for the game, let's stop and look at something else, the way some of the Jets' players really felt about the upcoming game and their opponents. These opinions, detailed by the players today, were not really publicized back then, but putting them in the context of the prevalent thinking in January of 1969, it really appears that the entire pro football world was not looking at the two teams fairly, unable to put aside the preconceived notion that the NFL had to be the better league simply because it had been in existence so much longer.

As a prelude, Namath made one statement in Miami that raised a swirl of controversy. He said that there were four or five quarterbacks in the AFL who were better than Earl Morrall. He included among them himself, Len Dawson, Daryle Lamonica, John Hadl, and Bob Griese of Miami. Then he added, "I study quarterbacks. I can assure you the Colts have never had to play against quarterbacks like we have in the AFL."

Knowing Namath and the way he liked to talk, most took his remarks as those of a cocky guy just blowing smoke. Okay, let's dismiss the four other quarterbacks for now and just stick with Namath. According to Don Maynard, who should know since he was on the receiving end of so many Namath passes, Joe offered up something that every team in the NFL should fear.

"When Joe first came up, I used to challenge him," Maynard said. "I used to say you can't touch the ball from the center and throw it out to me quick enough. So he began taking the ball from center, turning and throwing it early. The minute I turned my body and my head, I wanted the ball there to catch. The secret was to throw it early, something many quarterbacks are never taught. Joe got rid of the ball, boom, fast.

"If a passing attack is run right, a quarterback should be able to lineup in a shotgun formation and throw the ball so quickly that he doesn't even need an offensive line. If he throws it quickly, unblocked lineman won't reach him in time. Joe didn't line up in the shotgun, but he was never sacked by a safety or corner blitz. That's because he backpedaled when he retreated from center. He could backpedal faster than most quarterbacks who went sideways. He really worked at it. By backpedaling, he could release the ball quickly and accurately, and could also see the guy coming from the blind side. Sure, Joe and I were great on long passes, but he could whip that ball out to the sideline faster than anyone."

Why was that significant? Simple. In the eyes of the Jets, Joe could not only throw a pass that most NFL quarterbacks couldn't throw, but one that the Colts wouldn't be able to defend. "I remember Vince Lombardi saying that no team would beat his Packers except one that had a quarterback who could throw a great out," Al Atkinson said. "There wasn't one NFL quarterback who could throw that kind of out, but Joe could take a couple of steps back and throw a 30-yard dart to the outside. I think even Lombardi would have been leery if he had to go up against Joe and his quick arm."

But Namath wasn't the only reason. There was a two-week break between the championship games and the Super Bowl, and once the Jets reached Miami and began watching films of the Colts and reading the papers, the players all began reaching a different conclusion than was being predicted for them. Matt Snell remembers looking at the game from several different angles and always reaching the same conclusion.

"Baltimore played a zone defense," Snell said, "and they did that because they felt their cornerbacks couldn't hold up in man-to-man coverage. With them in a zone, we felt we could pick them apart. We had faced zones in the AFL week in and week out, and there are always certain holes and weaknesses. If the receivers go to an area and stop, we knew Joe could hit them. The purpose of the zone is to stop you from going deep, but that leaves a lot of areas under the zone open, 12, 15, 18 yards down field. We also knew Baltimore wouldn't change for us. They had played zone all year, then annihilated Cleveland, so we knew their ego wouldn't allow them to change.

"When we went to Florida, Weeb assigned us rooms for the first time. [Emerson] Boozer I roomed together and talked about the game a lot. We read in the local paper that the Colts were rated better than us at every single position but quarterback. They rated Joe [Namath] and Earl Morrall even. Well, I had played with their halfback, Tom Matte, at Ohio State my sophomore year, and I told Emerson there was no way Matte was better than he was, and I knew their fullback, Jerry Hill, wasn't better than me. I think things like that helped us psychologically.

"We also felt we had an advantage playing in the heat of Miami. We were the younger team. They had a number of players over 30, and we were hoping for hot weather because we felt they would be the ones who got tired. After a long season, the heat in Miami has to affect you. We felt we had to play good, solid, basic football. If Joe could avoid interceptions and we could establish a running game, we would be fine. We didn't want to put Joe in a position where he felt he had to win the game and begin throwing it all over the place. We also couldn't allow their defense to get momentum. Mike Curtis, their middle linebacker, was usually all over the place, and big Bubba was a great defensive end. We knew, however, that Dave Herman would fight him tooth and nail, but if you just stand back there and pass, and do nothing else, Bubba is gonna get you."

How did Dave Herman plan to stop a behemoth like Bubba Smith? Having moved from guard to tackle for the Oakland game, where he neutralized Ike Lassiter, Herman prepared very carefully for Bubba.

"Bubba was a freshman when I was a senior at Michigan State," Herman said. "We had run into each other, but didn't really know each other. What I did know was that Bubba was very athletic despite his great size. He was big, strong, quick, and fast. He had all the skills and outweighed me by about 70 pounds. So I devised a plan to get into him right away. At 6'8", there was a big gap in his three-point stance between his front foot and back foot. My plan was to attack him while he was moving that back foot forward. Make him go through me to get to the quarterback or running back. Get underneath and right into his middle. It worked great. I would attack on both running and passing plays when he had that back foot moving. The interesting thing is that all he had to do was move off the ball half a yard, either to the outside or backward, and it would have made it easier because I couldn't have gotten to him as quickly. But he never adjusted."

John Elliott said the defense also devised a very solid plan to stop the Colts. "The Colts averaged about 30 points that year," he said. "Yet we knew we had a better defense than they had offense. We ran an overshifted line that they hadn't seen before. If their tight end was on the right, they had just the guard and tackle on the left. Verlon would line up outside the shoulder of the tackle on the right. I'd be head up over center with Al Atkinson right behind me. They didn't know which way I was going. If they had two guys block me, then there would be just one on Al. If I went left, I tied up both the right guard and center. If the center hesitated a second to watch me, it gave Al a step advantage to go where he wanted to go. We relied on our quickness and always got that half step. That put us in pretty good shape right away. We also knew they had two quarterbacks who couldn't throw a 20-yard out and who couldn't throw deep downfield with any zip on the ball. So if we shut down their running game early and made them pass, we were pretty sure we had them."

As the game approached, the Jets' confidence grew. The more they watched the films, the more they scoffed at the 17-point spread. In fact, some began to think that maybe it should have been the other way around.

"The 17-point underdog thing never even entered my mind," Don Maynard said. "I never even thought about who the favorite was, but I knew this: I had been playing professional football for ten years, and after watching the films, I knew that if we didn't make any mistakes I could guarantee that we were gonna kick these guys. I was more confident in that game than any other game I ever played in my life. I've thought about it many times since. I never had any doubt. But the key was not making any mistakes.

"Even though they had beaten Cleveland, 34-0, I just couldn't see them doing that to us. The way I saw it, we had as great a passing attack as any team in either league. We had a fine running attack, a great offensive line, and the best defense in the league. Then there was Jim Turner, a clutch field goal kicker who had set a scoring record. We're watching film all week, and at one point Pete Lammons just flat out told Weeb, 'If you don't stop showing this film we're gonna get overconfident.' Other guys guaranteed a win in that same meeting. The defensive backs said they would intercept five passes. Honestly, that's how confident we became before the game even started."

There was one other guarantee that would make headlines. It came from—who else?—none other than Joe Namath, who got into an after-hours debate with Colts place kicker Lou Michaels, brother of Jets coach Walt. After that incident received widespread publicity, Broadway Joe went one step further. Three days before the game he appeared before the Miami Touchdown Club and brashly announced to the audience, "The Jets will win on Sunday, I guarantee it."

That pronouncement made headlines. Where did Namath get the nerve? Johnny U. would never do something like that, but Namath loved to stir the drink. Many felt that he had given the Colts the perfect blackboard fodder to further motivate them. Were the Jets worried that their quarterback had gone too far? Not really.

"Weeb put newspapers under our doors every morning," Matt Snell said, "so we all saw right away what Joe had said. No, it didn't bother us at all. The way I saw it, if Baltimore needed something like that to get them psyched, they were in trouble."

Namath loved being the center of attention and loved to get reactions to the things he said. Did it get the Colts to thinking? Probably, at least just how much they wanted to flatten him on the field. Coach Shula tried to keep things cool. But he picked up on Namath's statement that there were four or five AFL quarterbacks better than Earl Morrall.

"I don't know how Namath can rap Earl," Shula said. "After all, Earl's number one in the NFL, he's thrown all those touchdown passes (26), he's thrown for a great percentage without using those dinky flare passes to build up his average, and he's been voted Player of the Year. But, I guess Namath can say whatever the hell he wants."

Then, however, the Baltimore coach praised Broadway Joe's ability and showed that his scouts had done a good job. For in his praise, he mentioned some of the very qualities Joe's teammates had cited as reasons Baltimore wouldn't be able to stop him.

"He's a helluva thrower and a fine quarterback," the Colts' coach said. "He has a quick release and sets up with good depth. Namath backpedals more than most quarterbacks in our league and that helps give him such good vision for spotting his second and third receivers. He doesn't get caught with the ball very often, and the big problem against Namath is just trying to get to the guy.

"He has what we call fast feet. [That gives] him the ability to move back from the center quickly, and once he's in the pocket he can move from side to side to get out of the rushing lanes. And he knows where to go with the football."

So the stage was set. As expected, Earl Morrall would be starting for the Colts, but John Unitas said he was ready if needed. There were 75,389 fans at the Orange Bowl on January 12, 1969, to watch the third championship meeting between the AFL and the NFL, and at game time, the Colts remained the overwhelming favorite. Many just felt the men from Baltimore would simply push the Jets all over the field. The don't-make-mistakes theme was repeated by Coach Ewbank who, in a final reminder, told his team;

"Don't lose your poise."

Finally, the moment of truth had arrived.

Because he had played in the NFL and for the Colts, the Jets sent John Sample out for the coin toss in place of Namath. There,

# MIRACLE YEAR, 1969
## AMAZING METS AND SUPER JETS

Quarterback Joe Namath was undoubtedly the Jets' leader in 1968. All eyes were on the familiar number 12 when the Super Bowl began, especially after he "guaranteed" that his New York Jets would defeat the 17-point-favorite Baltimore Colts. *Icon SMI*

With a strong offensive line geared to protect him, Namath could pick apart any team with his powerful right arm and lightning release. Several members of the Jets were confident of victory because they felt Broadway Joe could throw passes not normally seen by NFL defenders. *AP/WWP*

Early in Super Bowl III the Jets established a running game that would help open the field for Namath's passes. Here the quarterback hands the ball to fullback Matt Snell (41), who would end up with a then-Super Bowl record of 121 rushing yards. *Icon SMI*

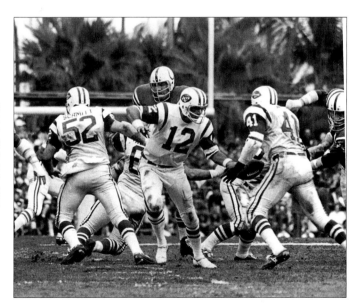

# MIRACLE YEAR, 1969
## AMAZING METS AND SUPER JETS

Jets tackle Dave Herman had the unenviable task of keeping mammoth Colts defensive end Bubba Smith away from Namath. This is one of the few times Smith (78) almost got to Namath, but Joe had already thrown the ball. On the whole, Herman was able to effectively shut down the fearsome Smith. *AP/WWP*

As Namath drops back to pass, tackle Herman once again stops Bubba Smith in his tracks with a hard block. Unlike many NFL quarterbacks, Namath normally backpedaled when he dropped back, allowing him to see the entire field and get the pass off more quickly. His teammates said he could backpedal faster than most quarterbacks could retreat sideways. *Icon SMI*

Throughout Super Bowl III, the Jets continued to successfully mix the running and passing games. Here Namath hands off to running back Billy Mathis (31) as veteran guard Bob Talamini (61) prepares to throw a block. *AP/WWP*

Baltimore's frustration continued to grow as the game progressed because they could not get to Namath. Once again, Namath gets the pass off before the Colts defenders can nail him for a sack. *AP/WWP*

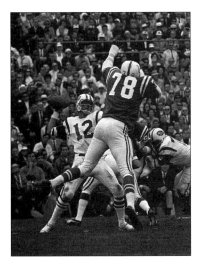

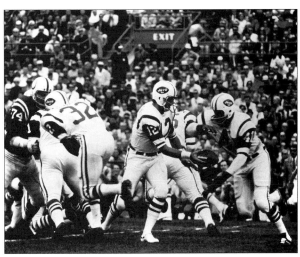

A fraction of a second too late again, the 6'8" Bubba Smith leaps in the air in an attempt to block a Namath pass. Tackle Herman has said that Smith never adjusted to his blocking technique and he was able to keep the NFL star off Namath all afternoon, but it wasn't an easy task. *AP/WWP*

The Jets' well-oiled running attack kept going off-tackle and gaining yards. As left guard Talamini blocks Colts tackle Billy Ray Smith (74), halfback Emerson Boozer (32) prepares to throw a block of his own to help spring Snell (41) for yet another good gain. *AP/WWP*

# MIRACLE YEAR, 1969
## AMAZING METS AND SUPER JETS

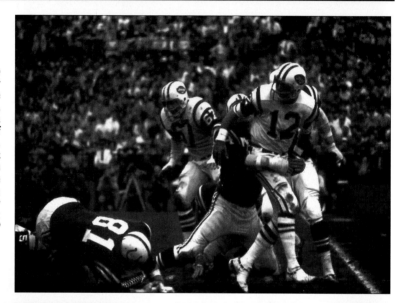

The Jets serve up more frustration for Baltimore. As was the case all afternoon, Namath was always a few seconds ahead of his adversaries. Though a Colt defender finally got his arms around Joe, the ball was already in flight and headed for an open receiver. *AP/WWP*

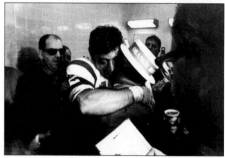

**ABOVE:** The final 16-7 score enabled the Jets to become the first American Football League team to defeat an NFL rival. Here, MVP Namath embraces his father in the winners' jubilant dressing room following their great upset victory. *AP/WWP*

**LEFT:** Years after his retirement, Joe Namath continues to be a recognizable celebrity wherever he goes. Here, he waves to a crowd in Canton, Ohio, during the 2003 ceremonies to celebrate the latest inductees into the Pro Football Hall of Fame. Namath was inducted in 1985. *Aaron Josefczyk/Icon SMI*

# MIRACLE YEAR, 1969
## AMAZING METS AND SUPER JETS

A clutch relief appearance by young Nolan Ryan allowed the Mets to clinch the National League pennant with a three-game sweep of the Atlanta Braves in the first-ever division playoffs. Catcher Jerry Grote rushes to embrace Ryan after the final out. *AP/WWP*

The Mets' improbable pennant brought pure joy to the clubhouse. Here, Jerry Grote (left) and Rod Gaspar give New York City mayor John Lindsay a champagne bath. The mayor doesn't seem to mind at all. *AP/WWP*

Mayor Lindsay (right) is on hand again at LaGuardia airport to wish manager Gil Hodges and the Mets luck as they get ready to fly to Baltimore for the first game of the World Series. *Bill Sauro/New York Times/ Getty Images*

# MIRACLE YEAR, 1969
## AMAZING METS AND SUPER JETS

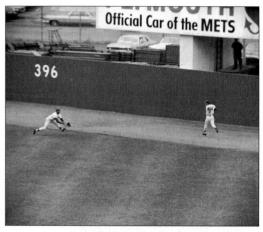

Mets center fielder Tommie Agee makes a great catch of a drive by the Orioles' Elrod Hendricks in the fourth inning of Game 3. Agee raced to the wall in left center to make the "snow cone" grab of the ball, which can be seen at the edge of his glove. Backing up the play is Mets left fielder Cleon Jones (21). *AP/WWP*

Agee's second great catch in Game 3 came off the bat of Baltimore's Paul Blair in the seventh inning and with the bases loaded. This time he raced into the right center field gap to make a diving grab as right fielder Ron Swoboda races to back him up. The two circus catches made more and more people feel that the Mets were a team of destiny and simply couldn't lose. *AP/WWP*

First baseman Donn Clendenon was a midseason acquisition who gave the Mets a legitimate power threat. He proved his worth by belting three home runs in the World Series. The one shown here came in the second inning of Game 4. *Meyer Liebowitz/ New York Times/ Getty Images*

# *MIRACLE YEAR, 1969*
## AMAZING METS AND SUPER JETS

Southpaw Jerry Koosman cuts loose against the Orioles in Game 5. After giving up three early runs, Koosman settled down and pitched the Mets to a 5-3 victory and their first-ever world championship. *AP/WWP*

More destiny awaits the Mets as the normally light-hitting Al Weis crosses home plate after slamming a home run to tie the score in the fifth and final game of the World Series. Greeting him at home plate are teammates Tommie Agee (20) and Rod Gaspar (17). *Robert Walker/New York Times/ Getty Images*

Champs at last! Mets fans race onto the Shea Stadium turf seconds after Cleon Jones caught a fly ball for the final out, giving the New Yorkers the title. The turf at Shea might have taken a beating, but no one seemed to mind after the team's miracle finish. *AP/WWP*

# MIRACLE YEAR, 1969
## AMAZING METS AND SUPER JETS

The years have not dimmed the glory of 1969 or the adulation for the Mets' heroes of yesteryear. Here, Tom Seaver waves to the Shea Stadium crowd during ceremonies in 1999 honoring the 30th anniversary of the Mets' first World Series triumph. Seaver won 25 games in 1969, more than 300 in his career, and is now a member of baseball's Hall of Fame. *Ray Stubblebine/Getty Images*

**ABOVE:** Fun-loving Tug McGraw shouts his "You Gotta Believe" maxim at the Mets' 30th anniversary celebration in 1999. McGraw's war cry led the Mets to another pennant in 1973 and he later helped the Phillies win a world series with his clutch relief pitching. Sadly, McGraw died in January of 2004. *Ray Stubblebine/Getty Images*

**LEFT:** Manager Gil Hodges and his wife, Joan, ride in the lead car as the city of New York holds a ticker tape parade for their heroes following the Mets' triumph over the Orioles. *Ernest Sisto/New York Times/Getty Images*

he shook hands with old friend Lenny Lyles from his Colts days. Then Sample called the toss correctly and elected to have the Jets receive. As he turned to walk away, he said to Lyles quickly, "The first one goes to us."

With more than 75,000 fans at the Orange Bowl and millions more watching on television all on the edge of their seats, Lou Michaels kicked off and Earl Christy brought it back out to the 25. Namath and the offense came out on the field for the first time, Joe shuffling in that stiff-legged gate of his. Matt Snell remembers a pact he and fellow running back Emerson Boozer made before the game.

"We knew we had to get the running game going," Snell explained, "and we decided to make a pact. Whichever one of us got it going, the other guy would block his tail off and do whatever it had to do to make it work. We shook hands on it, not knowing which one of us would end up running more.

"We had our basic off-tackle play, called a 19 straight. If I get the ball, Emerson blocks the outside linebacker, [offensive tackle] Winston Hill blocks the defensive end, and I option off them. If Sauer isn't going deep, he blocks the corner. His role confused their corner who didn't know after a while whether to cover George or support the run."

That's how the Jets opened. On the first play, Snell carried for three yards over left tackle. Namath came back with it again and the big fullback rambled for nine yards and a first down. In addition, he hit safety Rick Volk to hard that Volk had to be helped off the field to recover. After that, however, the drive stalled, though Namath did complete a nine-yard pass, also to Snell. Curley Johnson punted, and the Colts got the ball for the first time at their own 27.

Morrall didn't waste any time. He dropped back and immediately hit tight end John Mackey for a 19-yard gain and a first down. On the second play, halfback Matte ran a sweep around right end and gained 10 more for yet another first down. Here we go, many thought, the Colts are going right through them. The ball was already in New York territory at the 44. It was looking easy. Then three more running plays produced yet another first down at the Jets' 31. A third-down pass to second tight end Tom Mitchell gained 15 more, giving the Colts a first down at the Jets' 19. They were knocking at the door midway through the first period. If this initial drive resulted in a touchdown, many felt, the rout would be on.

But suddenly the drive stalled. Willie Richardson dropped a pass, another to Mitchell was overthrown, and then Morrall was caught by Al Atkinson for no gain when he couldn't get the pass off. Lou Michaels came out on the field to try a 27-yard field goal, close to a chip shot. But the left-footed Michaels was kicking into a tricky wind, and his field goal try went wide right. The Colts had moved the ball but had come up empty. Would the momentum swing over to the Jets?

Taking over at the 20, Namath tried a short pass to Snell that was dropped. After throwing for just two yards to Pete Lammons, Joe backpedaled again and hit Billy Mathis for 13 yards and a first down at the 35. Now Namath decided to go for it. Several days before the game, Joe was watching films and told Don Maynard.

"I found a key. Every time they line up this one way, we can go for it."

Maynard shook his head and said, "Okay." He takes up the story from there. "Right after the first down Joe spotted the defense he saw on the films and checked the play off at the line of scrimmage. I saw it and sprinted down the right sideline. I was already five yards behind everyone when Joe threw. The ball was just slightly overthrown and ticked off my fingertips. Just a little less mustard on it, and we would have had a score. But that play scared them. I lined up so wide that they had to show zone coverage, and Joe could see that as he walked from the huddle to the center. And after that near miss they began doubling and tripling me. Joe could see it. I would run deep, taking the corner and safety with me and that opened things up for Sauer and for Snell."

This time the Jets had to punt again, and Baltimore took over at its own 42, but went three and out and had to punt as well.

The Jets were pushed back to their own four and after Snell gained nine on two running plays, Joe threw a short pass to George Sauer going for the first down. Sauer grabbed it at the 13, but when it was hit by linebacker Dennis Gaubatz, he fumbled and Colts linebacker Ron Porter recovered it at the 12. Remember what the Jets' players had said, "We can't make mistakes." Now they had made a major one. Instead of a first down, they had turned the ball over to the Colts at the 12. It was inconceivable that the Colts would come away empty this time.

On first down, Tom Matte ran a sweep to the left and gained seven yards before being stopped at the five. Now Baltimore was knocking at the door. Morrall dropped back and looked into the end zone. He threw over the middle in the direction of Tom Mitchell, but linebacker Al Atkinson tipped the ball just slightly and it bounced off Mitchell's shoulder high in the air. Cornerback Randy Beverly went after it and made a diving interception in the end zone. The Jets rejoiced. They had gotten the turnover right back and, for a second time, kept the Colts from scoring in close. By this time the first period had ended, and when Namath came out to start his team at the 20, he was determined to set the tone for the rest of the game.

He began by running Matt Snell four straight times for gains of one, seven, six, and 12 yards. That brought the ball all the way out to the 46 with another first down. Then Joe changed pace and went to the air. After a pass to Sauer was broken up by linebacker Don Shinnick, Joe completed three straight, one to Billy Mathis for six and two more to Sauer for 14 and 11 yards, giving the Jets a first down at the Baltimore 23. Suddenly, it was the Jets' turn to knock on the door. Everyone waited to see how the New Yorkers would react to the pressure. After all, the Colts had come up empty twice.

From the 23, Boozer ran for two yards, but then Namath dropped back again and hit Snell for 12 as Dennis Gaubatz again made the tackle. First and goal on the nine. This may have been the play that Don Maynard spoke about when he said, "I went down deep one time, again taking the corner and safety. This time middle linebacker Curtis also ran toward me to stop the deep square in. What he didn't see was that Snell had already caught a pass and was running with it right behind him. Curtis didn't even see him. That's how quickly Joe got rid of the ball. He certainly wasn't about to throw to me under those conditions."

Was Namath starting to outthink the Colts defense? It was beginning to appear that way. From the nine it took just two Snell carries, the first over right tackle for four yards and the next over left tackle and into the end zone. The Jets had scored, driving 80 yards in 12 plays and taking 5:06 off the clock. When Jim Turner kicked the extra point, the Jets had themselves a 7-0 lead as many watching couldn't believe what was beginning to happen.

Following the kick, Baltimore mounted a mini-drive, but it ended when Lou Michaels missed a long field goal from the 46. The Jets returned the favor when they drove from the 20 to the Baltimore 34, but then Jim Turner missed from the 41. So it was still 7-0 with 4:13 left in the half. Then, it looked as if the Colts would get a break. On the second play of their next drive, Tom Matte broke a sweep for 58 yards, taking the ball all the way to the Jets' 16. For the third time, Baltimore was tantalizingly close to the Jets' end zone. After a short gain on the ground, Morrall dropped back and threw toward Willie Richardson near the goal line. Only this time veteran Johnny Sample dashed in front of the receiver for the Jets' second interception of the game.

"Here it is, here's what you're looking for," taunted Sample, holding the ball up for Richardson to see.

Once again the Colts had been blunted, and now NFL rooters were seeing a painful pattern develop. It would only get worse. The Jets got the ball at the two-minute warning, but after a three and out, Curley Johnson had to punt from his end zone. Dual penalties led him to punt a second time, and Baltimore got the ball at the Jets' 42 with just 43 seconds left. After a one-yard completion to Jerry Hill, the Colts tried a trick play. Morrall gave the ball to Matte, who started into the line, then stopped and lateraled back to Morrall. It was the old flea-flicker. Morrall looked downfield and threw toward Jerry Hill over the middle at about the 12-yard line. This time it was strong safety Jim Hudson who was Johnny on the spot, darting in front of Hill and picking off the pass. It was the Jets' third interception of the half, and as time ran out, the Jets had a 7-0 lead as football pundits everywhere scratched their heads wondering just what was happening.

But that wasn't all. When Morrall got the ball back from Matte, he failed to see wide receiver Jimmy Orr standing at the 10-yard line, unguarded and waving his arms for the ball. Morrall confirmed that he didn't see him, later saying that he had to turn to his right to take the lateral and that Orr wasn't in his line of vision. Others said that Orr blended in with the blue uniforms of a marching band, whose members were standing behind the end zone preparing to perform at the half. Whatever happened, people have pointed to that play for years as a major turning point, claiming that had Morrall seen Orr it would have been an easy touchdown, leading to a 7-7 score at halftime, something that might have altered the final outcome of the game. Don Maynard, for one, doesn't agree. He saw the play differently and later confirmed what he had seen.

"Most films of that play isolate on Orr waving his arms," Maynard said. "There wasn't anyone around him then, but I also saw the play from a wide-angle film that showed much more than just Orr. What I saw was our free safety, Billy Baird, not that far from Orr. Billy was the second fastest man on the team next to me and a very smart player who would sit in the hole back there and wait. I know from that wide angle that Billy could have gotten over there before Morrall could have thrown the ball that distance to Orr. It would have been about a 40-45 yard throw. Had he seen Orr and thrown it, I was sure Baird would have been over there in time to get the ball or knock it down."

Halftime in the Colts locker room must have been a solemn scene. Supposedly, Coach Shula told his team they were blowing it. "We're making stupid mistakes," he was quoted as telling them. "We're stopping ourselves. You've got them believing in themselves. You've got them believing that they're better than we are."

Many of the Jets had believed that all along. What happened in the first half only confirmed it.

"We had the feeling early on that this was going to be our day," John Elliott said. "As soon as we scored that touchdown in the first quarter you could see some of the wind go out of them. It was as if this can't be happening to us."

"I always felt that the flea flicker that Hudson intercepted psychologically destroyed Earl Morrall," Matt Snell said. "We felt it we didn't give up a big play early in the second half, we had the game in the bag. I also think our running game was wearing them down. The more Winston [Hill] blocked Ordell Braase, the more tired he became. Curtis began getting frustrated because our guards were blocking him. He was known for his speed and filling the holes, yet we were getting past him. We ran mostly to the left, because big Bubba was on the right. And it was working."

There was, however, an x-factor. Johnny Unitas, a miracle man so many times in his career, had deemed himself ready to play. The thought was that the Colts would turn to the legendary Johnny U. to begin the third quarter and that had some of the Jets worried.

"Did we fear Unitas?" Matt Snell asked, rhetorically. "Oh, man, tell me about it. Anyone around the game knew of the Johnny Unitas mystique. We knew he hadn't played much all year and didn't know how good his arm was. But we were fearful just knowing he was on the sideline. I prayed that Morrall would start the second half."

In the Colts locker room, Shula toyed with the idea of going to Unitas immediately. Unitas apparently had admitted that he was only about 80 percent recovered from his arm injury, but being the kind of competitor he was, he had told people he was disappointed that he hadn't been given the starting assignment. Finally, just before the teams came back on the field, Shula decided to give Morrall one more chance to get his team moving, planning to let him play at least one more series.

But the second half started no better for the Colts. They took the kickoff back to the 25, and on the first play from scrimmage, Tom Matte fumbled at the end of an eight-yard gain and Ralph Baker recovered for the Jets. Eight plays later, Jim Turner kicked a 32-yard field goal, and the Jets had a 10-0 lead. Now, it really began to look as if the New Yorkers were on the way. Morrall came in for one more series and the Colts could do no better than three and out. They had to punt.

The Jets started from their own 32 and marched all the way to the Baltimore 23. Namath tried another one to Maynard, who caught the ball this time but was barely beyond the end line when he pulled it in. Incomplete. On that play, the Jets suffered a potentially serious blow. Namath was hit after releasing the ball and went to the bench, holding his oft-injured right thumb. Babe Parilli came in, threw one incomplete pass and then Turner kicked his second field goal of the afternoon, this one from the 30, giving the Jets a 13-0 lead. But would the complexion of the game now change? Not only had Namath gone to the sidelines, but behind the Colts bench, Johnny Unitas was warming up.

Sure enough, as soon as the kickoff was ruled a touchback, the familiar number 19 shuffled out onto the field with the Baltimore offense.

"I can envision Unitas coming in as if it were yesterday," said Dave Herman. "I saw him play when I was a kid, and when I saw him trot onto the field that day my heart stopped for about 10 seconds. Here we go now, I thought. We all knew what he had done in the past. He had had so many, many outstanding games. But as soon as we saw there was little to no improvement in their offense, I kind of forgot about it and relaxed."

Matt Snell also remembers what was, at the time, a very dramatic moment in the game. "You could hear the fans cheering as soon as Unitas began warming up," Snell said. "We didn't relax until we saw him come out and throw. His passes were fluttering and just didn't have any velocity. He had the psychological advantage when he first came in, because we had all seen him do it so many times in the past. But you could see right away that his arm wasn't the same. In fact, it was horrible."

Unitas's first drive was a three and out when Orr dropped a pass. Namath had returned for the Jets, his thumb okay, and began moving the team once again. Mixing the run and pass, he took the Jets from their own 37 all the way to the Baltimore two-yard line, the big play a 39-yard pass to George Sauer. By the time Jim Turner kicked his third field goal, a nine-yard chip shot, the third quarter had ended. The kick gave the Jets a 16-0 lead with just 13:26 remaining in the game. Now no one was thinking about the 17-point spread. That was long by the boards. Jets fans were beginning to count the minutes as it became more and more apparent that they were about to win the game. For Colts fans and NFL stalwarts, the only hope was that the Jets would make a mistake, and that Johnny Unitas might have one more miracle in his once magical right arm.

Starting at their own 27, the Colts suddenly began moving, but most of it was on the ground. Unitas completed just two short five-yard tosses in the drive that finally reached the Jets' 25. On first down, he looked for Willie Richardson, but the pass was overthrown. On second, he looked for Jimmy Orr in the end zone. But once again the pass didn't have enough zip on it, and Randy Beverly got over in time to make his second pick of the game, remaining in the end zone for another touchback. Now, as Namath came out once more, there was just 11:06 remaining in the game.

The Jets then held the ball for about four and a half minutes, taking it from the 20 to the Baltimore 35. From there, Turner missed a 42-yard field goal and Johnny U. came out once more, taking over at his own 20. This time the old master stuck to the air, throwing seven straight passes, including a clutch, 17-yard completion to Orr on fourth down from the 20. Then a third-down toss to Mackey gained 11 more. A personal foul resulted in a first down for the Jets. After a one-yard run by Matte, Unitas dropped back again. He spotted Richardson and hit him for 21 yards, bringing the ball to the 15. Two plays later and an 11-yard pass to Orr gave the Colts a first and goal at the Jets' four. It took five plays, aided by a New York penalty, before Jerry Hill ran it over from the one. The Colts had scored. Finally! The kick made it 16-7 with 3:19 left.

Not surprisingly, Baltimore tried an onsides kick and Tom Mitchell recovered for the Colts at the Jets' 44. Even though his arm wasn't great, Unitas seemed to be finding the touch, the one that enabled him to move teams and hit clutch passes. A quick score now would make it a ball game, or at least a dramatic ending. When Unitas hit his first three passes, bringing the ball to the Jets' 19, it looked as if it was finally happening. But then, as suddenly as Unitas seemed to catch fire, he lost it. One pass to Richardson was broken up by Sample, the next to Orr was underthrown and a fourth-down try, again to Orr, was thrown too high. With 2:21 left, the Colts and Unitas had lost the ball on downs.

Now all the Jets had to do was run out the clock, or come close to it. Not surprisingly, Namath kept the ball on the ground. Snell carried three straight times off tackle to give the New Yorkers a first down at the 31. On his next carry, the Jets were penalized for being off sides. Ball back to the 33. Snell gained one, then a delay-of-game penalty brought the ball back to the 24. On third down Snell ran a rare sweep but gained just three. However, the job was done. The Colts called time out with just 15 seconds left. Curley Johnson's punt took the ball to the Colts' 34-yard line. With just eight seconds to go, Unitas threw two more passes. His second and last was good for 15 yards to Richardson, but the gun sounded. The game was over.

The Jets had won it, 16-7. The impossible had happened ... in the eyes of everyone except the Jets players. They had done what most of them had thought they could do. As they left the field, there was the indelible image of Namath, walking toward the tunnel, head down, but wagging his right index finger in the air, very conspicuously. *We're number one.* Yes, they were.

Namath, who had completed 17 of 28 passes for 206 yards, was named the game's Most Valuable Player. But he had plenty of help. Snell had gained a then-Super Bowl-record 121 yards on 30 workhorse carries. George Sauer, open all day because Maynard was being double-and triple-teamed, caught eight passes for 133 yards. Then there were the four interceptions by the defensive backs. Remember, they had predicted five. The Colts had none.

While Unitas maintained steadfastly over the years that "I just didn't have enough time," it's doubtful the Colts could have won. It just wasn't their day. In fact, veteran defensive tackle Billy Ray Smith, who had said he would get Namath, found he had nothing but praise for the brash young quarterback.

"He did it all," Smith said of Namath. "He threw the ball short a little. He threw the ball long a little. He ran the ball a little. He had it all going, and so they won. I just couldn't quite get to him."

As for Namath, he knew that it took a team effort and made that clear. "We beat 'em in every phase of the game," he said. "If ever there was a world champion, this is it. I always had the confidence we would win. But I didn't know what to expect. I had a good time, though. When you go out and play football, you're supposed to have a good time."

Coach Ewbank simply said, "Ball control did it. We didn't make any errors. Joe Namath called a great game. He was fabulous and he had great pass protection."

Looking back now, the Jets players still have fond memories of that magical moment that would usher out the turbulent 1960s in the world of pro football.

"I remember being totally exhausted after the game," Dave Herman said. "I was so tired having to block Bubba all afternoon. I remember Pete Roselle coming in with the trophy and saying to him, 'Guess what, Pete. That's ours now, not yours.'"

Matt Snell said the game was reflective a different era. "If it happened today, the money would be astronomical," he said. "It was our greatest year financially because we made the extra $15,000 for winning the Super Bowl. But I don't think we realized right away what we had accomplished. The night after the game we had guys from the AFL who played in the first two

Super Bowls come to the hotel to shake our hands, thanking us for finally getting it done. It meant a lot to people like Daryle Lamonica, Ben Davidson, and Buck Buchanan, and it meant something to us to have them thanking us for winning. Then when we got back to New York we were told we were going to be welcomed by the mayor. I think when we went to city hall, that's when it finally settled in psychologically."

Defensive tackle John Elliott was another who said the magnitude of the victory didn't sink in immediately. "The game wasn't hyped as much as it is now, and no one thought we were gonna win," Elliott said. "After we won, people didn't know how to deal with it. We didn't even have a party. When we came back to the hotel guys were asking where's the party. They said, what party? There was no team get together after the game, probably because Weeb would have had to pay for it. I remember being in my room by midnight. The funniest thing I remember is when we left the hotel the next day. They forgot the trophy, left it in the hotel safe. I took it out and brought it to the team bus, and that was the only time I ever held it.

"The next week I played in the AFL All-Star game at Jacksonville and that's what made it sink in. I went into the locker room and Billy Shaw, who was a longtime guard with Buffalo, told me how proud he was for what we did for our league and for pro football. He said he couldn't sleep that night because he was so hyped. I said, heck, was it really that big a game? But looking back now, it actually means much more to me than it did then. Maybe that was because our coaches did such an excellent job of keeping us on an even keel."

Don Maynard agreed somewhat with Elliott. "At the time it wasn't a big deal to me," he said. "We had no idea how big a game it was. Some guys were anxious to get the ring, but I just wanted the $15,000. That extra money meant a lot in those days. Looking back now, it was obviously important and had historical significance since we were the first AFL team to win. I went to the AFL All-Star game the following week and saw that other guys from around the league were the happiest guys in America.

They were all so complimentary, so happy we had won, had finally beaten the NFL. After that, I just drove home to El Paso."

There are a couple of things that made the game even more special. Though they had a great team, the Jets never got there again. Though the team won the division in 1969 with a 10-4 record they were beaten in a new inter-divisional playoff by Kansas City, 13-6.

"We had four key injuries that year," Don Maynard said. "I broke a foot when I was leading the league in receiving yardage. Philbin dislocated a shoulder and tried to play with it in a harness. Both guards were hurt, and Bob Talamini retired because he and Weeb were about $3,000 apart on a contract to bring him back. He was so much a part of teaching our young linemen how to block and pass block the year before, I said I would have paid to have him back. After that, the leagues merged, Joe got hurt, and the face of the team began changing. So it was a one-shot deal, but what a deal!"

The following year, the Kansas City Chiefs upset the Minnesota Vikings, 23-7, to give the AFL its second victory. After that, the leagues merged, and the AFL identity was slowly absorbed into one, big National Football League. Looking back, Dave Herman has his own take on what it could have meant if the Jets had been able to repeat.

"We came close, losing to Kansas City in the playoffs the following year," he said. "The Chiefs were a wild-card team that year, yet destroyed Minnesota in the Super Bowl. Wouldn't it have been great if we had gotten back there and won? Then those first four Super Bowls, the AFL-NFL Super Bowls, would have had a real nice ring. They would have read, Green Bay two, the New York Jets two. Only it didn't happen."

Yet in the minds of New Yorkers and AFL fans everywhere, nothing could replace that moment, when Joe Namath left the field waggling that finger in the air, having made good on his guarantee. It was one time when once was more than enough. In fact, it was perfect.

# JETS
# THROUGH THE YEARS

As mentioned earlier, the Jets never made it back to the title game, or to the Super Bowl. The team won the AFL East handily in 1969, with a 10-4 record. But as Don Maynard explained, several key injuries kept them from being quite the same team. When they were beaten by Kansas City, 13-6, in the new playoff system that had the divisional winners playing the runner-up from the opposing division, it signaled the end of an era. A year later, Namath was hurt; Snell was hurt, and the team crashed to a 4-10 record in the revamped National Football League that saw the Jets playing the Eastern Division of the American Football Conference. The AFL as a separate entity was no more, and the Jets would not challenge for a playoff spot again for more than a decade.

So the Jets did not go on to become a dynasty as others had. Looking back at pro football, the Packers are considered the team of the sixties, the Pittsburgh Steelers the team of the seventies, and the San Francisco 49ers the team of the eighties. In the nineties, there were a number of dominant teams, but the Jets were never among them. So the 1968 Jets remain the franchise's only Super Bowl champion, and it could not have occurred under better circumstances.

More and more it seems that the 1968 Jets were simply a team that "happened," achieved a kind of magical greatness for just a single season, when everything went well, there were few injuries, and the team got the breaks as well as making big plays. There's no doubt that the club had some fine football players, but many had their careers eventually shortened or curtailed by injury. Proof of the pudding is that only two members of that Super Bowl-winning Jets team are in Pro Football's Hall of Fame. Not surprisingly, they are Joe Namath and Don Maynard.

Namath played until the 1977 season, staying with the Jets until the final year, when he was a part-time quarterback for the Los Angeles Rams. By then his knees were shot and he had lost much of his mobility. Knee injuries also sabotaged a number of other seasons during his career. In the end, the strong-armed quarterback completed 1,886 passes in 3,762 attempts for 27,663 yards. His completion percentage was just 50.1 percent, and he threw for 173 touchdowns as opposed to 220 interceptions. Going by statistics alone, he doesn't approach quarterbacks like John Unitas, Joe Montana, Terry Bradshaw, John Elway, or Dan Marino.

But it was a different game then. Quarterbacks, especially those coming out of the AFL, threw downfield more and completed fewer short passes than those who came later. Namath didn't always have a strong running game to support him, and when teams knew he had to throw just to play catch up, they were ready for him. Even when the Jets were winning, his interceptions often came in bunches. But "Broadway" Joe always had a mystique about him. He was a flamboyant personality who was perhaps the single most driving force in putting the AFL on the map and forcing the eventual merger. In addition, his brilliant play against the Colts will never be forgotten. He was voted into the Hall of Fame in 1985 and fully deserves the honor.

Don Maynard remains one of the greatest deep receivers to have played the game. His career average of 18.7 yards a catch is one of the best ever. Starting with the NFL New York Giants in 1958, then joining the original Titans in 1960, Maynard played until 1973, spending his final season with the St. Louis Cardinals. He wound up with 633 catches for 11,834 yards and 88 touchdowns. Fans in New York will never forget the sight of Maynard streaking down the sideline, catching one of Namath's long passes in full stride and taking it into the end zone. He was elected to the Hall of Fame in 1987.

Weeb Ewbank coached the Jets until retiring after the 1973 season. He'll always be remembered for two championship games, coaching the Colts to that great overtime win over the Giants in the NFL championship in 1958, then leading the Jets past his old team in Super Bowl III. Both of those games changed the face of pro football in America. The 1958 game is still remembered as the game that put the NFL squarely on the national sports map and is still referred to as "the greatest game ever played." The Super Bowl III victory showed the world the AFL was more than ready to compete with the NFL and that the upcoming merger was a good thing. His election to Pro Football's Hall of Fame in 1978 was also well deserved.

As for the other members of the Jets, many of them had fine careers, making various all-pro teams and playing in the Pro Bowl. None of the others, however, has been deemed good enough for enshrinement in the Hall. Some, perhaps, deserve it, but many had their careers shortened by injury or by choice. Let's look at a few.

Matt Snell, the powerhouse fullback who set a Super Bowl rushing record of 121 yards against the Colts, wound up with only 4,285 career rushing yards. In fact, the 1969 season was the last in which he was able to play almost a full schedule. Injuries relegated him to part time after that and he retired after the 1972 season. Emerson Boozer had a similar career. He played until 1975 and retired with 5,135 career yards. Both running backs were fine, all-around players who could block and catch, as well as run, but injuries slowed them, and because of that, neither is looked upon as an all-time great.

George Sauer, the talented wide receiver who played opposite Maynard, retired after the 1970 season, apparently losing some of his passion for the game. He wound up with 309 receptions for 4,965 yards, a 16.1 receiving average and 28 touchdowns. Yet the Colts couldn't stop him when it counted, in Super Bowl III. Defensive back Johnny Sample never played again after the Super Bowl, but he had the distinction of playing both for the 1958 Colts and 1968 Jets. For him, there were no more worlds to conquer.

As a point of reference, some of the other cornerstones also left the game fairly soon after the greatest win of their lives. Offensive lineman Dave Herman retired after the 1973 season, linebacker Al Atkinson played until 1974, defensive tackle John Elliott left after 1973, while linebacker Larry Grantham's last year was 1972. The team's two fine defensive ends also left soon after the Super Bowl victory. Verlon Biggs and the Jets parted ways after the 1970 season, and he finished his career with the Washington Redskins, retiring after 1974. Gerry Philbin left the Jets after 1972 and finishing his career with the Philadelphia Eagles a year later.

Even in the days before free agency and the salary cap, it wasn't easy to keep an NFL team together for any length of time. Lombardi was able to keep his core group of Packers in tact for almost a decade, but that was an exception. For the Jets, it didn't happen. Yet their victory over the Colts is still viewed as one of sports' greatest upsets and is remembered today.

"We really had a unique team," defensive tackle John Elliott said. "If you lined our guys up now and compared them to the players today, none of us would make today's team. But I'd venture to say that no team before or since had a bigger heart than that one."

Don Maynard, the slim Texan who ran his way into the Hall of Fame, loves the New York fans and adds, "Whenever I go back there today there are still plenty of people who remember me and remember the game. And they love to talk about it."

But perhaps it was Dave Herman, the offensive lineman who stopped Bubba Smith in Super Bowl III, who put the victory into the clearest perspective.

"First it took a while to really sink in," Herman said. "I slowly began to realize how big it was. And it keeps getting bigger with people over time. I see Joe [Namath] all the time and the number of people who come up to him and want to talk with him is still overwhelming. When Joe was playing, the younger generation could identify with him. How they're 45 or 50 or 55 and running the country, and they still look back at that game as being so monumental. It's as big today as it was then around the New York area."

# PART TWO
# THE 1969
# NEW YORK METS

# 7
# LOVABLE LOSERS
# FILL A VOID

It's very easy to make a case for New York City being the Mecca of Major League Baseball in the early to mid-1950s. The Yankees, of course, were always the Yankees, and at that time had another of their powerhouse dynasties. From 1949 to 1953, the mighty Bronx Bombers won five consecutive pennants and all five World Series that followed. The team was managed by the venerable Charles Dillon "Casey" Stengel, and continued to win while making the superstar transition from Joe DiMaggio to Mickey Mantle. Though the Yanks missed in 1954, finishing second to Cleveland despite winning 103 games, they returned to win pennants again from 1955 to 1958, adding another pair of World Series triumphs to their growing dossier.

For all their success, however, the Yankees were not the only game in town. New York in the 1950s had two other major league baseball teams, making it the only city in America to sport a trio of ball clubs. The National League New York Giants and Brooklyn Dodgers also had outstanding teams during the same period. The Giants won the pennant in 1951, making that great stretch run against the archrival Dodgers, culminated by Bobby Thomson's shot-heard-round-the-world home run that won the third and final playoff game in the ninth inning, converting what seemed to be a 4-2 defeat into a 5-4 victory. Though they lost to the Yanks in the World Series, the Giants came back in 1954, winning the pennant and upsetting the Cleveland Indians in four straight games to win it. Those were the Giants of Willie Mays and manager Leo Durocher, a great and colorful ball club.

Then there were the Dodgers, the beloved Bums, a team looked upon with near-religious fervor in the borough of Brooklyn. The Dodgers had one of the great teams ever in those years, winning pennants in 1949, 1952, 1953, 1955, and 1956. It was a star-studded cast with Jackie Robinson, Pee Wee Reese, Gil Hodges, Duke Snider, Roy Campanella, Carl Furillo, Billy Cox, Preacher Roe, and Carl Erskine. Each time the Dodgers won the pennant, they had the misfortune to face the Yanks in the World Series, breaking through only once, in 1955, to become champions, and finally shedding the wait-'til-next-year chant that had become oh-too-familiar to their fans.

What a great time to be a baseball fan in New York. From 1949 through 1958 there was a New York team in the World Series each year, and on six occasions two New York teams. The term "subway series" became synonymous with the Big Apple, and fans had plenty of occasions to ride those subterranean rails. The Dodgers and Giants may have had the most heated rivalry in sports, while the Bronx Bombers continued to be baseball's dominant team. Plus there were all kinds of sub-stories going on, from Jackie Robinson breaking baseball's so-called "color line" in 1947 to which team had the best center fielder. Was it Mickey, Willie, or The Duke? This was simply a period in baseball that could not and would not ever be duplicated again.

Unfortunately, it didn't end because the teams suddenly lost their stars. It ended because two of the teams left, saying good-bye to New York. After the 1957 season, Dodger owner Walter O'Malley and Giants' owner Horace Stoneham, both announced that they would be relocating their franchises to the west coast prior to the 1958 season. It began major league baseball's great geographical expansion, making the sport a coast-to-coast adventure. But for the fans of New York this was akin to a Greek tragedy. Who in their right mind could fathom the *Los Angeles* Dodgers or the *San Francisco* Giants? It didn't make sense. The words simply wouldn't roll off the tongues of thousands of shocked and angry fans. What would happen to those great old baseball shrines, Ebbets Field (in Brooklyn) and the Polo Grounds? New York was the biggest city in the world, and suddenly it had lost two of its three baseball teams.

At that time, both O'Malley and Stoneham had made economically feasible moves. Both teams would ultimately be a huge successes on the west coast, and both old New York stadiums would eventually be razed so that housing projects could be built. But in the meantime, what was New York to do? Despite the success of the Yankees since the 1920s and the parade of stars that had come to the Bronx from the days of Babe Ruth, many had always considered New York a National League town. Almost to the day the Dodgers and Giants left, talk began about how to bring a senior circuit team back to New York.

It would take five years, which is not a real long time in terms of the history of baseball. When the Dodgers and Giants left, baseball was still a 16-team sport, eight teams in each league. It had been that way since the formation of the American League in 1901. Soon, however, there was talk of adding new teams. More and more cities wanted big-league ball clubs. The fan base seemed to be there, television was beaming the sport to all corners of the land, and the ever-increasing population of the country meant there would be more players available. Expansion seemed inevitable. Plans were put in place, and in 1961, the first expansion occurred in the American League. That year, the Washington Senators franchised moved to Minnesota and became the Twins. Immediately, a new team was put into Washington, and a second new club, the Los Angeles Angels, was situated on the west coast. The junior circuit now had 10 teams for the first time.

A year later, a similar expansion came to the National League. Major League baseball came to Texas for the first time as the Houston Colt 45s (later the Astros) played their first season in

1962. The second new team that year had some big cleats to fill. National League baseball was finally back in New York. The team was officially called the New York Metropolitans. But to the fans and everyone else, they would now and forever be known as the Mets. In those days, new teams were stocked by drawing from a player pool made available by existing teams. Obviously, they didn't have farm systems from which to draw. All that had to come later. There was no way any of these expansion teams could be competitive from day one.

The Mets immediately looked to bring some tradition to New York with them. For openers, they would begin play at the ancient Polo Grounds, former home of the Giants. And when the team named its first manager, they brought back one of the most beloved figures in New York baseball annals. The Mets wasted no time in appointing 71-year-old Casey Stengel to be their first manager. The Yankees had unceremoniously dumped Old Case after winning his 10th American League pennant in 1960. Shortly after the Yanks were beaten by the Pittsburgh Pirates on Bill Mazeroski's Game 7, walk-off World Series home run, Stengel got the ax. So when the Mets hired him, Casey had only been out of the game for one year. Now he was back managing a team decidedly different from the ultra-successful Bronx Bombers.

The talent pool available consisted of some aging veterans, well past their primes, marginal players who never quite made it and who were pretty much cast-offs, and some young players not considered top prospects in their original organizations. The Mets consciously tried to pick up veteran players with New York roots. By tabbing a guy like Gil Hodges the first year, then picking up Duke Snider in 1963, the team quickly allowed fans to conjure up memories from those great Brooklyn Dodgers teams, though both players were well past their primes and were just finishing their careers in part-time roles. Among the other vets picked up the first few seasons with some previous connection to the city were Don Zimmer, Roger Craig, Gene Woodling, Charlie Neal, and Yogi Berra. Other vets who had been both productive and even great players included Warren Spahn, Richie Ashburn, Gus Bell, Clem Labine, "Vinegar Bend" Mizell, Jim Piersall, Frank Thomas, and Felix Mantilla. Unfortunately, none had enough left to transform the team to even near winners.

Then there were untried youngsters. Some, like pitchers Jay Hook and Al Jackson, and outfielder Jim Hickman, would have their moments, but others like Elio Chacon, Choo Choo Coleman, "Marvelous" Marv Throneberry, Chris Canizzaro, Hobie Landrith, "Hot" Rod Kanehl would become symbols of futility, players forever associated with a team that lost more than any other at the beginning of its history. Ed Kranepool, who played briefly with the 1962 Mets before embarking on a long, 18-year career with the team, feels the Mets did some smart things in the early years, knowing they couldn't put a winning product on the field.

"I always felt that New York was a National League town," Kranepool said, "and that none of the old Dodger and Giant fans went over to the Yankees. They remained loyal to the National League and, as a result, greeted the Mets with a tremendous out-pouring of affection, were very loyal, and supported the team through all the lean years. Playing in the Polo Grounds the first two years was also a great thing, because fans identified with the ballpark, and whenever the Giants and Dodgers came to town there were sellouts.

"The team also intentionally chose the old Giants and Dodgers players who had name recognition. That was another good move to bring back the fans quickly. In those early years it was more about having fun at the ballpark than about winning. No one expected to win then, but National League baseball was back."

There was little doubt that the team's first superstar was Stengel. The "Old Perfessor," as he was called, would entertain the media for hours on end, telling his stories from the old days, poking fun at his futile team, and saying things in his own special way, a twist of language dubbed "Stengelese" by the media. And when he uttered his plaintive, "Can't anyone here play this game?" call to action, that told everyone just what kind of team the Mets had. But no one really had to be told. It was there for all to see. In their first season, the New Yorkers set a record for futility, winning just 40 games and losing 120. They finished a record 60 1/2 games behind the pennant-winning Giants in a 10-team league. Heck, the Cubs lost 103 games and still finished 18 ahead of the cellar-dwelling Mets. A year later, with basically the same cast of characters or, at worse, interchangeable parts they weren't much better, finishing with a 51-111 mark.

Then in 1964 the team finally abandoned the old Polo Grounds and moved to spanking new Shea Stadium in Queens, built right alongside the World's Fair. The new ballpark brought more excitement for the fans, but no better results on the field. The Mets improved only by two games, to 53-109, and still had no stars, no homegrown talent that gave any indication of making a difference. In fact, the team continued its ignominious tradition of having a 20-game loser on its pitching staff. In 1964 it was Tracy Stallard. Before that it had been Roger Craig (twice) and Al Jackson. All the records were the negative kind, and the losing continued unabated as the 1965 season got underway. Still, Casey Stengel entertained the media and fans, taught, cajoled, and sometimes shamed his players to make them win and still thought, "Can't anyone here play this game?"

Ron Swoboda was a Mets rookie in 1965, a player who quickly endeared himself to the fans with a spate of early-season home runs. He had a chance to observe Casey Stengel in action for a good part of the season and saw that the venerable old skipper was a lot more than the class clown.

"Casey was very much the manager and very much in charge," Swoboda said. "He understood exactly what was happening. Expansion back then didn't give you access to much talent and, because there was no free agency, teams couldn't buy their way to respectability. That's the way the game was designed, and it made it very difficult for expansion teams to win. But I always felt that Casey, in his heart of hearts, was still very much a manager who was trying to win. He just understood that the franchise would be pathetic for a while and, that being the situation, he was the perfect guy for the job. He had so much personality. He changed from the guy who had managed the Yankees to ten pennants to one who took on much of the public relations and media relations for the Mets. He wooed the writers, told them stories, and in doing so took the attention away from the futility on the field. It probably hurt his ultimate reputation in a way, going from all those World Series wins with the Yankees to the worse team ever with the Mets."

Swoboda can also relate a couple of personal stories that proves old Case was still very much the manager and a baseball man of long standing. "Early in the 1965 season the Mets were playing in St. Louis and had a rare, 3-0 lead. I was playing left, and late in the game the Cards had the bases loaded with Dal Maxvill up. He hit a dying quail and because I didn't have sunglasses on, I lost it in the sun and it cleared the bases, tying the game. Then in the top of the tenth with the game tied, I popped out with a chance to do something. When we were getting ready to go out for the bottom of the tenth I was so angry with myself, almost in a rage that I tried to stomp my batting helmet, which was lying on the steps of the dugout with the open end up. It cracked open and my foot got stuck inside it. Casey had a cast on his hand then because he had broken his wrist, and I remember he came bouncing up the dugout steps like a 20-year-old. He grabbed me by the shirt and said, 'God damn it, when you missed that fly I didn't go into the locker room and throw your watch on the floor. I don't want you busting up the team's equipment when you screw up.'

"Well, I thought I had ruined my career right there. He took me out of the game and I thought he was going to crack me with that cast on his wrist. It was the low point of my rookie season, because I had totally messed up a baseball game. And I learned quickly that day that you didn't mess with Casey."

There was another incident in spring training that year that proved how, no matter what the situation, Casey Stengel demanded total respect from all his players. Again, Ron Swoboda was there and remembers it well.

"We had gone on a road trip to West Palm Beach [Florida] to play some games. At that time, it was customary for the team's owner, Mrs. Joan Payson, to buy everyone dinner. So one night we went to a steak house and they had these bottles of Lancer's wine on the tables, in his little crock-type bottles. Well, we all got into the Lancer's pretty good and Casey went up to the podium to make a speech. His theme was ways we could take care of ourselves and improve.

"'Always think about tomorrow,' Casey said. 'When you go out to have a couple of drinks, don't go out with six guys, go out with two. If you go out with six, by the time you buy back, all of you will be drunk.' We had a journeyman outfielder name Duke Carmel there, who was trying to make the team. Duke was a New York guy and feeling pretty good that night. When Casey said that, Duke suddenly piped up in a loud voice, 'I've seen you out with ten guys.' Well, Casey didn't laugh and suddenly, the whole room quieted. 'I've seen you, too, Mr. Carmel,' he said, 'when you didn't see me. And remember, you haven't made this team yet.'

"The very next day Carmel's locker was empty and he was gone. The lesson was clear. You don't show the old man up. Casey may have been in his 70s then, but he had been around the game since about 1912 when only tough guys made the majors. Though he was known for his sense of humor, he still had pride and an ego. In a nutshell, Casey was still pretty much one tough sonofabitch."

Unfortunately, Casey didn't finish the 1965 season. His Mets career ended after the game of July 24. That night, he went to a party at Toots Shor's restaurant in Manhattan to honor those invited to the Old Timer's Game at Shea the following day. At the dinner, Stengel took a fall, resulting in a broken left hip. After 3,766 games as a manager, including a 31-64 mark in 1965, Old Case retired. Former New York Giants catcher Wes Westrum was appointed to succeed him, and the Mets finished the year with a

50-112 record, last again. In their first four years of existence, the team had made little, if any, progress, losing 120, 111, 109, and 112 games. The New Yorkers seemed as bad as ever, yet the fans continued to come out to Shea. If nothing else, they could once again watch National League baseball, still welcome the Dodgers and Giants back, and feel comfortable with the knowledge that there was another game in town besides the New York Yankees. Ironically, after winning five more pennants between 1960 and 1964, the Bronx Bombers had suddenly faltered and finished the 1965 season with a 77-85 record.

A year later they would tumble to last, and it would be several more years before they even contended again. Maybe that was a good stroke of fortune, because it also opened the city up for the New York Mets.

The question was when would the team begin to get better? Under Westrum in 1966, there was a glimmer of hope. The team not only had its best season to date, finishing at 66-95, but also emerged from the cellar at the same time, finishing ahead of the Chicago Cubs. The Cubs, now managed by Leo Durocher, were last at 59-103. Though no one knew it then, both these ball clubs would be part of a summer-long drama just three years later.

Why had the 1966 Mets suddenly improved, losing fewer than 100 games for the first time ever? It wasn't that new manager Westrum was more of a genius than Old Case. Nope. Finally, the new farm system was taking hold and the team was beginning to grow some good young players of its own. Young Ed Kranepool was a year older and hit 16 home runs. Scrappy second-sacker Ron Hunt became the team's first bona fide all-star selection. Outfielder Cleon Jones looked like a potentially strong hitter, batting a solid .275. A trade with Houston brought catcher Jerry Grote, just in his second full season and already an outstanding receiver who would also develop into a fine handler of pitches. Veteran standout Ken Boyer gave the team a stability at third, though his career was winding down. The pitching staff still wasn't very solid, but there was enough talent for the team to escape the cellar. Could the team finally be ready to move up the National League ladder?

Not quite. Though everyone went to spring training in 1967 with renewed hopes, it would turn into a season of mixed emotions. On the one hand, the ball club seemed to take a backward step, finishing the season at 61-101, once again in last place and eight full games behind the ninth-place Houston Astros. The club even lost its manager when Wes Westrum resigned with 11 games left in the season. It was really a season of turmoil. Bing Devine was the new club president that year, and he swung into action, making one roster move after another. During the season, the team used a record 54 players, including 27 pitchers, not exactly the way to achieve stability. Westrum also came into conflict with some of the younger players, notably Jones, Grote, and Kranepool, all of whom were looked upon as being part of the club's future. There were also some disappointments, players who didn't live up to advance billing. They quickly joined the revolving door that was the roster that year. Coach Salty Parker managed the club the final 11 games until, mercifully, it was over.

But wait! There was a bright spot in 1967, an event that is still looked upon today as the first step in changing the face of the New York Mets' franchise. It was the arrival of 22-year-old right-handed pitcher Tom Seaver. Seaver went from pitching for Fresno State in 1965, to Jacksonville of the International League in 1966, right to the Mets a year later. But the fact that the Mets had him at all proved the fortunes of the franchise were changing. They landed Seaver thanks to some good, old-fashioned dumb luck.

It was the Atlanta Braves that first drafted Seaver in January of 1966. However, the Braves had made a mistake. They inadvertently violated a Major League Baseball rule that prevented the signing of players who were college juniors or seniors once their collegiate seasons had begun. Seaver had pitched for Fresno State the year before but had just joined the team at the University of Southern California as a transfer. Though Seaver never pitched for USC, the team had begun play when the youngster signed a contract with the Braves that included a $50,000 bonus. When the baseball commissioner's office voided the deal but at the same time ruled that Seaver was ineligible for further collegiate action, his father threatened a lawsuit. That's when an unusual ruling was made. The rights to Seaver would be given to any team willing to match Atlanta's original bonus offer.

Three teams stepped forward—the Phillies, the Indians, and the Mets. Amazingly, the winner would be decided by a name being drawn from a hat. Slips of paper with the names of the three teams were put in, and when the winning slip was pulled out, New York Mets was written on it. Tom Seaver was theirs.

It didn't take the Mets long to see that they had a polished pitcher, a young kid with great mechanics and leg drive, a power pitcher who knew how to pitch and brought a maturity to the team well beyond his years. In fact, his manager at Jacksonville in 1966, veteran baseball man Solly Hemus, noticed Seaver's maturity almost immediately.

"He has so much poise," Hemus said. "Tom reminds me of Bob Gibson out on the mound. He's in command all the time, and the kid is only 21 years old. Tom Seaver has a 35-year-old head on top of a 21-year-old body. Usually, we get a 35-year-old arm attached to a 21-year-old head."

It didn't take Seaver long to establish himself as a big-league pitcher. He himself said he wasn't about to accept the losing mentality that seemed to permeate the team. Like other great pitchers, the whole team seemed to pick up when he walked out to the mound.

"When you saw Tom Seaver, right out of the box you saw a very good, complete major league pitcher," Ron Swoboda remembers. "He didn't need any time to assimilate; he arrived the complete package, a great pitcher the day he showed up from the minors. Seaver was the golden boy, a kid who was in command of himself and the game from the get go. You knew whenever Seaver was out there you could score three runs and have a chance to win."

Bud Harrelson remembers it the same way. "From day one Tom showed he could pitch," Harrelson said. "He was a lot like Johnny Bench, who came up the same year. Both of them took charge immediately. Tom was simply ahead of his time. He wasn't overly cocky, but despite his age, he sure knew how to pitch."

Though the team lost 101 games in 1967, Tom Seaver finished with a record of 16-13, and with an earned-run average of 2.76. He completed 18 of his 34 starts, fanned 170 hitters in 251 innings and spun a pair of shutouts. The Mets had been a bad team for six years now, but suddenly they had a pitcher they could build upon. No wonder Tom Seaver was soon given the very complimentary nickname of "The Franchise."

# 8

# GIL AND THE GUYS

The 1967 season was one of mixed emotions. On the negative side, the team had slipped back into the National League basement and had again lost more than 100 games. They had also lost another manager with the resignation of Wes Westrum. Salty Parker was just an interim, no doubt about that, so the team would be seeking its third permanent skipper to pilot the team in 1968. On the positive side were Tom Seaver and his 16 victories. If the club could build on that, put together a pitching staff around their young right-hander and continue to bring in some talented young players, well, then improvement should come. But naming a manager was the first order of business. In what now would seem to be a strange move, the Mets actually traded a player to get themselves a manager.

Prior to the start of the 1968 season, the New Yorkers announced they had sent pitching prospect Bill Denehy along with $100,000 to the Washington Senators in return for their manager, Gil Hodges. It was a brilliant move for two reasons. The first was that Hodges was a New York icon, a prominent member of those great Brooklyn Dodgers teams that won so many pennants in the late 1940s and 1950s. A power-hitting first baseman with great defensive prowess, the big guy had 370 home runs in his career.

He was a solid .273 lifetime hitter and drove in 100 or more runs seven years in a row. Hodges played briefly for the Mets in both 1962 and 1963, giving the fans a last glimpse at a legend. Then he retired only to resurface as the manager of the Senators a year later, being named for the final 121 games of the 1963 season and going from there.

Though the Senators were an expansion team (the original Senators having moved to Minnesota), Hodges had them improving each year. By 1967 the team had a 76-85 mark, and respect for the big guy as a manager and handler of players was growing. He was the man the Mets wanted and they got him. But in truth, New York was the place he wanted to be. He still maintained a home in Brooklyn, a place where he would always be looked upon as a hero, a beloved figure forever associated with the Dodgers, the team fans still felt had been stolen from them 10 years earlier. As for the Mets players, Hodges made an immediate impression on them, as well.

"All of us knew Gil, knew who he was and what kind of ballplayer he had been," shortstop Bud Harrelson said. "He brought credibility to the team as soon as he arrived. Because he had come from the American League, he kind of just let us play in 1968 and didn't presume he knew everything about the league and the Mets. But you always knew he was in charge. Gil was a big, strong man, and I don't think anyone wanted to find out how strong. He also had huge hands, one of the reasons he was such a great first baseman. I remember being introduced to him at a Christmas party. He put out his hand, and I wasn't sure if I wanted my hand inside that huge thing that was there. I'm kidding, of course, but I think both of my hands could have fit inside one of his."

Left-handed pitcher Jerry Koosman, who had come up briefly in 1967 but made the team as a starter the next year had some preconceived notions about the new manager before he even met him. "I remember Hawk Harrelson, the old ballplayer turned broadcaster, had written a book in which he described Gil as pretty much a tyrant. I hadn't read it, but that was the word," Koosman said. "When Gil came to the Mets, a lot of us expected that kind of guy. Well, in 1968, Gil was just the opposite. I found him to be a fun person, joking around a lot, a good guy all year. He had a light attitude, would kid around with individuals and small groups. He was feeling the club out, seeing what kind of personnel he had. Once 1969 rolled around, however, he got a lot tougher.

"Maybe it was because he felt he had a team that could win. He became stricter that year, didn't have as many of those light conversations with the players. But he was always fair and knew what he was doing."

Ed Kranepool felt that one of the reasons the team went out and got Hodges was that they knew the fans, who had supported the Mets since the beginning, were starting to tire of losing. "I always felt that the New York fans were and are the greatest in the world," said Kranepool. "They were always knowledgeable, knew the game, and by 1967 last place wasn't fun any more. The team's marketing strategy had always been to make it fun, no matter how many games we lost, but by 1967 the fans began to wane a bit and wanted to see productivity. They began to expect the club to win. I could begin sensing the frustration. People can accept excuses for a while, but not forever.

"Gil was a strong disciplinarian and a tough manager. You played it his way or took to the highway. He always made decisions based on what he felt was right and that was it. He had one set of rules and didn't divert from them. It was apparent that he was the right man for the job at the time. He had the New York connection and the marquee name, but he knew he also had to remold the ball club. It wasn't a matter of just showing up any more after Gil arrived. So many guys were used to losing that they had negative habits. It's contagious. Gil wanted to put an end to that immediately. He set goals, and his first was to get the club to .500."

Ed Charles was a 34-year-old veteran when he was traded to the Mets from Kansas City in 1967. He had been around longer than most of the young players, and he, too, saw the change immediately when Gil Hodges took command of the team.

"Hodges changed the losing mindset," Charles explained. "He was an upfront type of manager, very knowledgeable about the game, very firm in what he expected from the players. He told us when we were out there he expected 100 percent effort. If we couldn't give it because of a physical reason, he wanted us to tell him, because he wouldn't put us on the field. A few guys were prima donnas when he took over and there were some early confrontations. But he established the fact immediately that he was the boss and that things wouldn't be like they were in the past.

"It was his whole demeanor and his approach to the game, the way he interacted with the players. He made it known there would be no favorites and that he expected everyone to do the job. If you couldn't, he didn't want you out there. Once he established that he was the boss the guys took notice in a hurry. I remember him getting mad once and telling us he would bring up the whole Tidewater (triple-A) ball club if he had to. We believed him."

So Hodges was step number one. Step number two was better ballplayers. The new manager wanted to solidify the roster and stop the revolving door of players. His method was to establish a core of young, scrappy players surrounded by a few seasoned veterans, such as the aforementioned Charles. Kranepool was already a veteran at first, though still in his early 20s. Young Bud Harrelson was beginning to establish himself at shortstop as was Grote behind the plate. Cleon Jones and Ron Swoboda were in the outfield, while young pitchers Jerry Koosman, Nolan Ryan, Dick Selma, and Jim McAndrew joined the pitching staff. Hodges then picked up veterans like Phil Linz, Al Weis, Art Shamsky, Don Cardwell, Cal Koonce, Ron Taylor J.C. Martin, and another young veteran in center fielder Tommie Agee to change the face of the team.

The biggest addition in 1968 would turn out to be left-hander Koosman, who had signed with the Mets in August of 1964 and had worked his way up through the minors. He had a cup of coffee in 1967, but by 1968 was ready. All Koosman did was take his place alongside Seaver and give the team a potent one-two punch, a righty and a lefty who both had the potential to be front-line starters and big winners.

"I got two starts when I came back at the tail end of 1967," Koosman recalls. "I probably wasn't on the same level as Seaver then, but I felt a kinship with him. The team wanted me to work more on a change and my curve, and felt I needed more seasoning. But once I returned, I think Tom and I learned from each other. We were both power pitchers. He, of course, had the lead role and developed into the spokesman for the club, both on and off the field. Tom was always well spoken and handled the media very well.

"I felt we had a pretty good ball club in 1968, but the other teams just seemed to be better. We were still lacking in the hitting department and often didn't score enough runs. Here I was, pitching against the likes of Mays, Stargell, Clemente, Aaron, Banks, Williams, and when I looked around, we didn't have any guys like that. The National League was so much different then. Teams looked to develop their own players from their farm systems, rarely looked to get players from the American League. The feeling then was that the American League was more of a curveball league, while the National had better fastball hitters. So not many players changed leagues in those days."

One case in point might have been new center fielder Agee. In his first full season with the Chicago White Sox in 1966, Agee batted .273 with 22 homers and 86 RBIs. He also swiped 44 bases. Joining the Mets prior to 1968, Agee had the misfortune of being beaned by the Cards' Bob Gibson in spring training. When he came back he went into a terrible slump and wound up hitting just .217 in 368 at bats, with only five homers, an anemic 17 RBIs and only 13 stolen bases. Clearly, he wasn't the same player he had been with the White Sox. Maybe changing leagues had something to do with it. The beaning didn't help, either, but Hodges decided to stick with him as his center fielder in 1969.

Because he didn't have star players at many positions, Hodges began a practice in 1968 that would pay dividends the following year. He platooned at various positions, playing the left-right percentages in an effort to put the best team possible out on the field every day. One player who didn't like this and because of it sometimes clashed with his manager was Ron Swoboda. Looking back, the brutally honest Swoboda admits that much of the fault was his.

"Gil brought authority with him when he joined the team," Swoboda said. "He was a big, strong guy who was very much in charge, and he had complete command of what he wanted to do as a manager. He and Rube [Walker] would talk a lot. Rube was the pitching coach, but was also like the bench coach today. Gil had a lot of confidence in his coaches, and we had a pretty damned good staff. When Gil got there I was coming off my best year in 1967, thought I had arrived as a major leaguer, and probably thought I was a little more important than I should have.

"For some reason, Gil and I began to grate on one another. It wasn't a lack of respect, just hardheadedness. I had things I liked to do and he had his way of doing things. For example, I used to take a lot of fly balls, grounders and liners in the outfield. One of our coaches, Eddie Yost, used to hit to me and I'd do a lot of my throwing during that drill. I don't think Gil liked that. He didn't have much regard for me as an outfielder, but I felt this was a way to make myself better, which I was determined to do. But the clashes were really my fault. He was the manager and I needed to understand that. For some strange reason, I've always struggled with authority figures. It shouldn't have happened that way. He just wanted us to do things his way and play the game the right way. He wasn't being unreasonable or asking anything extraordinary. There were just times I wanted to do something one way, and he wanted it another way.

"I just wish I could have learned those lessons a little earlier, because it ruined my relationship with him, and one of the things

I regret most from my time in the big leagues was not having a solid relationship with Gil. But I wanted to be playing all the time. Maybe that wasn't in the cards, but I wasn't ready to give it up. Sometimes you get hot when you're sitting. You can tell in batting practice. So not playing sometimes was very frustrating to me. My attitude was let me play more and I'll be a better hitter. I just couldn't get through the platooning. I was just never cool with it, but in the end Gil proved that he knew what he was doing."

Under Hodges in 1968, the Mets once again escaped the cellar, but didn't go any higher than ninth. They finished with a 73-89 record, best in franchise history, due largely to the one-two punch of Seaver and Koosman. "Tom Terrific," as he would become known, had a second consecutive 16-win season, finishing at 16-12 with a 2.20 earned-run average in 35 starts. He had 14 complete games and fanned 205 hitters while posting five shutouts. With more run support, he might well have been a 20-game winner that year. There was little doubt that this young power pitcher with the command and presence of a ten-year veteran, was the real deal.

As for the rookie Koosman, all he did was finish the season with a 19-12 record, almost becoming the team's first ever 20-game winner. Koosman had an impressive 2.08 earned-run average with 17 complete games in 34 starts. He had 178 strikeouts in 263.2 innings, and threw seven shutouts. Though 1968 would become known as the year of the pitcher—when the great Bob Gibson threw 13 shutouts and had a 1.12 earned-run average while Detroit's Denny McLain won 31 games—there was little doubt in the minds of most baseball people that the Mets had found themselves an incredible pair of young hurlers.

But those same experts saw little improvement in the rest of the team. After Seaver and Koosman, the only other pitcher with a winning record was reliever Cal Koonce at 7-4. No other starter won as many as ten. As for the hitters, they finished dead last in the National League with a .228 team batting average. The leading hitter was young Cleon Jones, who batted .297. Veteran third-sacker Charles led the team in homers with 15, while the sometimes-disgruntled Swoboda actually had the most RBIs with 59. But it simply wasn't a big year for hitters. No National League batter had as many as 40 home runs, and only four players hit 30 or more. Only one, the Giants' Willie McCovey, knocked in more than 100 runs. He had just 105. There were similar numbers in the American League, which produced just a single .300 hitter, batting champion Carl Yastrzemski at .301. No wonder the lords or baseball decided to lower the mound and compress the strike zone in 1969.

There was one other major change prior to the 1969 season. With expansion, the 10-team format was already a bothersome situation to some. There could only be one pennant winner, which meant nine teams wouldn't make it. Baseball was planning to expand once more—with two new teams in each league—and anything larger than a 10-team league would be near impossible. It was the American League that first announced it would break into two, six-team divisions. At first, the National wanted to hold at 12, but eventually followed suit. So at the outset of the 1969 season, each league would have two, six-team divisions and an extra playoff series to determine the pennant winner. The teams finishing first in the two divisions in each league would meet in a best-of-five series to determine which continued on to the World Series. In such a tradition-conscious sport, this change was akin to a major earthquake.

The Mets were part of the National League East, joining Montreal, Philadelphia, Pittsburgh, Chicago, and St. Louis. The West had the Giants and Dodgers, Houston, Cincinnati, Atlanta and San Diego. Montreal and San Diego, of course, were the new teams. There would be the same 162-game schedule, but each team would host those within its division nine times, and the six teams in the opposing division only six times. The Mets opposed this, at first, because it would limit the number of times the Dodgers and Giants came to town, and the two west coast teams still had legions of fans in New York. By coming to town only a half-dozen times instead the previous nine, the Mets felt they would lose three potential sellouts. But finally they agreed.

When the Mets came to camp prior to the 1969 season Las Vegas oddsmakers didn't think too much of the team. Strictly second division, lucky if they reach .500. Bottom line, the odds of the New York Mets winning the National League pennant were set at 100-1.

"I thought we'd be better in 1969," Ron Swoboda said, "that we could go out and play with almost anybody. We had been a little better in 1968, and I wanted to be even better than that, to take the next step. Only I didn't know what it was. Reaching .500 would be a step forward, winning 80 or 81 games. In fact, I thought that would be a big step forward. And while it didn't seem out of reach, I don't think anyone came out of spring training aiming at the moon."

Bud Harrelson remembers something Gil Hodges said to the team during spring training. "One day he got us together and said very quietly and straightforwardly, 'You guys lost 36 one-run games last year. If you had won half of them, you'd be in contention. If every pitcher on the team won just one game more than they lost, the team would be 10 games over .500.' It was logical, but simplistic. Of course he knew that Seaver would be more than one game over .500; Koosman, too. But Gil was trying to set the tone for the year. He wanted everyone to be just a little bit better."

Ed Kranepool agrees, though he felt the initial goal in 1969 was just to get the team to .500. "In other years we just showed up," was the way Kranepool put it. "Gil had his sights set on getting to .500. He expected improvement and wanted us to learn how to win, to be able to find ways to win."

For Ed Charles, it was the leadership of Gil Hodges that made things different at the beginning of the 1969 season. "Gil knew how to get the most out of his players," Charles said. "It didn't take him long to go to a platoon system as a number of positions. Some of the players didn't like it, the fans didn't like it, and even the press got on him for it. But he started it right away and stayed the course. By 1969, I think we had all adjusted to it. Then we responded."

Though the Mets were far from a star-studded aggregation at the outset of the 1969 season, the team had slowly put more pieces together. Hodges wanted every one of his 25 players to be available and serviceable. There would be no deadwood just taking up space. Everyone would have a role. Here's what the team looked like going into the season.

Pitching was again going to be the strong suit. If Seaver and Koosman were able to improve on their 1968 performances, the ball club would have a pair of aces capable of beating anyone. A pair of right-lefty power pitchers was tough to come by, and some were already looking back at the Koufax-Drysdale tandem of the early and mid-1960s to find a basis for comparison. That might be a stretch, but these two guys both appeared to have the potential for greatness. Hopefully, the two stars would have some backup now.

Rookie right-hander Gary Gentry was looked upon to follow the top two guys to stardom. Another power pitcher, the reed-thin Gentry was described as "fearless," a kid who went after hitters hard and wouldn't back down from a challenge. The fourth starter was veteran Don Cardwell, who had been in the majors since 1957 and with the Mets since 1967. He wasn't great, but steady, and usually gave his team a chance to win, a good guy to have in the four spot. A pair of young righties was also available to start and relieve if necessary. They were Jim McAndrew and Nolan Ryan. Ryan was especially intriguing. He had a blazing fastball and great stuff but was often wild. The fact that he had to spend several weekends a year with a National Guard unit always seemed to retard his progress. Ryan was a kid the word *potential* was created for. The question was would he ever fulfill it?

The relief corps also appeared solid, with righties Cal Koonce and Ron Taylor, a pair of seasoned veterans, and young lefties Jack DiLauro and Tug McGraw. McGraw was another intriguing pitcher. A free spirit, he had been with the Mets since 1965, and the prevailing opinion was that he'd be a starter. In fact, he was the first Mets pitcher ever to defeat Sandy Koufax. But after several up-and-down seasons, in which he often had to leave for military commitments, Tug spent all of 1968 pitching at Jacksonville in triple-A. Now he had made the team once again with the plan being to use him almost extensively out of the bullpen. In those days, there were no set-up men and closers, no specialists, so Hodges and pitching coach Rube Walker would have to decide where and when to use the relievers. Taylor figured to be the guy used primarily in what they call save situations today, though Koonce was also reliable enough to finish a game. As the rest of the National League would soon learn, this was a deep and effective pitching staff.

The everyday lineup wasn't exactly Murderer's Row. Here's how the lineup shook out after some early-season adjustments. Ed Kranepool was playing first. Young Ken Boswell, potentially a fine hitter, alternated at second with veteran Al Weis. Weis could also spell shortstop Bud Harrelson, who was coming off a knee injury. The veteran Charles, a righty swinger, alternated with left-handed hitting youngster Wayne Garrett at third. Jones in left and Agee in center were considered everyday players. In right, Swoboda wanted to be, but would find himself platooned with lefty swinging Art Shamsky. Hustling young Rod Gasper made the team in the spring and saw time in right and also at the other two outfield spots. Jerry Grote, considered one of the best defensive catchers in the league and a fine handler of pitchers, would do the bulk of the catching. Veteran J.C. Martin, a lefty swinger, was there to spell him, and young Duffy Dyer served as a third catcher. Infielder Bobby Pfeil was also available to play third and second, giving Manager Hodges still another option.

What the team lacked at the outset of the season was the big slugger, the guy who was a constant threat to knock the ball out of the park and had 100 RBIs potential. That's why Hodges felt he had to platoon, have everyone ready to play. No one on the 1969 Mets would get rusty and bored. All 25 players had to be ready to contribute in any way the manager felt best.

"We knew going in we had a pretty good defensive ball club," Jerry Koosman said, "and we could make some plays other teams couldn't. Do you give away some of those good defensive players to get offense? In fact, we had all kinds of good pitching and defense in the entire organization, and I think upper management decided to take on the rest of the National League that way. They felt they could do it because of Gil, and what he could bring to the table as the manager. It wasn't the worst formula in the world. The Dodgers had built a championship team around pitching and defense. So we all knew it could be done."

And what about the National League of 1969? The league was really at the tail end of a great era that began in the 1950s, when a ton of outstanding players began coming into the game. The National League had been much quicker than the American to sign the best African-American and Latin players, something that most felt gave them an advantage over the junior circuit. As the Mets prepared to take on the rest of the league, they knew they would be facing star-studded teams in both divisions, with the exception of the newer expansion teams. Because the league had grown from an eight to a 12-team circuit over the past eight years, there was some dilution of talent. But the superstars were still predominant. Let's take a quick look at just what the New Yorkers would be facing as they traveled and entertained teams from around the league.

From a hitting standpoint, some of the players those young Mets pitchers would be facing included Ernie Banks, Ron Santo, and Billy Williams in Chicago; Roberto Clemente, Al Oliver, Matty Alou, and Willie Stargell in Pittsburgh; Joe Torre, Curt Flood, and Lou Brock in St. Louis; Dick Allen in Philadelphia; Hank Aaron, Orlando Cepeda, Felipe Alou, and Rico Carty in Atlanta; Willie Mays, Willie McCovey, and Bobby Bonds in San Francisco; Johnny Bench, Pete Rose, Tony Perez, Lee Maye, and Alex Johnson in Cincinnati. There were others, of course, but these were some of the best hitters not only of their time, but of all time. They didn't make it easy on pitchers.

As for the opposing hurlers, there were plenty of them, as well. Remember, just the season before was the one known as "The Year of the Pitcher," when hurlers dominated. The Mets knew they didn't have a great hitting team, and that was the one area in which the team felt it still lacked. Here are just a few of the top arms the Mets would be facing in 1969: Ferguson Jenkins, Bill Hands, and Ken Holtzman in Chicago; Bob Veale and Steve Blass in Pittsburgh; Bob Gibson, Steve Carlton, and Nelson Briles in St. Louis; Phil Niekro and Ron Reed in Atlanta; Juan Marichal and Gaylord Perry in San Francisco; Jim Maloney in Cincinnati; Claude Osteen, Bill Singer, and Don Sutton in Los Angeles; and Larry Dierker in Houston. Those were just some of the top starters. A number of teams also had good secondary starters and deep bullpens. Taking all of this into account, it wasn't surprising that the Mets had those 100-1 odds against them winning.

Ironically, there was a cloud hanging over the season before the players even reported to spring training. The Players' Association threatened to strike unless the owners agreed to raise pension money. It was one of the earliest disputes in what would become almost the norm for the game for the next 30 years and would eventually result in the cancellation of the 1994 season in August, the only year there were no playoffs or World Series in nearly a century. An agreement to settle the threatened strike finally came on February 16, almost two weeks after pitchers and catchers were due to report to their respective camps.

The Mets also announced in February that their two top pitchers had both been given raises. Tom Seaver signed a new contract that would play him $35,000 in 1969, a raise of $10,000 over the previous year. Koosman, coming off his 19-win rookie season, was given a merit raise from the league minimum of $10,000 at the end of the 1968 season and would be earning $25,000 in 1969. Think about what the players are making today, and you'll see how far they have come and how they had to fight for everything back then. At the time, both Seaver and Koosman were happy, and so were the Mets. As general manager Johnny

Murphy said, "These are the two guys we call our untouchables, and they are worth the money."

By March 1, the final pair of unsigned players—Swoboda and J.C. Martin—inked their contracts for the coming year, and the team was complete and ready to go. The Mets had some notable spring games. In the space of three days, they not only defeated both teams that had been in the 1968 World Series, they buried them. First they dropped the World Champion Detroit Tigers, 12-0, then banged out 22 hits in beating the St. Louis Cardinals, 16-6. Suddenly, instead of the pitty-patter Mets, they were looking like the Queens Bombers. Were they the real Mets? Probably not. No one was kidding themselves about the Mets' hitting. Hodges just hoped it would be enough.

There was one other major question going into the 1969 season, and that was Hodges's health. On September 24, 1968, the Mets were playing in Atlanta, finishing out the season. During the game, Hodges began feeling poorly and decided to go back into the clubhouse. Jerry Koosman remembers.

"I started the game that night and remember it was very hot," Koosman said. "It wasn't one of my better games and I was knocked out about the sixth inning. Gil had gone back into the clubhouse about the fourth or fifth inning, and when I got back there he was laying on the trainer's table, his face very red. I asked him how he was and he answered a quick, 'I'll be all right.' They took him to the hospital for tests, and we soon learned he had suffered a mild heart attack. Rube Walker became the interim manager for the rest of the season, and I believe Gil remained in the hospital down there for several weeks. Once he was discharged, we all felt he would be all right."

Naturally, there were questions that spring. The manager tried to put them to rest when in an open letter to baseball writer Red Foley on February 18, in which he talked about the state of the team, he also addressed the issue of his health.

"I know the question of my health still has some people wondering about Gil Hodges's immediate future as Mets' manager," he wrote. "Well, all I can say is that I've never felt better, and the doctors, who are pleased with my progress, assure me I can look forward to managing the Mets this season. And believe me, that's just what I'm going to do."

As far as anyone could tell, Hodges was fine. He continued to do all the things he had done before and that a manager should do. The issue of his health would not come up again for some time, including the entire 1969 season.

Just prior to opening day, there was another interesting story. Back in 1969, the home computer was unheard of, something that was still almost part of the science fiction world. But there were big, huge computers that were already doing amazing things. One of these computers was asked to analyze data from all the baseball teams and come up with potential pennant winners for the new season. Not surprisingly, after analyzing a brace of statistical date, the computer predicted that St. Louis and Detroit would repeat as league champions. But there was another prediction that came out of the computer that had many baseball people scratching their heads. How dare could the computer say something like this?

According to the data digested by the computer, the Mets were a "dark horse" in the National League East. It said that defensively, the Mets were second best in the league to the Cardinals and acknowledged their fine young pitchers. To really challenge for a divisional title, according to the computer analysis, the Mets would need to score about 100 more runs than they had scored in 1968. Now the next part was really interesting. The computer pinpointed the Mets' inability to win close games as a major factor in their ninth-place finish in 1968.

Why was that so interesting? Remember what Bud Harrelson said Hodges had told the team about 1968. He reminded them that they had lost 36, one-run games that year, telling them that if they had won half, they could have been in contention. So maybe the computer wasn't that far off. Maybe there would be some surprises coming out of Shea Stadium in 1969. Not too many people agreed, but the games always have to be played on the field, and nowhere else.

# 9
# A Better Than Usual Start

The Mets had lost every single opening-day game in their short history. Maybe that shouldn't have been surprising considering the amount of losing the team had always done. It was symbolic, a losing start to another losing season. In 1969, the Mets were opening up at home against an expansion team, the Montreal Expos. They would have Tom Seaver on the mound and many felt this was one opening day game they would win. The starting lineup for the New Yorkers in game one was as follows:

**Tommie Agee, cf**
**Rod Gaspar, rf**
**Ken Boswell, 2b**
**Cleon Jones, lf**
**Ed Charles, 3b**
**Ed Kranepool, 1b**
**Jerry Grote, c**
**Bud Harrelson, ss**
**Tom Seaver, p**

There were a couple of surprises in manager Gil Hodges's batting order. Rookie Rod Gaspar, who had scrapped and hustled his way onto the ball club, got the start in right field. Ken Boswell, considered a good hitter but not a big power guy, was batting third. To some, that showed the weakness in the ball club, the lack of big bats in the center of the lineup. The team, as of opening day, didn't really have a three, four, or five guy in their lineup. In fact, the player with the most home-run potential on the team was center fielder Agee, who had hit 22 with the White Sox in 1966. Yet Hodges wanted him leading off. Ron Swoboda remembers.

"We didn't have a whole lot of speed on our team," he said. "Gil felt that Agee could give us offense at the head of our line-up, speed and power. He wasn't a typical leadoff hitter, but he could steal a base and that's where Gil wanted him. Looking back, he had him in the right place."

On April 8, some 44,541 fans came out to see baseball's first international game ever. It was the inaugural game for the expansionist Montreal Expos, making the Mets the veteran team, a kind of reversal of roles. The mayor of Montreal, Jean Drapeau, was there to throw out the first ball amid the pageantry that was opening day and the beginning of what would be an unforgettable season. But when the rag-tag Expos scored a pair of runs off Seaver in the first inning, many of the Mets faithful wondered what was going on. The Mets fought back, however, and by the time Seaver left after throwing 105 pitches in five innings, the Mets had a 6-4 lead.

Only the relievers made it look as if it was 1962 all over again. Veterans Al Jackson and Ron Taylor couldn't do the job, and by the time the Expos' Rusty Staub hit a solo homer and Coco Laboy slammed a three-run shot, both in the eighth inning, the Expos had an embarrassing 11-6 lead. The fans couldn't believe what was happening. "Same old Mets," many thought. Now they can't even beat an expansion team. It didn't matter that the New Yorkers rallied for four runs in the ninth, highlighted by a three-run pinch homer by young Duffy Dyer. In fact, they wound up with runners on first and second before Rod Gaspar fanned to end the game. The final score was 11-10, and the Mets had lost on opening day for the eighth straight year.

The next night the two teams were at it again, only this time just 13,827 fans pushed their way through the Shea Stadium turnstiles. Hodges tabbed young Jim McAndrew as his starter, and again it wasn't a pretty game. There were runs scored by at least one of the teams in eight of the nine innings. The Mets grabbed an early 4-0 lead, but McAndrew quickly faltered, Hodges yanking him after the Expos loaded the bases with none on in the second. In came Tug McGraw, who promptly shut the door. The young lefty then threw goose eggs before tiring in the eighth. Nolan Ryan came in at the finish, wasn't real sharp, but the Mets won the game, 9-5, thanks to their hitters who produced for a second straight day. The Mets had 12 hits, including a homer by Boswell, while Jones, Grote, and Kranepool drove in two runs each.

In their first two games, the supposedly anemic offense had scored 19 runs, while the potentially outstanding pitching staff had already yielded 16 runs. The team had split its first two games, but had done it in the topsy-turvy fashion, with hitting instead of pitching. That wasn't the way it was supposed to be. The next day, they reverted somewhat to form. Young Gary Gentry got his first career start and, helped by a pair of Tommie Agee homers, defeated the Expos, 4-2. That was more like it.

That was also the end of playing an expansion team for a while. Next on the agenda was the defending-champion St. Louis Cardinals. It was against this kind of team this early in the season that the Mets usually started going south. It was no different this time. The Cards won the first one, 6-5, defeating Jerry Koosman in his first start, then took the second, 1-0, despite a brilliant six-hit effort by the veteran Don Cardwell. The third game was a battle of right-handed aces as Tom Seaver went up against the highly competitive Bob Gibson. Once again, Seaver was roughed up early. Lou Brock went after Seaver's first pitch and doubled to right center. Curt Flood promptly singled him to third, and both runners came around to score before the inning ended.

Gibson, in the meantime, began mowing the Mets down with seeming ease. The New Yorkers didn't get a hit until Kranepool doubled in the fifth. He would come around to score on a Harrelson single, but that's all the Mets would get. Gibson went the distance to send the Mets to a third straight loss, 3-1, running his lifetime record against the New Yorkers to an amazing 22-3. He joined the Giants' Juan Marichal (21-2) and the Dodgers' Don Drysdale (23-6) among the most devastating Mets killers in the National League. Not surprisingly, all three pitchers are now in the Hall of Fame. At the end of the day, the Mets were already in fifth place in the new National League East with a 2-4 mark, three games behind the division-leading, 5-1 Pirates. It was not the start the team had hoped for. Jerry Koosman said they knew by then that the pitchers had to pick things up.

"Early in the season we realized we had to win low-scoring games," Koosman explained. "You simply had to pitch your butt off. If you got one run, you had to try to win the game. If you got two, then you *had* to win. If you got three or four, you were expected to win. If you couldn't win those games, you might well lose your spot in the rotation. Once we really got into the season we realized we had to pitch like that for the team to succeed."

But this wouldn't exactly be the formula in the early weeks of the season. There were a lot of up-and-down, low-scoring, then high-scoring games. The team was still hitting better than expected but not pitching as well as everyone thought they would. In fact, even Koosman was having trouble living up to his own formula. After splitting a pair with the Phillies, the team traveled to Pittsburgh where the Mets' lefty went up against the Pirates' Bob Moose. Pittsburgh promptly batted around in the first inning and scored four runs. The closest the Mets got was 5-3 in the fourth, but Moose put out the fire and went on to fan 11 in an 11-3 rout. Nolan Ryan was also knocked around in relief as the young pitchers seemed to be learning tough lessons.

When the Pirates took the second game of the series, 4-0, the New Yorkers found themselves already in a 3-7 hole.

For the remainder of April, the Mets looked like little more than a slightly improved version of their team from a year earlier. After winning a pair from the Cards, they lost two of three against Philly and Pittsburgh. Then Cubs beat them three of four in the first head-to-head meeting of the year. Leo Durocher's charges defeated Seaver in the opener, dropping Tom Terrific's record to 1-2. Then they bombed Don Cardwell, 9-3, and pinning a loss on reliever Koonce, 8-6. Finally Tug McGraw stopped the bleeding in the final game, winning it 3-0. That left the Mets with a 7-11 record, not much to write home about. In the meantime, the Cubs had sprinted out into the division lead, setting up a major rivalry between the clubs that would play out over the next five months.

From there the team went to Montreal, and in their first ever game in Canada suffered a potential loss that could have sabotaged the entire season. They won the game, 2-0, but that wasn't the big story. Jerry Koosman started and was throwing a two-hit shutout in the fifth inning when he suddenly summoned his manager and trainer to the mound.

"I was facing John Bateman," Koosman recalls, "and with two strikes on him threw an inside fastball just to brush him back a bit. As soon as I threw the pitch my arm went numb. Gil wanted to play it safe and quickly took me out. I remember going into the trainer's room and saying I'm okay, my arm is fine. They sent me to New York where I was examined, but doctors couldn't find anything wrong. The team went from Montreal to Chicago and I rejoined them there. But as soon as I tried to throw, the pain got so bad that tears came to my eyes. I couldn't even reach home plate.

"I remember our GM, Johnny Murphy, coming in and saying that he had a similar problem when he pitched for the Yankees years earlier. He reached over and touched a spot just behind my armpit saying when he had it the pain was right there. Boom, the tears came to my eyes again. That was the spot, all right. There was a small muscle located there that had become knotted. It wasn't something you could operate on. I don't even know if they would treat it any differently today. The only thing they could do then was to rub it and put pressure on it. Believe it or not, it took nearly a month to work it out and get it back to where I could pitch."

When he was hurt, of course, no one knew how long Koosman would be out. It goes without saying that the team didn't want to lose its 19-game winner from a year earlier. That would be an irreplaceable loss, one that would mean kissing the season goodbye, or at least the part of it that said the team could finish at .500 or better. The day after Koosman was hurt, Seaver topped the Expos, 2-1, evening his record and allowing the Mets to finish April at 9-11. Koosman wouldn't pitch again until May 24, meaning he was out nearly a month, but when he returned the team was almost exactly where they were when he went down, two games under .500.

It was a month of ups and downs. Early on the team lost Nolan Ryan to the disabled list with a groin pull, and Jim McAndrew missed a start or two with a sore finger. But in a May 15, game against the Braves, "the Amazins'," as they were sometimes called, scored eight runs in the eighth inning to win, 9-3. So the team was doing things that previous Mets clubs hadn't done, but still not showing the kind of consistency needed to make a move. The Cubs, in the meantime, were solidifying their hold on first place, and Leo Durocher's ball club was beginning to look like the team to beat. The one bright spot all month long was Cleon Jones. The left fielder appeared to be coming into his own as a hitter, leading the National League with a scorching .390 mark just after the middle of the month. The team had never had a hitter like that before.

On May 21, the Mets topped the Atlanta Braves, 5-0, behind Tom Seaver's three hitter, his fifth straight win, which gave him a 6-2 mark on the year. The victory brought the team to .500, at 18-18, the latest point in any season that they had been at the break-even mark. Jones drove in a pair of runs and raised his batting average to .391. The team was now a half-game behind the Pirates for second and five and a half behind the front-running Cubs (25-14). In addition, Jerry Koosman was beginning to work his way back, having pitched five innings in a minor league game in Memphis, striking out 10.

"He looked good," pitching coach Rube Walker said. "There was no sign of anything wrong with his shoulder. He came straight overhand, and about 75 percent of his fastballs were very good."

Koosman was optimistic about his return and about the club's chances. "Now all we need is for Nolan to come back, and we'll give those Cubs a battle," he said. "I don't think Chicago can play that good all year long. Somebody is going to start catching up with them, and I think we will the next time we [meet] them."

Of course, right after reaching .500 the team got walloped by the Braves, 15-3, with McGraw taking the shellacking. Gentry was then beaten by Houston, 7-0, putting them two games under before Koosman was set to make his return against those same Astros. Houston had been an expansion club in 1962, same as the Mets, but for some reason had always given the New Yorkers fits. This year seemed no different. Maybe the returning Koosman could turn it around? Gentry had been erratic, showing a tendency to make bad pitches at the worst time, while McGraw, who had done well in some spot starts, seemed more suited to being a long reliever.

Koosman joked about being on a 100-pitch limit and not being allowed to go nine. He shouldn't have worried. Houston beat him decisively, 5-1, and when the Astros beat Seaver the next day, 6-3, and then the Padres defeated McAndrew, 3-2, the Mets had lost five straight. After cresting at .500, the team had returned to its losing ways and suddenly saw it slipping away again at 18-23. Now the Mets were at a crucial part of the season, maybe the most crucial part. They had fought their way to .500, only to watch any elation dashed by the five-game losing streak. Worse yet, the game against the Padres was the first of 16 straight they would be playing against west coast teams. After entertaining the Padres, the Giants and Dodgers were slated to visit Shea before the New Yorkers hopped a plane to the west coast to meet those three teams again. Not only had the Giants and Dodgers, especially, always given the Mets fits, but west coast trips had often proven disastrous, sometimes fatal. The Mets' west coast home-and-away odyssey would span 16 games. If the Mets, for example, lost 10 of them, they would come home 11 games under .500, and any hopes for a special season would be pretty much dashed. They had already dropped the first one to the Padres.

Now it was Koosman's turn again. The young lefty went back to the mound to face the Padres in the second game of the series, this time pitching on just three days' rest. Any concern about the lingering effects of his shoulder injury suddenly disappeared. He was the Koosman of old, throwing smoke and making the San Diego hitters look like little leaguers. No pitch count this time. After nine innings, the game was still scoreless, but the tall south-paw had fanned 14 Padres. When he struck out his 15th hitter in the top of the tenth, Koosman had set a new Mets record, top-ping Nolan Ryan's previous mark of 14. Tug McGraw pitched the top of the 11th and benefited from a great play by catcher Grote, who pounced on a bunt attempt like a cat and fired to second base to begin a nifty double play. The Mets finally pushed across a run in the bottom of the 11th and won it, 1-0. McGraw got credit for the win, but it was the pitching of Jerry Koosman that had the Mets elated and enabled them to end their losing streak.

The Padres were only in for a pair of games. Now it was the Giants' turn, and it was always exciting when Willie Mays returned to Shea. The "Say Hey Kid" still had legions of fans in New York and always performed well against the Mets. It wasn't easy to count all the game-winning hits he had against the New Yorkers over the years. Maybe the most memorable came in 1965, when the great Warren Spahn joined the Mets at age 44 to finish out his amazing career. One night, Spahn hooked up with Giants ace Juan Marichal, and the two hurlers kept shutting down hitter after hitter and posting nothing by zeroes on the scoreboard. The game finally went into extra innings, 11, 12, 13, 14. At one point, Giants manager Herman Franks asked Marichal if he wanted to come out of the game.

"If that old man can keep going out there, so can I," Marichal said, referring to Spahn.

The game went into the 16th inning when Mays reminded the fans at Shea and Warren Spahn how great he was. He blasted a solo home run, and the Giants won the game, 1-0. Ironically, Mays's first major league hit back in 1951 was also a home run off Spahn. The two future Hall of Famers had come full circle.

So Mays was always the featured attraction when the Giants came to town. Waiting for them this time was Tom Seaver. Seaver pitched well, as usual, got some late-inning help from Ron Taylor and won it, 4-3. The next day Gary Gentry shut the Giants down, 4-2. The win gave the Mets a 12-12 record for the month of May and brought their overall mark to 21-23. Seaver had won six of his last seven starts and was developing into a true ace at 7-3. But there were once again both ups and down as the team fought to get to .500, a first step before trying to go even further. They were both winning and losing the close games, dropping 3-2 decisions for the Expos and Cubs, then beating the Cubs twice by 3-2 scores in a doubleheader behind Seaver and McGraw. Twice during the month the offense exploded for 11 runs, but they were also shutout on two occasions. Young Gary Gentry was proving to be a solid number-three starter, but he had a tendency to pitch a real strong game followed by a mediocre one. At this point, the Mets were showing all the earmarks of a .500 team at best.

But once again they were flirting with .500. Then the next night they completed a rare sweep. Jim McAndrew started, but left in the second inning with a blister on his middle pitching finger. This time, however, the relievers held the fort while the Mets twice came from behind with two-run innings against Giants starter Bob Bolin. A two-run triple by Grote and RBI singles by Kranepool and Swoboda did the job. Ron Taylor got the win in relief when Giants pitchers walked four straight Mets in the ninth inning, the final one being Swoboda, forcing in Bud Harrelson with the run that gave the New Yorkers a 5-4 victory.

The game was significant for several reasons. It was the team's fourth straight victory, bringing them within a game of .500 again, and it marked the first time ever that they had swept the Giants in a three-game series. Jerry Koosman, for one, felt that all the preparation demanded by Hodges was paying off.

"Gil wanted everyone executing the fundamentals," explained Koos. "To minimize mental errors and poor execution, he instituted a system of fines. If you didn't cover first base in time, it was a fine. If you failed to bunt a guy over—fine. There were fines for everything, and the next day he had you doing extra work. We had rehearsed these basic plays over and over in spring training. The fines were his way of making the point that you have to execute.

"He also had all the pitchers participate in base-running drills more than other clubs. Most teams get their pitchers out of the way and let them do their work in the outfield. But Gil wanted more guys able to do more things. In the National League at that time you sometimes had to use your entire roster to win a game. If there was an extra pitcher in the bullpen, a guy who wouldn't get in the game that day, Gil might have him serve as a pinch runner. He wanted to be able to use all the bodies at his disposal."

After sweeping the Giants, the Mets had the next group of visitors, the L.A. Dodgers. Jerry Koosman was back on the mound facing lefty Claude Osteen. It turned into a pitchers' battle. The Mets got a break when Jerry Grote's pop to third got caught in a swirling Shea Stadium wind and eluded third baseman Bill Sudakis. That led to a pair of runs and was all Koosman needed. As he had said earlier, in close games you pitch your butt off, and that's just what he did, completing the 2-1 victory that brought the team back to .500 at 23-23. Afterward, he admitted he did it with less than his best stuff.

"I didn't have my good curve and my fastball, while it was good, [it] wasn't going where I wanted it to," he said. "I didn't have my rhythm, but I will say when they got that man to third I was able to reach back and fire."

The next night Tom Seaver took center stage and trimmed the Dodgers, 5-2, running his record to 8-3, taking the Mets a game over .500, and running the win streak to six games, second longest in team history. When the National League standings were posted on the morning of June 5, the Mets were in a very unfamiliar position, tied for second place with the Pittsburgh Pirates and a game and a half ahead of the defending-champion Cardinals. The only bad news—if there could be bad news about a Mets team over .500 in June—was that the Chicago Cubs were on fire. Leo Durocher's charges, led by their middle of the line-up power with Billy Williams, Ernie Banks, and Ron Santo, were playing at a .686 pace, their 35-16 record giving them a huge, nine-game lead over the rest of the field. If there was going to be a chase it would have to start soon.

Suddenly, however, the Mets were winning every which way—big, small, and come from behind. After Seaver took the measure of the Dodgers, the Mets completed the week with a 1-0, 15-inning classic, Ron Taylor getting the win. The streak was now at seven as the club took a day to fly out to the west coast. Could they now duplicate their success away from Shea? First up was San Diego. The locale might have been different, but the result was the same. Gary Gentry whipped the Padres, 5-3, as the Mets came from behind to set a new franchise-record win streak, eight straight. The other good news was that Nolan Ryan was activated before the game, his groin injury healed. Everyone was healthy again.

The streak continued. Koosman beat the Padres, 4-1, evening his record at 3-3. Then Seaver won his ninth, a 3-2 win over San Diego for the team's 10th straight victory. Finally it was Don Cardwell winning the opener against San Francisco, 9-4. That one marked the Mets' 11th win in a row and gave them a record of 29-23, by far the team's best June 10 mark in history. Tommie

Agee belted a pair of homers and Cleon Jones had one in support of Cardwell's pitching. All good things, of course, have to end, and the next night the streak became history as the Giants won, 7-2. The club then lost two of three to the Dodgers, all close games. In fact, though Koosman lost, he gave up just a single run, the 1-0 game, proving he was all the way back from his arm problem earlier in the season. The team finished its west coast trip at 30-26 and ready for more good things.

By now, people were beginning to notice that these weren't the same old Mets. Dodgers manager Walt Alston noted that "the Mets have grown up. They no longer beat themselves. They hold on to one-run leads and they make the big plays."

Sportswriter Joe Trimble called the Mets the "best expansion team in major league history, beyond a doubt." He went on to point out that some 178 players had donned the Mets uniform since the club began play in 1962, but that they finally had a very solid product. "It took eight years and much patience by the fans as well as the front office," he wrote. He also pointed out that the team's entire roster, with the exception of Agee and Grote, had been home grown through the team's farm system, a further tribute to an organization that had done things right.

The success the team had in the home-and-away series against the west coast teams also began to convince the players that what they were doing was no fluke. "I think those two series against the west coast teams was the biggest turnaround," Bud Harrelson recalled. "Up to then, we had never played well against west coast teams, especially the Dodgers and Giants. They always kicked our butts. This time they came in and we beat them in New York, then went out to the coast and beat them again. And that's when we began to say, 'Hey, we're competitive. Things are different.'"

Ed Charles remembers something else about that west coast trip, something that also changed the tone for the remainder of the season.

"We had about two free-for-alls that year," Charles said, "with Cincinnati and Houston. As usual, it involved brush-back pitches or hit batters. When we went to San Francisco on that west coast trip we had a team meeting. Tommie, Cleon and I were kind of the ringleaders. A lot of our guys, especially Tommie and Cleon, were being brushed backed and hit. Up to then, we didn't feel our pitchers were retaliating, and we were annoyed. We told them flat out if they didn't start protecting us, don't expect a lot of runs. We needed someone to step up to the plate. It was Jerry Koosman who set the tempo for the staff. He began knocking guys down left and right, retaliating as soon as someone tried to intimidate us. The other pitchers just fell in line. That sent a message that the Mets wouldn't be intimidated, something that was very important back then. And seeing our pitchers step up like that gave us a feeling that we were gonna kick butt if everyone did his job."

Ron Swoboda confirmed what Charles said, alluding to games with the Cubs where pitchers from both sides had to knock hitters down. "Durocher and Hodges had a history from Brooklyn Dodgers/New York Giants days," Swoboda said. "When we played them, they were always tough games, knock-down games. They tried to knock our hitters down, but our pitchers came right back. Koosman would throw a baseball right through you. Seaver would hit you, and Gentry was fearless. Our pitching staff showed up and that was protection for everyone."

No one could complain about the way the Mets were playing. Everyone was contributing. Agee was showing power at the top of the lineup, and Jones was among the two or three top hitters in the league. Though Hodges continued to platoon at several positions, he seemed to be pushing the right buttons. Because everyone was contributing and the team was winning, no one complained. But good ball clubs don't stand pat. If there is a good deal staring them in the face, they pull the trigger. The day after they finished their west coast trip, the Mets announced they had obtained 33-year-old first-baseman Donn Clendenon from the Montreal Expos for four young players from their farm system. The plan was to have the righty-swinging Clendenon platoon with southpaw swinger Ed Kranepool at first.

Clendenon had spent the first eight years of his career with Pittsburgh, hitting over .300 twice and showing very good power. He wasn't considered one of the top sluggers in the National League, but in his best season, 1966, he batted .299 with 28 homers and 98 RBIs. The 6'4" Clendenon wasn't happy in Montreal and talked about quitting. He was hitting just .240 when the Mets picked him up, but he gave the team a dimension it had lacked before. Looking back now, several of the Mets feel the trade for Clendenon was the final piece of the puzzle.

"Clendenon was very important," Ed Kranepool said. Knowing full well he would lose playing time, the Mets veteran still welcomed the newcomer. "Donn gave us experience. He had that personality from being in Pittsburgh, loud and boisterous, and he performed when given the opportunity. It didn't take long for him to become a leader."

Ron Swoboda was another who welcomed Clendenon's presence, fully appreciating all the attributes the former Pirate brought to the ball club.

"Clendenon was the only offensive change that year, but he was a good one," Swoboda said. "It wasn't only his offense, but his personality, as well. He was one of those wonderful characters who could get on your nerves, but did it in a way that was fun. He rode everybody in a fun way, had nicknames for everyone. He was an elder statesman who could lead. He had the authority to go up to someone and tell him he was doing something the wrong way, though he would say it with rather colorful language. We all knew that Donn had played on some great teams and would be a huge addition to the Mets."

As for Bud Harrelson, he was another who saw the importance of the trade. "Clendenon's acquisition completed the team," said the shortstop. "He was a real power guy, and no part of the ballpark could hold him. He became the first legitimate guy who could turn the game around for us with one swing. Agee and Jones could do it, too, but Clendenon added veteran stability. When he hit one good he used to tell the pitcher, 'You threw it right where I was swinging.'"

As for Clendenon, he was happy to be with the Mets for two reasons. Not surprisingly, one of them was Gil Hodges, who he had met years earlier when Gil was managing the Washington Senators and Clendenon was with the Pirates.

"I was having some trouble in the field back then," Clendenon said, "and before an exhibition game with the Senators I worked up the guts to go over and ask him to help me. I think that he's the best guy for any right-handed first baseman to copy. He's also the kind of man who won't walk over and offer advice, but if you ask it, he will give you all the help he can. I had 'stiff hands' and was always told to use both hands when taking throws. Gil said it wasn't necessary and showed me how to relax my hand and catch the ball with the glove."

He was also happy to be out of Montreal and back with a team that was getting awfully close to contending.

"I don't think I ever really fitted into [Montreal's] plans," he said. "They took me in the expansion draft, then when they were in a long losing streak they didn't play me much. I don't see how a .280 lifetime hitter who has knocked in a lot of runs should be sitting on the bench of an expansion team which was losing."

Clendenon was a guy who didn't like to lose and came to New York ready to play. Returning from the west coast and with Clendenon in the lineup, the Mets continued to pick up the pace. In fact, Clendenon made an immediate impact by driving in the leading or winning run in his first 16 games. Not too shabby. The club took three of four from the Phillies, then three of four from the Cards, faded a bit and lost four of their next seven to Philly and Pittsburgh, and as June turned into July, the club split a four-game set with St. Louis. The Mets finished June with a 19-9 record and on the morning of June 30, they had a 39-32 record, eight games behind the Cubs, who were still playing well at 49-26. The Mets, however, seemed to be firmly ensconcing themselves in second place. They had a three-game bulge on the Pirates and led the Cards by six.

When Tom Seaver pitched the Mets past the Pirates on June 29, he ran his record to 12-3 for the year and hadn't lost a game in more than a month. His victory tied Atlanta's Phil Niekro for most wins in the league. Better yet, it was his 44th lifetime victory. In not quite two and a half seasons, the hard-throwing right-hander had become the winningest pitcher in Mets history.

With the halfway point of the season approaching, the Mets continued their amazing run. Seaver and Cardwell whipped the Pirates in a doubleheader, 11-6 and 9-2, as the Mets batters kept surprising everyone with their run-scoring ability. A third straight victory over Pittsburgh ran the team record to 45-34. The Mets were now 11 games over .500 and counting. But a big series was now looming with the front-running Cubs coming to town for a three-game set. The Chicagoans had been slumping a bit and when they rolled into New York, Leo Durocher's charges had just a five-game lead over the Mets. In the opener, Jerry Koosman would be facing the Cubs' ace, Ferguson Jenkins.

Koosman pitched very well, only for much of the game Jenkins was better. The Chicago right-hander was a workhorse who was on his way to a third straight 20-win season. Jenkins began mowing down the Mets right from the beginning. By the ninth inning the Cubs had a 3-1 lead, both pitchers still in there. The lone Met hit to that point was Ed Kranepool's seventh home run of the year in the fifth inning. Now Jenkins was just three outs away from a victory. But these weren't the Mets of 1962, 1965, or even 1968. These Mets didn't seem to know the meaning of the word quit. Three straight doubles to open the inning brought two runs home to tie the game as a huge Shea Stadium crowd of 55,096 fans exploded with joy.

But it wasn't over yet. With Cleon Jones on second, the Cubs walked the next hitter to set up a potential double play. A ground out to the right side enabled both runners to advance. Now Ed Kranepool was up. Jenkins tried to work him carefully, keep the ball on the outside of the plate, but Kranepool reached out and poked a bloop single to left, driving in Jones with the winning run. Players and fans went crazy. The Mets had won another nail-biter and had moved within four games of first place. It was really beginning to look as if something special was happening with this team that had been a laughingstock for so long. Nothing was stopping them. With Koosman going the route again and pitching so well, the club now had two outstanding frontline pitchers at the top of the rotation. They would show that to the Cubs once more in a very special way the next night.

With a record crowd of 59,083 fans jamming into the six-year-old ballpark in what was suddenly a very big game, Seaver took his 13-3 record out to the mound to face the good Cubs hitters. Only on this night, none of them were hitting, and the reason was simple. Seaver had great stuff and was mowing them down with ease. There was a one-two-three first and then a one-two-three second. It stayed that way through the third, fourth, fifth, and sixth innings. That's when the excitement began building. Seaver was still perfect. A one-two-three seventh, then a one-two-three eighth. During their short history, no Mets pitcher had ever thrown a no-hitter, let alone a perfect game. Now, Seaver was just three outs away. He took the mound again, the Mets holding a 4-0 lead, but Seaver and everyone else were undoubtedly thinking about those last three tough outs.

Catcher Randy Hundley was first up in the ninth. The crowd was hushed, hanging on each pitch. Seaver had relied mostly on his great fastball and his ability to spot it on this night. He had great command and worked the hitters wisely and well. Hundley decided not to wait and tried to cross up the Mets' defense with a bunt. Seaver came off the mound quickly, scooped it up and threw to first. The crowd let out a huge roar. One out! Then they began booing Hundley for what they perceived as an attempt to get a cheap hit. But, hey, that's just part of the game, and if it started a rally, who knows. The Mets had rallied from 3-1 down in the ninth just the day before.

Next up was rookie center fielder Jimmy Qualls. Qualls was a switch-hitter playing in just his 18th big league game. Like Hundley, he decided not to wait. As expected, Seaver threw a fastball, a little high, and ticketed for the outside corner of the plate. Qualls swung, and in an instant a huge groan went up from the crowd. The rookie had lined a solid single to left center, breaking up the no-hitter and potential perfect game. After booing Qualls for a few seconds, the crowd rose and gave Seaver a standing ovation. Tom tipped his cap, then went back to business, retiring the final two hitters via popups and closing it out with a brilliant, one-hit, 11-strikeout gem.

The victory was their seventh straight and elevated the Mets record to a season best 47-34. The Cubs were at 52-33, giving them just a three-game lead with just one game difference in the all-important loss column. Now there was no denying what was on people's minds, something considered impossible at the beginning of the season. The New York Mets had a chance to win the National League East.

# 10

# LIGHTNING IN A BOTTLE

Tom Seaver's one-hit gem came in the Mets' 81st game of the season, the halfway mark. In a way, it marked a high point, the team's cresting for the first time. They were 13 games above .500 and just three games out of first place. The way things had been going, it almost seemed as if the team was ready to sweep past the Cubs, forge into first place and take it from there. After all, this was a Mets team that was suddenly firing on all cylinders. They had not one, but two pitching aces, a very strong defense, and were getting some surprising clutch hits. Manager Gil Hodges's plan was working. Everyone was contributing. Ron Swoboda talked about the formula that was making it work for the Mets.

"We had a very solid infield and not much fell in the outfield," he said. "When I was in right I always had a good relationship and good communication with Agee in center. We both had something in common, we always wanted the ball and didn't care what we had to do to get it. Cleon was the same way and got most everything in left. There weren't too many catchers better than Grote. He was great at throwing guys out and knew how to handle the pitching staff. He even developed as a hitter who could use the bat, was a little bit smarter at the plate than everyone thought.

"I always included pitching as part of defense. Nothing happens until your pitcher lets go of the ball. How you put it up to the hitters is related to what you do defensively. Our pitching staff put the ball in play very well, so we didn't have to make that many outstanding plays defensively. There were many more routine outs because of the way our pitchers threw. We all knew that many games were going to be close and, obviously, to win you just need one more run than the other guy. If your pitching staff is doing the job, and you have that solid defense behind them, then you don't feel the added burden of having to score a bunch of runs each night."

Swoboda also said that the surge of victories that had brought the Mets close to the division lead was a little daunting, especially for guys who hadn't been there before.

"It's pretty scary because when you've never had your hands on it before, you can't lose it. We were always lovable losers and we knew that would get better. But once you realize your arm is long enough to grab the ring, then you don't want to lose it. So it's scary and fun at the same time. I think by that point in the season we had hardened as a team. Because of the great run we had to get us in the race, we began to have a strong sense of ourselves. It had happened at the right time because it began to tell us we were good enough."

However, the euphoria brought about by Seaver's gem was short lived. The next night the Cubs managed to salvage the third game of the set, parlaying a five-run fifth inning against Gary Gentry into a 6-2 victory. Still, Hodges was pleased, only he didn't like losing a sloppy game. "Anytime you take two of three it has to be considered a good series," he said. "We made some mistakes in this one, and Gentry simply didn't pitch as well as he's capable of pitching."

The loss began a stretch of games in which the Mets' magic began to fade. It wasn't a major slump, but from 47-34 on July 9, the team went to 64-51 on August 16, and they had to beat the

San Diego Padres in a doubleheader that day to get there. That meant they had played just .500 ball (17-17) over a five-week period. What's more, the Cubs had rebounded, and the defending champion Cardinals had come to life. When the National League East standings appeared on August 17, the Cubs were first with a 74-44 mark, still playing .600 ball (.627) and a full 30 games over .500. The Mets were at 64-51 and now eight and a half games off the pace. To make matters worse, they were just a percentage point ahead of St. Louis, which had a 66-53 record. Now, if the Cubs faltered, it could be a hot Cardinals team that would steal the division. The Mets' chances certainly appeared just a bit dimmer than they had been a month or so earlier.

During this stretch, there was a nine-game losing streak and even their vaunted pitchers were taking some cruel and unusual punishment. At one point, Seaver lost four of five starts, including an 8-5 defeat by the Reds after which the ace right-hander complained of some stiffness in his pitching shoulder. Any discomfort in an arm, elbow, or shoulder of a pitcher is cause for concern. And it wasn't the first time. Some three weeks earlier doctors had checked Seaver's shoulder because of some discomfort and stiffness. Nothing amiss was found, and he continued to pitch.

That same night, Nolan Ryan pitched a gem in the second game of a twin bill against the aforementioned Reds, beating them 10-1 for his first victory since June 20. The bad news section of the good news was that Ryan had to leave for another two-week stint of military duty, something that always seemed to set him back a bit, and no one was sure just how much the fast-balling righty could be counted on for the rest of the season. With Ryan, it was a case of *when he was good he was very, very good, but when he was bad ... well, you know the rest.*

Koosman was long recovered from his early-season arm woes and had pitched some brilliant games. But after his loss to the Astros, 8-7, on August 12, his record fell to 9-8. And when rookie Gary Gentry lost to Houston the very next night, 8-2, he was sporting a 9-10 mark. It didn't take a mathematician to realize that put together, Koosman and Gentry were pitching just .500 baseball. That wasn't good enough for the number two and three starters on a team that wanted to contend. To make matters worse, the Mets had now lost 10 straight games to their fellow expansion team from 1962, the Astros. Houston seemed to have the Mets' number for the entire twin histories of their franchises. It was hard to figure.

The real low point came on August 14. After spending 72 straight days in second place, the Mets emerged on the backside of a Houston three-game sweep that not only left them trailing the Cubs by nine and a half games, but also saw them slip behind the Cards into third place. That was when the euphoria that had crested when the team cut the Cubs' lead to just three games on July 9—the night Seaver pitched his near-perfect game—had all but disappeared. In the spring, Hodges had talked about the team winning 85 games. For a brief period of time, it looked as if the New Yorkers could do much better than that. But after that nine-game slide and 34-game stretch of playing .500 ball, the goal had become much more modest once more.

Was the near-incredible run over? If it was, the New Yorkers had certainly earned respect and credibility. These were surely not the Mets of old, not the Mets of Casey or Marvelous Marv, or Choo Choo. They were no longer the lovable losers of the early and mid-60s. No, these Mets were a baseball team that even Gil Hodges was proud of, as he confirmed after a July victory over the Cubs that had brought them to within three and a half of the top.

"I think these boys have made their mark to the Cubs and to everyone else," the manager told the press. "You don't cinch a pennant in July, not with two and a half months of tough baseball to play. But they certainly are a contender now. Ask any of them. They believe. It has been a tremendous team effort. But we really began to win when Tommie [Agee] began to hit. It's a great thing to get that leadoff hitter on base, and it's even better when he homers or starts out with an extra-base hit.

LIGHTNING IN A BOTTLE 161

"The big difference in this team and last year's is the fact that a number of players have begun to live up to their potential. Jones was a .300 hitter in 1968; now he's a .340 hitter and an All-Star. Agee is now a strong .280 hitter, where he had to rally last season to reach .200. It's a team where everyone can pick us up at one time or another."

Even members of the opposition saw the change in the team. Ron Santo, the captain of the front-running Cubs, also admitted that his club's prime rival was no longer the pushovers of the past. "They fooled me," Santo said. "They're much better than I thought they were. In fact, they're harder for us to beat than any other club."

During the Mets' losing streak, some of the attention was diverted by something people once considered impossible, and still nothing short of a miracle. On July 21, American astronauts Neil Armstrong and Buzz Aldrin became the first men ever to step on the surface of the moon. This amazing accomplishment, viewed then as the first step in the ultimate exploration of space, took the nation's attention away from the attrition caused by the Vietnam War and even that other mode of escape, the baseball season.

"We were all aware of what was going on in the country," Jerry Koosman recalled. "I remember us watching the moon landing on television in a Montreal airport. So much was happening then, with Vietnam and all the demonstrations and protests at home. Yet as a team, I don't recall us talking much about politics. Our conversations always revolved around baseball. After games, no one ran for the showers. We all stayed around the clubhouse and talked baseball—to the reporters and among ourselves."

Both Ed Charles and Ed Kranepool felt the Mets, and their surprising success, offered the people of New York an escape from the turmoil going on within the country and in Southeast Asia, thousands of miles away.

"Baseball has always been an escape," Charles said. "We were quite conscious of what was happening in the country with the war and the demonstrations. But baseball has never been a political thing. Fans came to see the games and I remember feeling that at least for that day or that night the New York fans could drift away from all the problems and just focus on what was happening at Shea and with the Mets. The feeling overflowed from Shea into New York City and for the moment, people forgot about the war."

"People were looking to relax and get away from their everyday troubles," was the way Kranepool put it. "The Mets were an escape. 1969 was a crazy year with the war, then the moonwalk, and all the demonstrations. We provided a release for the New York fans. As you walked around the city, there was a tremendous atmosphere created by the team, and it was a good feeling."

Ron Swoboda confirmed that the players were all aware of world events, but around Shea and on the road it was always baseball. The individual players often thought about and discussed politics away from the game and the ballpark.

"I was very much aware of the protests and the war," Swoboda said. "I had gone to Vietnam in 1968 as part of a USO tour, and places I had been were always popping up on the news. When the Tet Offensive began in 1969, I knew just where that was and I knew what Saigon looked like, so it was hard to ignore what was going on. I had friends away from the team, friends who were in the arts, and I would talk to them about the war. New York was a tough place *not* to be aware. There were peace marches all over the city. I remember Tom Seaver once quoted as saying if the Mets can win the World Series, America could get out of Vietnam."

Yet no matter what was happening in the world, the baseball season had to continue, and the Mets were surely at a crucial point in their season. If they wanted to continue to contend, they had to break the win one, lose one, .500 mold they had been cast in for the past five weeks. The doubleheader sweep of the Padres on August 16 that brought them to 64-51 was a stepping-off point. The next day they beat the Padres in another twin bill by identical 3-2 scores, Koosman and Cardwell the winning pitchers. Now the Giants and Mays came in again. The first two games were both shutouts, the Mets winning 1-0 and 6-0, with McGraw and McAndrew the winning pitchers. They lost the finale, but then whipped the Dodgers three straight and followed that up by flying to the west coast and sweeping the Padres. Seaver ran his record to 18-7, and Koosman brought his to 12-8 in that series. Both aces were suddenly on a roll again as was the team. The Mets had gone from 64-51 to 74-52, winning 10 of 11 games and climbing back into the fray.

Once again they were winning with great pitching, very solid defense, and timely hitting, the same formula that led to their surge in July. When the Mets beat the Dodgers, 7-4, on August 24, they did it with a seventh-inning rally, which was becoming typical of their season. Cleon Jones opened the seventh with his third hit of the day. Art Shamsky followed with his second hit. Ken Boswell then attempted to bunt the runners over to third. But when Dodgers pitcher Jim Brewer elected to go to third to force Jones, his throw was late. Boswell had a base hit and the sacks were loaded for Ron Swoboda. Ron promptly slammed a double to left, clearing the bases, then scored himself on a base hit to center by Jerry Grote. The four-run explosion was enough to make a winner of reliever Cal Koonce.

That victory completed the sweep of the Dodgers and gave the Mets a 9-1 home stand. It also gave them a 21-5 record for the year against the three west coast teams and once again had them firmly in second place and hot on the heels of the slumping Cubs. The ebb and flow of the season was continuing, and finally Gil Hodges admitted that his team had a chance to win.

"Yes, we're a contender," Hodges said quickly, answering a reporter's question. Reminded that he had predicted the Mets would win 85 games, the manager grinned. "I might have to change it once we get to 85."

Like the players, Hodges was taking it one day at a time. On August 30, the Mets went up against the Giants at Candlestick Park. They had lost the night before and now had to face the tough Gaylord Perry. Don Cardwell started for the New Yorkers, and it was a strange game with sloppy plays being mixed with spectacular ones by both teams. Rod Gaspar saved the game for the Mets in the ninth by making a great throw from right to cut the potential winning run down at the plate. In the tenth, with Perry still pitching, Donn Clendenon blasted a long home run to give the Mets a 3-2 lead. Tug McGraw made it stand up, retiring the Giants in the bottom half of the inning to give the Mets yet another one-run victory.

On the morning of August 31, a look at the National League East standings painting an undeniable picture. With about a month left, it had become a two-team race. The Cubs were still first with an 81-52 mark, and the Mets were just three and a half games back at 75-53. They had shaved five games from the Chicago advantage in just two weeks. The Cards had fallen off the pace and were now nine games back, a half-game ahead of the Pirates. For those teams to win, both the Cubs and Mets would have to collapse. That was highly unlikely. Nope, at this point in the season it was almost a sure thing that the National League East winner would come either from Chicago or New York. The only question was which one. The Mets served some quick notice when that night Tom Seaver shut out the Giants, 8-0, for his 19th victory of the season and enabling the Mets to complete their August games with a 21-10 mark. At this point the *flow* belonged to New York, the *ebb* to Chicago. If the Cubs didn't turn it around soon, the Mets might just sneak past them.

After Seaver's 19th, the Mets dropped the finale to the Giants, then lost two of three to the Dodgers, including a 10-6 defeat in which Koosman didn't pitch well at all. Though they had won six of 10 on the coast, those couple of losses dropped them five and a half games behind the Cubs. Kranepool had been sidelined with a bruised hand, but Donn Clendenon had been hot during the west coast trip, hitting .393 with five homers and eight runs batted in. Still, Hodges had the choice of playing either Art Shamsky or J.C. Martin at first. Both were left handed-hitters and gave him that option to platoon, though he would likely stick with the hot hitter. But just having those options showed what a

LIGHTNING IN A BOTTLE 165

well-rounded and versatile team the Mets had. Every single player could fill a role, maybe two, and was available whenever the manager needed him.

The first game of the home stand was a doubleheader against the Phillies, and in the opener Tom Seaver made Mets history. He became the first pitcher in franchise history to win 20 games in a season, beating the Phillies, 5-1, and running his record to 20-7. Unfortunately, the team lost the nightcap, 4-2. But now the most crucial part of the season was looming. After two more games with the Phils, the Cubs would be coming to town for a pair of games. This would be a great time for the Mets to make a frontal assault on first place. They started their drive by winning the final two games against the Phils, 3-0, behind Don Cardwell, and 9-3 with Nolan Ryan getting the victory. Ryan's win in the series finale cut the Cubs' margin to just two and a half games, the closest the Mets had ever been. And they had the perfect setup for the Cubs, who came in sporting a four-game losing streak. Their two starting pitchers would be Koosman and Seaver. It was as if the stars were all in alignment. You couldn't have asked for it to be any better than this.

Right hander Bill Hands was the Cubs' starter against Koos in game one. With nearly 49,000 fans at Shea on a rainy night, Hands set the tempo immediately. As soon as Tommie Agee led off in the Mets' half of the first he had to hit the dirt as a Hands fastball sailed over his head. This wasn't shocking for a Leo Durocher-led team. When Leo was managing the Giants and playing the archrival Dodgers in Brooklyn/New York days, one of his favored verbal instructions to his pitcher was "Stick it in his ear!" The two teams often wound up playing bean ball on many occasions. So the low-bridge to Agee was no surprise to longtime New York fans. The Mets didn't score in the first, and Ron Santo came up to lead off the Cubs' second.

Koosman stared down Santo, wound up and threw. Almost everyone heard the thud as the fastball smashed into Santo's forearm just above the wrist. These certainly weren't the Mets of old. No amount of Durocher's intimidation would work. As Ron

Swoboda had said, Koosman would throw the ball right through you. The way the game was played in 1969, this was simply good old-fashioned hardball, an even-steven, tit-for-tat game, and it didn't always result in free-for-alls between the involved teams. Sometimes, once a team retaliated, it was over. That's essentially what Koosman would say later.

"They threw at Tommie, and I had to do it to end it right there," he explained. "If I don't, they keep doing it, and they keep getting away with it. I've seen it. I've seen three, four, five of our guys get knocked down and our pitcher never came close to their men. Nobody had to tell me anything. I know I've got to do it, and I'll do it again. If Tommie doesn't think I'm working for him, he won't work for me—and I want Tommie Agee working for me. He and Cleon, they're the two best hitters I have out there. I want both of them working for me."

Agee confirmed that he didn't have to say anything to Koosman when he returned to the bench after Hands decked him. "If a guy's pitching, he's a pro," Agee said. "He knows what's going on. Down the stretch I'm gonna get thrown at more and more. Our pitchers can't let us get run off the field."

So that was settled fast. Now the two teams could get back to the business of baseball. Agee got some revenge in the third when he took a Hands fastball deep with Bud Harrelson on first. The leadoff man's 26th homer of the year gave the Mets a 2-0 lead. Koosman held the Cubs in check until the sixth when the visitors pushed across a pair of runs to tie it at 2-2. But in the bottom half of the inning, the Mets showed they could retaliate with runs as well. Once again it was Agee getting things started with a double to left. Young Wayne Garrett then rapped a single to right. As Agee sped around third, Cubs right fielder Billy Williams fired the ball to home. Catcher Randy Hundley grabbed it and lunged at Agee just as he hit the plate. Both looked up at ump Dave Davidson. Safe!

Durocher came storming out of the dugout as both he and catcher Hundley argued the call, but to no avail. The Mets led, 3-2, and Koosman made it stand up, striking out 13 Cubs in running his record to 13-9. The victory moved the Mets to within a game and a half of the Cubs. To the Shea faithful, who had waited eight years for this, the game and a half meant nothing. They expressed exactly how they felt in the final innings, chanting, "We're number one," over and over again. And why not? It was beginning to look as if these Mets just couldn't lose.

The next night the weather was better, and both teams were trotting out their aces, Tom Seaver against Ferguson Jenkins. Not surprisingly, there were 58,436 fans jamming into Shea. Every game counted now, counted big time. There were just over three weeks remaining in the season, and suddenly the Mets were within a baseball's throw of first place, something considered nearly impossible at the outset of the season, especially given the team's history of racking up games in the "L" column. Seaver had already won 20 games, and his confidence was sky high. On the other hand, Jenkins had control problems that night, and the Mets were quick to jump on him. Ken Boswell drove in a pair of runs, and by the time Seaver took the mound for the top of the second, he had a 2-0 lead. It would turn out to be more than enough.

As the Mets lead mounted, something happened that almost seemed symbolic, in view of the turn of events that had put the Mets so close to the Cubs' heels. Jerry Koosman remembers.

"Right in the middle of game one, one of the cats that lived under the stands came out on their side of the field. A black cat. He got scared and ran right across in front of their dugout," Koosman said. The fans saw it and began cheering and screaming, which scared the cat even more. He just kept running back and forth in front of the their dugout, and in seconds the whole stadium was rocking. Then the press picked up on it and portrayed it as another sign that the Cubs were done."

Ron Swoboda still laughs today when he thinks about the black cat incident. "It's almost a legend now," Swoboda said. "But then it was the most incredible thing you ever saw. It was like we hired the cat and trained him to run back and forth right in front of their dugout."

When Seaver and the Mets won the game, 7-1, the black cat episode seemed even more significant. The Mets had won both games of the series, drawing to within a half game of the Cubs, and now the two teams wouldn't meet again until the final two games of the season. Right now, they seemed to be two teams going in different directions and many questioned whether Durocher could rally his troops into making one more run. The Cubs had been so good, so solid for almost the entire season that it seemed for the first five months of the season that they were a shoo-in. With a seasoned, competitive, and resourceful manager like Leo Durocher, it wasn't likely that he would allow his team to falter. Not only was Leo a master motivator, it sometimes seemed as if he could will a team to victory. Fans in New York, especially, remembered how he brought his Giants from 13 1/2 down in August to catch the Dodgers back in 1951, the year that Bobby Thomson's shot-heard-'round-the-world home run won the pennant.

But that was long ago, and this was a different team and a different game. Some of the Mets players had their own theories as to why the Cubs wilted under the Mets' late-summer assault. Some of the beat writers, in fact, felt the Chicagoans were a tired team down the stretch.

"Whether we saw it or not, that was our belief," said Jerry Koosman. "You got to remember there were no lights at Wrigley Field then and they were playing day games in the hot sun. They said it didn't bother them and felt it gave them an advantage over visiting teams. Players will never admit they were tired, but I felt they were worn down more than some of the other clubs. Part of it was playing day baseball and part was Durocher playing the same guys every day. We might not have had as much man-to-man talent or as many stars as they did, but with Gil platooning and playing more night games, I think we were the fresher team."

Ed Kranepool agrees. "I think they got a stiff neck looking over their shoulders at us," he said, "and I think they got exhausted physically and the reserves couldn't do the job. We just kept winning and stayed strong right through the end, through the playoffs."

Ron Swoboda acknowledged that the Cubs played a lot of day ball, but feels it was the great play of the Mets that closed the gap. "I know a lot of guys on the Cubs felt they choked," Swoboda said. "But look how we played. We were winning every series, and I think we wound up playing over .700 ball the final weeks of the season. We were simply playing incredible baseball. So in the final analysis, I don't think it was a matter of them wearing out. We just did an incredible job and left it all on the field."

Ed Charles remembers when the Mets won two consecutive series from the Cubs in July, the first at Shea, and the second at Wrigley. It was apparent then that the Cubs were the Mets' bitterest rivals that year, and it was fitting that those two teams would ultimately battle it out.

"Ron Santo used to always tee us off," Charles said. "When they would beat us, he would jump and click his heels. When we beat them in New York he said wait 'til they get us in Chicago. Then we went to Wrigley and won two of three. We were all feeling good on the bus to the airport that day. We had to fly to Montreal, and the whole team was whooping it up, ragging on Santo and his cockiness. I remember Seaver hollering at me, 'Hey, Glider, you're a poet. Give us a poem.' And I said, 'East side, west side, all around the town. When October rolls around, the Mets will wear the crown.'

"I remember Seaver liked that. But in all honesty, I felt it was a little premature to come up with that, but I was beginning to feel we might have a chance. Our confidence level was so high then that we began to feel we would be tough to beat. And it stayed that way right until the end."

Sweeping the Cubs had the Mets closer than the team had ever been. The night after beating the Cubs behind Seaver, the team had a doubleheader against the Expos at Shea. The date was September 10, a date that would forever be etched in Mets history. The first game with Montreal was a tight one, neither team able to break it open. At the end of nine, it was tied at 2-2. By the time the Mets came up to bat in the bottom of the 12th, the scoreboard showed the Cubs losing to the Phils, 2-1, though the game was just in the fourth inning. Now the Mets began to rally. Cleon Jones started it with a single. Then Rod Gaspar drew a walk, bringing Ken Boswell to the plate. As he had done so many times already, the clutch-hitting Boswell came through, slamming a single to right past second baseman Gary Sutherland. Jones came racing home with the winning run, giving the Mets and Ron Taylor a 3-2 victory.

The fans began cheering the victory, but many of them did not realize what had happened at the precise moment that Jones's spikes hit home plate. The victory raised the Mets' record for the season to 83-57. The Cubs were still playing, so their mark stood at 84-58. That gave the Mets a .001 percentage lead. They were, technically, in first place, and that's what the big scoreboard at Shea flashed. Above the records it read: "Look Who's No. 1"

It wasn't over yet. The Mets won the second game easily, 7-1, behind Nolan Ryan's three-hitter. By then, 11:38 p.m., the Cubs had already lost to Philadelphia. At the end of the night the Mets had a full one-game lead. They were in first place for the very first time in franchise history. After the game the team held a small celebration in the clubhouse. There were even a couple of bottles of champagne passed around, though the team knew that nothing had been decided as yet.

"They're confident, but not overconfident," Hodges said.

"We were on a run all September," said Jerry Koosman. "It was great going into first place, but we all kind of felt we would get there. We were clicking and felt we had it all together. Gil had complete control of the club. We were excited, had momentum going, and felt nothing was going to stop us. The weather was getting cooler and you could start feeling the approach of fall at night. I think that helped revitalize us, especially the starting pitchers. The way I felt then was that we had gotten through the dog days of August and now we had a second wind. It was like a breath of fresh air blowing through and from that point on it was all downhill."

Ed Charles echoed what Koosman said. Looking back, the veteran third baseman had similar thoughts. "By September 10, we began to feel that nobody could beat us. Period. We were sky high. It was the same formula we used all year—great pitching, clutch hitting, good defense ... and having Gil Hodges. I just can't say enough about how much he did for us."

It didn't take the Mets long to open a lead. Gentry shut out the Expos the next day, then came a doubleheader with the Pirates. These two games might have well defined the Mets' season, in that at this point it was beginning to look as if there was no way the team could lose. Jerry Koosman started the first game and vet Don Cardwell the second. Both pitchers threw complete-game shutouts, won by identical 1-0 scores, and in each game it was the pitcher who drove in the only run. Two nights later, they beat the Pirates again, this time on Ron Swoboda's first ever grand-slam home run. And it came in the 10th inning. It was a different hero every day. Two nights later, the team went to St. Louis for a makeup game and faced young Cardinal left-hander, Steve Carlton.

Once again the game showed that the Mets were under a favorable star. Carlton had wicked stuff and from the start was striking out batter after batter. No one could touch him ... no one, that is, except Ron Swoboda. The bottom line was this. Carlton set a new strikeout record for a nine-inning game, fanning 19 Mets. In addition, the New Yorkers made four errors in the game. There was just one thing wrong with the picture. The Mets won the game, 4-3, on a pair of Ron Swoboda two-run homers. No wonder people were beginning to talk about the Mets as a "Team of Destiny."

Ron Swoboda has never forgotten that night in St. Louis, the events leading up to it or what happened afterward.

"In the days leading up to that game I wasn't feeling particularly solid at home plate," Swoboda said. "Plus I never hit Carlton very well. St. Louis was one of the few stadiums then that had a batting cage. When we got there I asked Ralph Kiner, who was one of our announcers then but who had been a great power hitter in his playing days, if we could go out to the cage and work on a few things. Ralph began feeding me some balls through the pitching machine and watching. He was a real student of hitting and helped me make some adjustments in my swing. We didn't have hitting coaches in those days, but after working with Ralph, I felt I was in a better space.

"Once we started playing the next night, you could see that Carlton had it from the beginning. Boy, was he ever doing it. He struck me out the first time I faced him. The second time there was a runner on first. They already had a one-run lead. He threw me a fastball and I got it, hit it into the upper deck, giving us a 2–1 lead. Later, they went up 3–2, and now he's going for the strikeout record. When I came up again in the eighth inning, Tommie Agee was on base. This time he threw me a slider—and he had a great one. It was a good pitch, but somehow I got it and hit a line drive that cleared the left field wall, giving us a 4–3 lead. How do you figure something like that out?"

Carlton went all the way, striking out 19 for a new single-game record at the time. But Tug McGraw came in and finished for the Mets, benefiting from Swoboda's second home run and getting the victory. After the game, Swoboda remembers being on the same postgame show with the Cardinal left-hander.

"Harry Caray had us on his show," Swoboda said. "I'm bubbling over and he looked like something just ran over his dog. I mean, he was having the greatest day a strikeout pitcher ever had, maybe the greatest day of his life. And looking at him, I just felt he was trying to figure out what happened. It was as if he was thinking, 'How could it be YOU? Anybody but you!'"

Bottom line: Despite Carlton's brilliance, the Mets had won again, running their record to 89-58 on the morning of September 16. The still-faltering Cubs were at 85-63, and were now four and a half games back. The Mets had now won 10 of their last 11 and now were playing .605 baseball. They were taking the bull by the horns and running with it. Many were reminded of something the great Jackie Robinson said when the Giants came from 13 1/2 down to catch the Dodgers in 1951.

"The Giants just caught lightning in a bottle," Jackie said then.

There were now just 15 games left, and barring a complete collapse, it certainly looked as if the Mets were going to make this impossible dream come true. Had they caught that same kind of lightning? It certainly seemed so. Everything was going right. In a four-day span they had won a doubleheader by an identical 1-0 score with the pitcher driving in the run both times. Then they had won a game in which the opposing pitcher struck out more batters in a nine-inning game than anyone in history. That night, the lightning came via a pair of two-run homers by Ron Swoboda. Barring an unforeseen catastrophe, the division title was firmly in sight, right around the next corner.

# 11
# A DIVISION TITLE AND A PENNANT

With just 15 games left, the Mets went back to work. There was no time to rest on their laurels, and no one was about to count any chickens. Gil Hodges wouldn't let them do that. Jerry Koosman followed up Ron Swoboda's heroics against Steve Carlton and the Cards by winning his 15th game with a 5-0 shutout at Montreal. A day later, Tom Seaver won his 23rd, also shutting out the Expos, this time by a 2-0 score. The Mets' two top pitchers were both on a roll, winning game after game. They were pitching as well as any two hurlers in the entire major leagues. With a 1-2 like Seaver and Koosman, the Mets would have a chance against anyone, especially in a short series.

"I think Tom and I won something like 18 of our last 19 starts that year," Jerry Koosman said. "By that time everyone on the club knew his place. For example, if Ken Boswell wasn't starting at second, he knew exactly when he would pinch hit. By then, we all knew just what Gil would do, how he platooned and used the players. All he asked of everyone [was] that we be ready to help the team. There was no screwing around. We all knew Gil's rules and how seriously he took the game, and how much winning meant to him.

"I always felt that Gil was the smartest manager in the league. The more time you spent around him the more you realized he was always one or two steps ahead of the opposing manager. If he noticed someone on the opposing club dropping his head and not paying attention, he would call a delayed steal. He would watch who the opposing manager had warming up in the bullpen. If it was a strong reliever, Gil would do something to try to get a run or two more off the guy who was still in there. Yet there was never any hollering or screaming. He might shake your hand or give you a pat on the butt. But mostly he sat quietly and ran the club on an even keel. He wouldn't let us get too high or too low. But by late in the season he did expect us to win."

So the Mets continued to move inexorably toward their first division title or, in reality, the first division title in National League history. Before 1969, if you finished on top, you won the pennant. But with divisional play, finishing first was only step one. But right now that was the immediate goal. Now fans were beginning to look at what has always been called "The Magic Number." In this case the magic number was any combination of Mets wins and Cubs losses that would clinch the title for the New Yorkers. By September 19, the number was seven, but a day later the Mets hit a slight roadblock. The Pirates' Bob Moose tossed a no-hitter at the New Yorkers, handing them their third straight loss. But a Cubs defeat that same night reduced the magic number to six.

The next day the club righted the ship again, sweeping the Pirates in a twin bill. Koosman won the first game, 5-3, his 16th victory of the season, while Don Cardwell pitched the Mets to a 6-1 victory in the nightcap. Cardwell, at 8-9, had been a big help, and the two victories cut the magic number to four with eight games left. Now it just seemed a matter of time. Seaver's 24th victory, 3-1, over the Cards cut the number to three. From that point, the Mets started to run the table. First they beat the Cards and Bob Gibson, 3-2, in 11 innings. Then Gentry closed out the series by shutting out St. Louis, 6-0. The rookie right-hander evened his record at 12-12, but the game meant much more than that. The victory clinched the division title for the Mets.

They had won it. They were National League East Champions. What's more, they had won it in front of the home fans in the last regular-season game at Shea for the year. A near-capacity crowd of 54,928 fans was on hand to witness the history-making event. The Mets said they didn't want to "back" into the title, by clinching it via a Chicago loss. Gentry made sure they didn't, throwing a four-hit whitewash. Ed Charles homered and Donn Clendenon blasted a pair. No, the Mets had not backed into anything. As they had done all year, they earned it.

Delirious Mets fans stormed onto the field and began tearing up sections of the turf, a new kind of souvenir they could take home. It was part jubilation, part vandalism, something that would increase in sports celebrations during the coming years. Fortunately, the team had to finish the season on the road. That would give the grounds crew a chance to repair the turf for the playoffs.

In the clubhouse there was mayhem, players hollering and swigging champagne, and taking turns congratulating Hodges. Jerry Koosman proposed a toast "to Leo," the venerable Cubs manager, and some of the veteran players raised their bottles in unison, shouting, "Here's to Casey!"

The celebration was pretty mild because everyone knew there was a long road ahead, but it was still euphoric, as Bud Harrelson recalls.

"It was a great feeling to clinch the division," Harrelson said. "You've got to remember that we had never been there before. But we also knew we had just climbed the first rung. Though we knew what kind of team we were by then, we still didn't think we had it made. Yet we finished so strong. I believe we were 32-10 in our final 42 games and we were beating everyone. In addition, we had two starting pitchers who could compete with anybody."

After the clincher the Mets just had to play out the string, but they also didn't want to lose the momentum that was building.

Koosman and Seaver threw back-to-back shutouts over the Phils, 5-0 and 1-0, then Gentry came back and produced the team's fourth consecutive shutout, his second in a row. The front-line pitchers seemed to be getting stronger. Suddenly, no one was scoring on them. Then the Mets went to Chicago for the final pair of games. It wasn't a happy group of Cubs. They probably didn't even want to play it out. The two rivals split, the Mets winning 6-5 and the Cubs taking the finale, 5-3. That didn't matter. No one had to be reminded of the final records. Amazing as it sounds, even today, the Mets had come from seven years of losing, and a ninth-place finish the year before, to win an even 100 games. They finished with a record of 100-62, winning the division by a full eight games over the fading Cubs and 12 over the defending-champion Cardinals. While in the eyes of some it was already a miracle, the best was yet to come.

Looking at the regular-season statistics, it was apparent that the pitchers led the way. Seaver had an incredible year, finishing at 25-7 with a 2.21 earned run average. "Tom Terrific" threw five shutouts and struck out 208 hitters in 273.1 inning, and was the top winner in the majors. Koosman was right behind. Despite missing a month with arm trouble early in the season, the big lefty finished at 17-9 with a 2.28 ERA. He had 180 strikeouts in 241 innings and tossed six shutouts. They were certainly a formidable one-two. Gary Gentry, who wasn't as consistent as the big two, still had a 13-12 record as a rookie, while veteran Don Cardwell as 8-10 and Jim McAndrew 6-7.

But the second group of pitchers really picked things up. Tug McGraw was 9-3 with 12 saves. Nolan Ryan, in a part-time role was 6-3, as was reliever Koonce. Ron Taylor compiled a 9-4 record to go with 13 saves. It was a good, deep staff.

The hitters didn't have quite the numbers. Cleon Jones, however, had his best season, finishing third in the league in hitting at .340. He had 12 homers and 75 RBIs. Agee had a great bounce-back year after his disastrous 1968 season. He hit .271 and, as a leadoff man, clubbed 26 homers and drove home 76 runs, both team highs. Clendenon hit just .252 as a Met, but belt-

ed 12 homers and drove home 37 runs in only 202 at bats. Art
Shamsky batted an even .300 with 14 homers and 47 RBIs,
while Swoboda finished at .235 with nine homers and 52 RBIs.
But many of his home runs came in clutch situations. Kranepool
hit just .238, but managed 11 homers and 49 RBIs. Even those
who didn't have the numbers managed to contribute in key situations.

To tell the truth, numbers didn't much matter at this point.
The name of the game in the playoffs is to win, and win quickly. In the first year of divisional play for the pennant, the series
would be a best of five, meaning the team that got off fast would
have a huge advantage. The Mets would be facing a hard-hitting
team, the Atlanta Braves, featuring the great Henry Aaron, who
batted .300 with 44 home runs and 97 RBIs. Behind Hammerin'
Hank were hitters like Orlando Cepeda, Felipe Alou, Clete
Boyer, Rico Carty, and Tony Gonzalez. They could score runs.
Knuckleballer Phil Niekro was the top pitcher at 23-13, but the
other starters—Ron Reed, George Stone, and Pat Jarvis—didn't
compare favorably with the Mets. The New Yorkers definitely
had the pitching advantage. In the eyes of many, however, these
were still the New York Mets. How could they be favored over
anyone?

Before the season had ended, there were a few extra pieces of
business. The final week of September it was announced that Gil
Hodges had been given a new contract for three additional years,
running through 1972. Though the terms were not announced,
most felt it was in the neighborhood of $70,000 a season, giving
the manager about a $10,000 raise. The raise was also retroactive
to 1969, a reward for a job well done. But it also shows how far
salaries have come. Today, the top managers are earning millions,
just as the players are.

On September 29, the Mets had an off day, at least as far as
National League opposition was concerned. They had to play the
annual Mayor's Trophy Game, which in those days pitted the
Mets against the Yankees for charity. The Mets even won that
one, 7-6, with Art Shamsky driving in five runs. The interesting

part of the game was the use of an experimental, "lively" base-ball, which supposedly had 10 percent more "hop" than the stan-dard ball. The so-called rabbit ball was used for five innings, dur-ing which time both teams banged out 16 of the 22 total hits. The odd part of this was that in later years there were occasion-al accusations that baseball was "juicing" the ball in order to liven up the game with more home runs. Back in 1969, it was an announced experiment but was not used in regular-season play.

The first ever playoff series was slated to open in Atlanta on October 4. In the American League, it would be the powerful Baltimore Orioles versus the Minnesota Twins. The Orioles, winners of 109 regular-season games were huge favorites against the Twins and the early favorite to win the World Series, no mat-ter which National League team they played. As for Mets-Braves, the oddsmakers installed Atlanta as 13-10 favorites, despite the fact that the Mets won seven more regular-season games, had beaten the Braves eight out of 12 times during the season, and had an outstanding pitching staff. In fact, opening-game starter Tom Seaver had gone 3-0 against Atlanta in the regular season, while Braves starter Phil Niekro was 0-3 against the Mets. Loveable losers. Maybe that image was still lurking in the backs of some baseball minds.

Before the playoffs began, some of the New York writers sought out an old sage for his prediction. As usual, Casey Stengel was quick to reply. The Mets' first ever manager was 79 years old but still had all his baseball wits and didn't hesitate to give his opinion. Here, in part, is what Old Case said:

"Let's get one thing straight at the start. The Mets will play all the way to the end of the World Series because they have more pitchers and they throw lightning. And you can look it up, that's best for a short series. ... Let's talk about the managers. They are two of the youngest that are well experienced. Both are the greatest, absolutely amazin' that Hodges has more experience. ... They got Aaron that's the best all-time ball player at the present time. I was in St. Louis for an old-timers game and I seen him win the most games against St. Louis, and Cepeda won the other always at the end of the game. ... Don't forget, I say it goes the limit to the World Series for the Mets."

As usual, Casey was talking in his own special way, in "Stengelese," but he got the point across. The Mets had pitching and they had Gil Hodges, and despite some great hitters on the Braves, the Mets would win. The way the playoffs were set up, the first two games would be played at Atlanta, and the next three—if three were necessary—would take place at Shea. But with the Mets' outstanding pitchers, many in New York who had followed the team predicted a low-scoring series.

Most of the Mets' players acknowledged that the Braves had the better offensive team, though they also felt their pitching staff was fully capable of neutralizing the Atlanta bats. As Ed Charles said, "We knew we had the best pitching in baseball, and we were gonna ride it all the way," he said. "There was a cohesiveness about the team then. We had molded into one unit and were very close as a team."

Charles continues to give credit to Gil Hodges for being the perfect manager for the Mets, the glue that brought it all together. He cites an early-season episode to show how the manager handled his players and potentially sticky situations, never allowing anything to get out of hand.

"Gil pinch hit for me in a game early on," Charles said. "I felt I was always best in the clutch, and this was that kind of spot, where the team needed a clutch hit. I was a little teed off about it and slammed my bat into the bat rack. Gil was sitting right there. After I collected myself I knew what I had done wasn't right. I was the senior member of the ball club and shouldn't have allowed the young guys to see me do that. My job was to help him settle the team down. But Gil let it go, didn't say a word to me.

"The next day I came to the ballpark early and went straight to his office. He looked at me and said, 'I knew you'd be coming in.' Then he added quickly, 'I knew you were mad, but I had to follow my hunch at that point.' Then he told me he really appreciated me coming in and apologizing, and after that I apologized to the other guys, as well. Gil and I had a very solid way of communicating. He knew me and knew what I was about. He was like that with everyone, just one heck of a manager."

Hodges wasn't going to change his pattern in the playoffs. With the right-hander Neikro starting, the manager went to what he called his left-handed lineup. Agee, Jones, and Grote were in the lineup, all right-handed hitters, but they played every day. The left-handed contingent included young Wayne Garrett at third, Shamsky in right, Boswell at second, and Kranepool at first. Harrelson, the shortstop, was a switch hitter. On the bench were righties Swoboda, Al Weis, Clendenon, and Charles.

The weather was perfect for game one of the playoffs. Unfortunately, the pitchers were not. The Mets got to Niekro early, scoring a pair of runs in the second inning. The way Seaver had been pitching recently, many thought that would be more than enough. But the Braves quickly countered with one in the second and two more in the third, to take a 3-2 lead. Niekro, however, couldn't hold it. The Mets came back in their half of the fourth to score another pair and retake the lead. Now would it be enough for Seaver? Nope. The Braves tied the game with a run in the fifth, and then took the lead in the seventh when Henry Aaron slammed a solo homer off the struggling right-hander. Atlanta had a 5-4 lead with just two innings left. Could the Mets pull yet another rabbit out of their bag of tricks?

Niekro was still on the hill in the eighth. That, in itself, might have said something about the Atlanta bullpen, because when a knuckleballer doesn't have it working, he usually doesn't have a great day. But Braves manager Lum Harris left him in the game. Wayne Garrett led off and promptly smacked and opposite-field double past Boyer at third. Then Jones looped a single to left, followed by a single by Art Shamsky. The game was tied once more. Niekro then caught Jones off second, but Cleon managed to roar into third and avoid Boyer's tag for a stolen base. Next, Kranepool grounded to Cepeda at first, but the throw home went wild and Jones scored, both runners advancing. After an intentional walk to Bud Harrelson to load the bases, Hodges sent up the veteran J.C. Martin to bat for Seaver.

Martin slammed what appeared to be a solid single to center. Two runs scored and when center fielder Tony Gonzalez let the ball get past him, Harrelson came around with the third run and fifth of the inning. The so-called punchless Mets had done it again, putting five big runs across the plate to take a 9-5 lead. Ron Taylor came in to pitch the final two innings, shutting down the Braves and allowing the Mets to draw first blood. Seaver got the win despite giving up five runs in seven innings, making him Tom Unsteady instead of Tom Terrific. But the bottom line was the "W," and the Mets had the immediate advantage. They hoped the win would pave the way for Jerry Koosman, who would be facing right-hander Ron Reed in game two.

"The Braves had stars all over the place," Ed Kranepool said. "But we showed right from the beginning that the team which plays as a unit and pieces it all together is stronger than a team of individuals."

In game two, the Mets jumped all over Ron Reed quickly. They scored one in the first, three in the second, two in the third, and two more in the fourth. Was this really the Mets, a team forging an 8-0 lead in four innings? Bet you couldn't count on your fingers how many times that happened during the season. And with Koosman pitching, it would appear that game was already over. The runs came in a variety of ways. A double steal and an infield hit did it in the first. An Agee homer and Shamsky single did the second-inning damage. There was a pair of unearned runs in the third and a Boswell homer in the fourth. The Mets were doing it every which way, and it didn't look as if the Braves had an answer.

Then the unthinkable happened. Like Seaver the day before, Koosman didn't have it ... or he lost it in the fifth. The Braves had gotten a single run back in their half of the fourth before the Mets ran their advantage to 9-1 in the top of the fifth. When Koosman came back out and got the first two Braves, it looked as if he had settled down. But then the amazing Henry Aaron did it again, belting his second homer of the series. Still, it was just 9-2. No sweat. Only then Koosman walked the next hitter, Cepeda doubled, and Clete Boyer had a two-run single. Before Ron Taylor came in to put out the fire, the Braves had score five runs and cut the deficit to 9-6. It was again a ball game, and for the second straight day the Mets' frontline pitchers had faltered.

But this time the Mets showed they had the better bullpen. Taylor pitched the sixth, then Tug McGraw came in and shut Atlanta down for the final three innings. The Atlanta relievers had already proved unreliable since the Mets had been unloading on them since starter Reed went out in the second. In the seventh they did it again. Cleon Jones belted a two-run homer to make the final score 11-6. The Mets had won again and were now just one game away from a pennant and their first appearance in the World Series. In a reversal of the norm, they were doing it with the bat, something that no one could have expected. With the two teams coming back to Shea, rookie Gary Gentry would try to clinch, while veteran Pat Jarvis would attempt to stave off elimination for the Braves.

On a sunny, cool October 6 afternoon, the Mets began play with the taste of a pennant in the air and a capacity crowd on hand to cheer them on. In the very first inning, Henry Aaron showed once again why the big crowd was watching a legend. He belted a two-run homer off Gentry to give the Braves the early lead. Gentry then got through the second, but in the third Tony Gonzalez opened with the single and the redoubtable Aaron promptly doubled him to third. Now the hard-hitting Rico Carty was up. Gentry worked the count to 1-2, but on his next pitch Carty slammed a hard drive deep down the left field line ... but foul. Hodges had seen enough. As Carty backed out, the manager made his way slowly to the mound, then signaled the bullpen.

Managers don't usually take pitchers out when they have a 1-2 count on a hitter, but Gil had been playing hunches all year. No sense changing now. He didn't like what he was seeing from Gentry. More than 50,000 pairs of eyes all went out to the Mets bullpen and watched as Nolan Ryan emerged slowly. There were cheers, but a sense of apprehension went with them. Ryan, with his great fastball, could be devastating, almost unhittable. But if his control wasn't there, free passes to first could abound. Everyone in the house was wondering which Nolan Ryan they would see.

Ryan came in and immediately blew a fastball past Carty. Strike three; one out! Next up was Orlando Cepeda, another dangerous hitter. Again manager Hodges made a move. He ordered Cepeda walked intentionally to load the bases and set up a potential double play. Clete Boyer, the former Yankee, was next. Ryan again got a pair of strikes on Boyer, then unleashed a fastball that was almost a blur. Boyer didn't even get the bat off his shoulder as the umpire shouted out, "Strike three!" Now two were down and rookie catcher Bob Didier up. Didier had a little more luck than Carty and Boyer. He actually got the bat on the ball, but lined out to Jones in left, ending the inning. Ryan left the field to a thunderous ovation.

Then the Mets went to work on Jarvis. Agee blasted a homer in the bottom of the third, and Boswell followed with a two-run shot in the fourth, giving the Mets a 3-2 lead. In the top of the fifth, Orlando Cepeda caught up with a Ryan fastball and drove it deep into the left field seats for a two-run homer. The teams were on the seesaw. Now Atlanta led, 4-3. But in the bottom of the inning the Mets dispensed with starter Jarvis and got into the shaky Atlanta bullpen. Once again Hodges made a decision. With the pitcher's spot due up first, he could have pinch hit for Ryan, put a better stick up there and had a fresh pitcher for the sixth. Instead, he stuck with Ryan who surprised everyone by stroking a single. With a runner on, Harris removed Jarvis and brought in lefty George Stone. Surprisingly, Hodges didn't counter with a right-handed hitter. He allowed Wayne Garrett to hit for himself, and the youngster responded with a two-run homer to give the Mets the lead once more. A Jones double led to a third run, and an inning later Boswell singled off Cecil Upshaw for run number seven.

From there, Nolan Ryan just cruised. At least for this one day he showed everyone just what kind of pitcher he could be, shutting down the Braves the rest of the way. His seven innings of relief was the highlight in the team's 7-4, pennant-clinching victory. At the end, the fans again went wild, swarming the Shea Stadium turf and leaving it in tatters. None of that mattered. The Mets had done the impossible. In a season where they began with the odds 100-1 against them, they had not only won 100 games, but had now emerged as National League Champions.

There was more. For a team that wasn't supposed to hit, the Mets had scored 27 runs and slammed out 37 hits in three games against Atlanta. Listen to some of the average of the starters. Agee .357, Jones .429, Shamsky .538, Garrett .385, Boswell .333. Talk about lightning in a bottle. There were the light-hitting Mets, a team that couldn't do it without great pitching. Well, they had just done it the other way, though Ryan certainly provided clutch pitching in the final game. The remembrances of that series are strong.

"When Nolan pitched those great seven innings of relief, it was huge," Jerry Koosman recalls. "It gave us another guy on our roster that we could go to with confidence, another body developed on our ball club. Nolan had been up and down all year, his season interrupted by both injury and military service. But Gil was doing these things throughout the year, showing us how to play the game, and because of him we found out we were capable of doing more than we knew we could. Remember, we were essentially a young club that hadn't been in this situation before, so much of it was unknown. When Nolan pitched the clincher like that, it gave the whole club confidence. If the situation arose again, we'd all welcome him coming out of that pen."

Like many others, the thing that most surprised Ron Swoboda was the way Atlanta handled the Mets pitchers. "Our pitching got battered in that series," he recalled, "but it was amazing the way we outhit them. Gil stuck to his guns and platooned, so I didn't get a single at-bat in the Atlanta series because of their predominately right-handed pitching. The Shamskys and the

Garretts and the Boswells did the job. For years I've been telling people that most of the players on the 1969 team were just guys who made themselves useful players in the context of the team. They weren't great players who will go to the Hall of Fame.

"Ryan's contribution in that final game was huge. In essence, he was a highball pitcher in a low-ball league. The key was whether he could get his breaking ball over for a strike. That's all he had to do to be successful because of the heat he had."

Ed Charles talked about the clutch nature of the entire team. "The playoff series against the Braves was one of the few times our pitchers had faltered like that and allowed an unusual number of runs," Charles said. "We were used to playing low-scoring games, but when we needed runs, our guys just responded. It was that way all year, someone always rising to the occasion when it was needed, different guys coming up with big hits."

For Bud Harrelson, the win over Atlanta was huge. It had to be because it gave the Mets their first pennant. Remembering now, the slick-fielding shortstop also feels the sweep gave the team something else.

"The feeling of having clinched the pennant was great, especially because none of us had ever been there before," he said. "But it was also just the first rung. We knew we would have a very tough nut to crack in the World Series, but there was a feeling of momentum building among us. It was almost spiritual, that we were just moving forward to the next place, that it was meant to be. Some people might have felt that if we lost, we lost, because it had already been a great run. But I can tell you even now that none of the players felt that way."

These Mets, of course, were looking back some 35 years, but right after the Mets had clinched, perhaps it was Cleon Jones who expressed the prevailing sentiment of the moment. Said Jones: "We're the greatest team in the world right now."

# 12
# HERE COMES BALTIMORE AGAIN

If Cleon Jones, and any others, felt the Mets were the best team in the world, then the Baltimore Orioles must have been the best team in the entire universe. On the same day the Mets eliminated the Atlanta Braves, the Orioles finished the job against the Minnesota Twins. Manager Earl Weaver's Orioles won in every way against the Twins, taking a come-from-behind victory, 4–3, in 12 innings; winning a pitching duel, 1-0, in 11 innings; and wrapping it up with an 11–2 laugher. The result was no surprise to the baseball world. These Orioles had won 109 games during the regular season. If the Mets were number one in pitching, the Orioles were 1A, right there with them. If the Mets had great team defense, the Orioles were every bit the Mets' equal. If the Mets were a weak-hitting team relying on clutch hits from a variety of players, the Orioles were an absolutely great hitting team, one that could do it all at the plate.

So the Mets had an opponent, and those in New York, and sports fans everywhere, quickly saw the irony in the match up. Just nine months earlier another New York team had surprised everyone by winning a league championship and had gone up against a supposedly superior team from Baltimore only to pull off what was considered one of the great sports upsets of all time.

That, of course, was the Jets' victory over the Baltimore Colts. Now it was the Orioles, installed as heavy favorites the minute the two pennants were decided. In an almost eerie coinicidence, New York would be matched up with Baltimore one more time.

And what about those match ups? Remember, when the so-called experts matched up the Colts and Jets nine months earlier, some gave the Colts the edge at every single position except quarterback, where Joe Namath and Earl Morrall were judged about even. But football is a different game. One defensive line may not perform the same way against a different kind of offensive line. So match ups don't really work all the time. Baseball, however, is a position-by-position game, and skills are skills. The only thing that can really change things is hot pitching and perhaps an untimely slump by a top hitter. In addition, the Super Bowl is a one-game, winner-take-all championship. An early injury to the quarterback can change everything. The World Series is seven games. Luck and breaks don't usually get it done.

But the match ups did give a good indication why most of the experts were picking Baltimore. Let's take a closer look.

**First base**—The Mets would continue to go with the left-right platoon of Ed Kranepool and Donn Clendenon. They had done the job during the second half of the season, and Kranepool got all three starts against the Atlanta lefties. But with the Orioles using a pair of southpaw starters, Clendenon would definitely play. The Orioles' counterpart was slugger John "Boog" Powell, a mountain of a man who could hit a ton. All Powell did during the regular season was bat .304 with 37 homers and 121 RBIs, second best in the American League. Everyone gave the edge here to the Orioles.

**Second base**—Once again the Mets would platoon, using Ken Boswell against righties and veteran Al Weis against southpaws. The O's countered with Davy Johnson, a .280 hitter who drove in 57 runs. As one writer said, "Johnson can outfield Boswell and outhit Weis." Chalk up another advantage to Baltimore.

**Third base**—This one was no contest. Again the Mets used a platoon, the veteran Charles against lefties, the youngster Garrett versus righties. The Orioles used just one player, maybe the best to ever play the position. Brooks Robinson had a magical glove, a fielder with few peers, and a guy with a flare for the spectacular. Brooks had an off year with the bat, hitting just .234, but still managed 23 homers and 84 RBIs. He could win a game with both his bat and glove. There was simply no comparison here.

**Shortstop**—This was a match up of two fine fielders. Many considered Bud Harrelson the best in the National League. Mark Belanger was, by far, the top glove in the American. The difference was with the stick. Harrelson hit .248 without a homer and with only 24 RBIs. Belanger had a fine year at the plate, batting .287 with 50 RBIs. Once again, the advantage had to go to the Birds, giving them a leg up at all four infield positions.

**Left field**—Chalk one up to the Mets. Cleon Jones with his .340 average gave him an advantage over the switch-hitting Don Buford. But Buford was no slouch. He batted .291 with 11 homers and 64 RBIs. Cleon had 12 and 75. So they were close. But Jones was also considered a slightly better outfielder with a stronger arm. This was one position where the Mets had the advantage.

**Center field**—Tommie Agee had a fine year, batting .271 with 26 homers and 76 RBIs. Well, listen to this. Baltimore center fielder Paul Blair hit .285 with 26 homers and 76 RBIs. So it was very close. But, again, most experts gave the advantage to the Orioles. Blair was the best center fielder in the AL. As good as Agee was, most felt Blair was a little better fielder, a little faster, had a little better arm, and hit 14 points higher. Another advantage for the Orioles, though just a slight one.

**Right field**—One more time there was a Mets platoon. Ron Swoboda would start against the lefties, Art Shamsky against right-handers. Both had moderate power, though neither was considered a great outfielder. Then look on the Orioles side. All the O's had in right was an all-time great, a future Hall of Famer, a great team player and leader. He was Frank Robinson, coming off a season where he hit .308 with 32 homers and 100 RBIs. Maybe Frank Robby had greater seasons, but he was still one of the very best. Oh yes, he could field and throw, as well. Advantage Orioles.

**Catcher**—This was the one position where the Orioles platooned. Andy Etchebarren usually played against lefties, while Elrod Hendricks started against right-handers. Both were average catchers and hitters, though Hendricks had 12 homers and 38 RBIs when he played. Jerry Grote hit .252 with six homers and 40 RBIs, but was a superior defensive catcher, the best in the league and close to Johnny Bench as a thrower. The Mets had the advantage here.

**Pitching**—Though pitching was the Mets' strong suit, this certainly wasn't a slam dunk. Everyone knew about Seaver, Koosman, and their surrounding cast. But a check of the team statistics showed that the Orioles staff actually had a lower team earned-run average than the Mets. The Mets' team ERA was 2.99, while the Orioles' was at 2.83. That certainly didn't give the Mets a clear-cut advantage. In addition, the Orioles had a pair of 20-game winners in lefties Mike Cuellar (23-11) and Dave McNally (20-7), and another star in right-hander Jim Palmer (16-4) who probably would have won 20 if he hadn't been hurt part of the year. Tom Phoebus (14-7) was the fourth starter during the season, while the middle relievers were Jim Hardin, Marcelino Lopez, Dave Leonhard and Dick Hall. Righty Eddie Watt (16 saves, 1.65 ERA) and lefty Pete Richert (12 saves, 2.20 ERA) were the short men.

Who, then, had the pitching advantage? If you asked the Orioles' Earl Weaver, he had a quick answer. "I hear the Mets have six good pitchers," said the Baltimore skipper. "Well, we've got 10."

It was almost a toss up, though some felt if both Seaver and Koosman pitched to the best of their ability, the Mets might have a slight edge. But the huge advantage the Orioles had at the other positions really made them a difficult team to beat, even for baseball's team of destiny.

Gil Hodges told the press he was not going to make any major changes for the series. He would continue to platoon at first, second, third, and in right, and he wasn't about to make any changes in his pitching rotation. He would use Seaver, Koosman, and the rookie Gentry, in that order. In those days, most teams went with three starters in the series, with the number one prepared to go to the hill three times if the series went seven games. Asked when he felt his Mets, such longtime losers, made the transition to winners, Hodges said: "I don't believe you can pick a specific day or event, or game, but I can single out a feeling. The Mets became winners when they began believing they could win. I think the Mets are an outstanding example of what a wonderful thing confidence is within yourself. That is the long look backward. Now, we look only ahead."

Down in Baltimore the fans waited in expectation. They loved their Orioles, of course, and looked for this super team to bring the city another champion. The Birds had won it back in 1966, upsetting the favored Dodgers—the Dodgers of Sandy Koufax and Don Drysdale—in four straight games. Now they wanted another. They also wanted the Birds to restore some pride to the Maryland city that had taken so much flak when the Colts were beaten by the Jets. Many fans were predicting a sweep, the feeling being that the Mets simply couldn't compete with their O's. Before the series even started, one newspaper headline in Baltimore read: "Miracle of Mets Near End."

To that, Tom Seaver answered, "What does that mean? We haven't played a game, and it sounds like we're behind, 3-0."

Like some others, Ron Swoboda felt the Orioles, as a team, were very certain they would win. "I sensed that the Orioles were overconfident," Swoboda said. "In fact, it would be inconceivable to think they weren't glad that we were the ones who made it out of the National League. They didn't know anything about us, so I can understand why they might have a little swagger. Why shouldn't they? But you have to remember that in a short series you consolidate your pitching. It's how good your top three are and what you have coming out of the pen. Seaver and Koosman were a given, and Gentry was tough and fearless. He had as good an arm as the other two. But I went in there thinking, 'Let's not embarrass ourselves if we don't win it.' At the same time, you have to play the games, and I wasn't conceding anything."

Finally, the time for talk was over. The Series opened on October 11, at Municipal Stadium in Baltimore. While there were some 50,429 fans at the ballpark, it was surprising to learn that there were nearly 2,000 unsold seats. For a city in love with its baseball team and seeking revenge for Super Bowl III, it would have seemed that they would be turning away fans by the thousands. At any rate, the starting pitchers for the opener were no surprise. Seaver, the majors' top winner with 25 victories, would get the call for the Mets, while 32-year-old Mike Cuellar, who won 13 of his last 16 en route to 23 victories would get the call for the Orioles. But before the game even started, there was a small, unpublicized controversy, but one the Mets felt had to be resolved and they took an immediate stand. Jerry Koosman remembers.

"During batting practice we found out that they had put our wives in the top deck down the right field line. We all got angry about that and decided that we wouldn't play until they moved our wives to seats comparable to where their wives would sit at Shea. They did it, moved our wives and families, and I think that was the start of a feeling that we wouldn't take anything from these guys. Gil was a huge family man, and no matter who they were, they weren't going to do that to our families. We were going to take care of our own."

Chalk one up for the Mets. But it was what happened on the field that would ultimately decide the champion. Before the game, Hodges had a final meeting with his team. "We all had nothing but respect for Baltimore," Ron Swoboda recalls. "Gil just reminded us that we were playing a very good baseball team. Then he reassured us, saying, 'You don't need to be anything but what you are, and have been. You don't have to be better. Don't try to get outside that envelope that's gotten you this far. Just get into it again out on the field and get the juices flowing.' It was a good thing to tell us."

But Swoboda couldn't help feeling something very different when he ran out on the field for the first time in the bottom of the first inning.

"Everything changes when you run onto that field in the first game," he said. "I've made a few parachute jumps in my life, and the first time you jump out of a plane you're absolutely petrified. But you do it, trusting the gear you have hanging on your back. The next time it gets easier, and you're more aware of things. That's how it was in the series. The first time I ran out on the field I felt like an absolute mechanical man, as if I've never been on a field before. The odd thing was that Baltimore was my hometown, the place where a little kid took his first swing at a baseball, and not that far from Municipal Stadium. That little kid is still somewhere inside you, and his eyes are as big as saucers. So you have to get him under control. I had this feeling of what the hell am I doing here and was pretty much overwhelmed by the event. At the same time you and your teammates have come this far, and now you're representing the National League, so you want to play ball."

Swoboda had no idea how soon he would be tested. After Cuellar set the Mets down in the first inning, Don Buford led off for the Orioles. Batting left-handed, he swung at Seaver's second pitch and hit a long drive to the right field fence. Swoboda went back, jumped, and then slumped to the ground as the ball sailed over the fence for a home run. It took just two pitches, and the Mets were behind, 1-0. As Buford circled the bases, and the fans roared, many felt that this was just the first small step in the Orioles burying the Mets in quick fashion. Swoboda still remembers that first-inning homer.

"I still had that mechanical man feeling when Buford hit the ball," he said. "It happened so quickly that I didn't have time to settle down. I still feel I should have caught it. I had no read on it, struggled back to the fence, and got there a second late. I just missed getting the ball."

Jerry Koosman had the same feeling. "When Ron went back to that fence, he didn't realize that if he pushed it would have given, allowing him maybe another foot or so. Had he known the way that fence was set up, he might have caught the ball."

But he didn't, and Baltimore had the lead. When the O's rallied for three more in the fourth after Seaver retired the first two batters, they upped the lead to 4-0, and this was one time the Mets' weren't going to come back. The cagey Cuellar scattered six hits with the Mets' only run coming on a sacrifice fly in the seventh. Seaver lasted just five, and the jubilant Orioles left the field knowing they had just beaten the National League's best pitcher.

"I had good stuff for three and two-thirds innings, and then lost it," Seaver would say.

The Mets also found out firsthand why Brooks Robinson was always getting raves for his play at third. Using his great instincts and quickness, Robinson made about a half-dozen fine plays at the hot corner, robbing the New Yorkers of several hits and proving all over again that he was the best in the business.

Ed Charles remembers how confident and optimistic the Mets were, and that the first game loss didn't destroy it. "After they beat us in that first game," Charles said, "I walked past their pitching coach, George Bamberger and said to him, 'George, this is the last game you guys are gonna win.' He looked at me, laughed, and said, 'You're full of shit.' But we knew we had the best pitching staff in baseball, and we were gonna ride it all the way."

Now Game 2 loomed large. It would be a battle of left-handers as Jerry Koosman took the mound against Dave McNally. Koosman was looking forward to his start and remembered something he had thought about for many years.

"One of my goals since I was a young man was not only to pitch a perfect game in the World Series but to get a hit every time up. So when I went out there, that was my initial goal. Why not think big, I thought then."

It wouldn't be easy. Baltimore lefty Dave McNally wasn't just a 20-game winner, he came into the fray with a streak of 21 consecutive scoreless innings in postseason play. That included a complete-game shutout of the Dodgers in the final game of the 1966 Series and then a 12-inning whitewash of the Twins in the American League divisional playoff the week before. He was a clutch pitcher, smart and cagey, because he didn't have overpowering stuff. But McNally knew how to keep hitters off balance and knew how to win. With him out there, the O's were confident they would go two games up on the Mets and take it from there.

But Jerry Koosman didn't come to lose. For three innings, the two southpaws matched serves and hung goose eggs on the scoreboard. Then in the Mets' fourth, big Donn Clendenon stepped in. McNally did the smart thing, working the outside of the plate, but Clendenon went out and got a fastball, taking it high and deep to right field for a home run. The Mets were on top for the first time in the series, 1-0. Now Koosman had a small cushion, but with the normally light-hitting Mets, he was used to that. He continued to roll, setting the Orioles down without a hit through six innings. It wasn't quite his childhood dream, but it wasn't far off.

Then, in the bottom of the seventh, the O's broke through. Paul Blair got the first hit off Koosman, a clean leadoff single to left. The speedy Blair then swiped second, and moments later scored the tying run when veteran Brooks Robinson slammed another base hit. The score was tied with both lefties continuing to pitch well. Neither team scored in the eighth, and when McNally retired the first two Mets in the ninth, it began to look as if Koosman would have to hold Baltimore in the bottom of the frame just to send the game to extra innings. Then Ed Charles singled. Jerry Grote was next. McNally went to work again, but Grote took that short stroke of his and banged another base hit, Charles stopping at second. Now, the normally light-hitting Al Weis was up.

Weis was a slick fielder who could play all three infield positions. He once batted as high as .296 in 135 at-bats for the White Sox in 1965. But a year later, getting 187 at-bats, he hit just .155. When he came to the Mets as a part-timer in 1968 he could only manage a .172 average in 274 at bats, and in 1969, platooning with Boswell, Weis hit just .215. He had hit only six home runs in his entire career, including a pair in 1969, and he might have been the least feared stick on the team. But all those stats went by the board quickly when he took a McNally pitch through the infield for a single, sending Charles home with the go-ahead run. Once again, the Mets had a potentially unlikely hero.

With a 2-1 lead, Koosman went out to try to close down the Orioles in the bottom of the ninth. He got the first two hitters, but now the dangerous Frank Robinson was up. Koos knew that Robinson could tie it up with one swing, so he worked carefully. The count went to 3-2, and then Robinson drew a walk. The O's were still alive. Earl Weaver sent Merv Rettenmund in to run for Robinson as another slugger, Boog Powell, came to the plate. Once again Koosman pitched carefully, and the scenario was exactly the same. The count went full and Koosman was off the plate with his next pitch. Powell had drawn a walk and the tying run moved to second.

That's when Hodges made a move. He hadn't made many wrong ones all year and now walked slowly to the mound. Then he signaled to the bullpen for Ron Taylor. As Taylor took his warmup pitches, the dangerous Brooks Robinson stood there waiting. A potentially dramatic confrontation was just seconds away. Then Taylor went to work. Knowing he was facing a dangerous, clutch hitter he worked carefully, just as Koosman had. Sure enough, the count went full. The runners would be moving on the next pitch.

Taylor came set, then delivered. Robinson swung and hit a hard grounder right at Ed Charles. Charles trapped the ball against his chest, then turned to run to third for the force out. But he saw Rettenmund already close to the bag and sensed he would lose a footrace. So he whirled and fired to first. Clendenon stretched way out and gloved the ball just before it hit the ground. Robinson, not the world's fastest runner, was out. The Mets and Koosman had won it, 2-1, and the series was tied. There would be no sweep, and now the Mets had the advantage of coming home to Shea.

One of the pressing questions after the game was a strange bit of strategy Gil Hodges used in the ninth inning. When Frank Robinson came up with two outs, Hodges had moved second baseman Weis into the outfield, in effect leaving three infielders and adding an additional outfielder. It became a moot point when Robby drew a walk, but reporters wanted to know just what Hodges was thinking. It was something most hadn't seen before, though those who covered the Mets had.

"There is a very solid baseball reason for what I did," Hodges said. "We were trying to shut off the extra base alleys. We were not trying to tempt the hitter, or taunt him. We were simply trying to keep the man from getting an extra base hit."

Hodges said he had done it before, against hitters like Willie McCovey and Richie Allen, power guys who can hurt a team with an extra base hit. He reminded everyone that a single would most likely require two additional base hits to get a run home, whereas a double or triple would require just one. When someone asked why Hodges just didn't throw him bad pitches and walk him, the manager replied, "To that, I say there's always a chance of getting him out, like we did the first three times today, when he hit the ball rather well."

So once again Manager Hodges had made an unorthodox move that didn't backfire on him. The biggest thing was the win. Visiting teams always like to come way with a victory in their opponent's backyard. They feel it takes away the so-called home-field advantage. That's just what the Mets had done.

"When we returned to New York tied at 1-1," Jerry Koosman said, "we all had the same thought. Let's win three games here and not have to go back to Baltimore again."

Game 3 had the rookie Gentry pitted against Baltimore's Jim Palmer, a 25-year-old coming star, who was a year away from the first of his eight, 20-win seasons in what would become a Hall of Fame career. But Palmer was 16-4 in 1969 with an outstanding 2.34 earned run average. He had 11 complete games and had hurled six shutouts. He wouldn't be easy. Gentry was 13-12 his first season, with the only knock against him being inconsistency. If the sharp Gentry showed up, the Mets would have a good chance to win.

Though no one knew it at the time, this game was over almost before it began, but it wouldn't end without some incredible heroics. After Gentry retired the Orioles in the first, Tommie Agee led off for the Mets. He worked the count to 2-1 and Palmer threw a fastball. Agee swung and sent the ball rocketing over the centerfield fence for a leadoff home run. That was one reason Hodges loved having Agee lead off, the chance to jump on top with a quick homer. It had happened again, only this time on baseball's biggest stage.

In the second inning, the Mets struck again. Palmer retired the first two hitters. But then Grote walked and Bud Harrelson followed with a single. Now Gentry was up. Not known for his bat, Gentry was hitless in 28 straight at-bats since his last hit on August 3. As for his RBI total for the year, well, he had driven in a long, solitary run. Everyone thought Palmer and the Orioles would get out of the inning. Only these Mets seemed to have some kind of magic touch. Palmer threw one of his trademark high fastballs and Gentry swung. The ball sailed out to right center in a high arc. Blair and Robinson converged, but the ball had eyes and hit on the warning track about 10 feet in front of the 396-foot sign. Both Grote and Harrelson scored as Gentry rambled into second. Now the Mets had a 3-0 lead.

In the fifth inning, Mets magic struck again. The Orioles had two men on with two out, and left-handed-hitting catcher Ellie Hendricks was up. The outfield was shaded to right, playing Hendricks to pull. Instead, he was slightly late on a fastball and hit a deep drive toward the left center field gap. The two Baltimore runners began circling the bases and Agee took off to his right and toward the wall at top speed. Agee, the ball, and the fence seemed to converge at the same time. After running about 40 yards, Agee reached across his body and caught the ball in the webbing of his glove just as it was falling past his waist. He hit the wall but held on, and the crowd of 56,335 fans roared. They had just witnessed one of the great catches in World Series history. The catch saved two runs, and maybe more, since Hendricks would have wound up on second or third.

"The ball almost went through my webbing," Agee said later, admitting he had barely caught the ball. But it was still an out, and the Mets maintained their 3-0 lead. Then in the sixth the Mets got another as Grote smacked a double to deliver Ken Boswell, who had singled and gone to second on a ground out. When Gentry took the mound in the seventh inning, he was still throwing a shutout. After two long fly outs, the young right-hander suddenly lost his control. In short order, he walked Belanger, pinch hitter Dave May, and Don Buford. Now the sacks were loaded, and Hodges made another of his slow walks to the mound. He signaled the bullpen, and out walked Nolan Ryan, hoping to continue the magic from Game 3 of the playoffs.

Paul Blair was the hitter as everyone in the ballpark and those watching on television knew what was coming—fastballs. Ryan was simply going to try to blow three of them past a good hitter. Blair took the first and it was over for a strike. Again Ryan wound and threw. Blair swung ... and missed. Strike two! Ryan stepped off to collect himself. Blair also stepped out, then got ready again. Ryan cranked and fired. Blair swung again and the ball rocketed in a line over the right field side of second base toward the gap. It looked as if it would clear the bases.

Once again Tommy Agee took off, this time running to his left. The ball wasn't that far from him, but it was traveling so fast he didn't know if he could get there in time. But he kept running and, at the last second, made a headlong dive, extending his arm and glove out in front of him. The ball settled in the glove just before hitting the ground. It was his second great catch of the game, the two of them combined saving five Oriole runs. The Mets got one more tally in the bottom of the seventh on a solo home run by Kranepool, and from there Ryan closed it out. The 5-0 victory gave the New Yorkers an improbable 2-1 lead in the Series. And for Game 4, they would have Tom Seaver ready to go again

Now, with the Mets leading and the third game highlighted by Agee's great catches, more and more people were beginning to see the Mets as a team of destiny, a ball club destined to win no matter what the opposition threw at them. At this point, it did seem as if the Mets always had the right answer, made the right move, got the key hit, made the big play. Ed Charles, however, wasn't that surprised by Tommie Agee's great catches.

"I knew Tommie from the American League," Charles said. "He had a lot of talent, but above all, he was always a go-for-broke type of player. Because of that, he never gave up on a ball in the outfield and had that propensity to make the great catch."

They were great, all right. Now if Seaver, their ace, could bring his "A" game to the ballpark, the Mets had the opportunity to take a 3-1 lead. Opposing Seaver once again was Mike Cuellar, the first game winner. Hodges remained consistent and went back to his right-handed platoon. As soon as the game began, it appeared that both pitchers had their stuff. Only in the second inning, big Donn Clendenon caught one, slamming a 3-2 Cuellar offering into the left field bullpen for a solo home run, his second of the Series. Once more, the Mets had taken the early lead, 1-0.

Seaver began setting down the Orioles. In the third, when plate umpire Shag Crawford called Mark Belanger out on strikes, Weaver came roaring out of the Orioles dugout. Maybe he was trying to light a fire under his team, or maybe he was just being Earl, but Crawford thumbed him out. Now the Orioles had lost their manager, and the way Seaver was pitching, they were losing the game. When the Orioles came to bat in the ninth, the Mets were still nursing the same 1-0 lead, and Seaver was working on a four-hit shutout. But that would change in a hurry.

With one out, Frank Robinson singled. When Boog Powell followed with a base hit to right, Frank Robby moved over to third, and now Brooks Robinson was up. The veteran third baseman didn't want to give Seaver a chance to work on him, so he went after the first pitch. He hit a sinking line drive toward right center. If it went through to the wall it would have been at least a double, maybe a triple, and both base runners would have scored. Only Ron Swoboda wasn't thinking about that. He was running hard toward the ball and, at the last second, made a headfirst dive along the turf, his left arm extended out with the glove turned in the backhanded position. Just before it hit the ground, the ball settled into his mitt. Robinson tagged and scored the tying run, but Powell had to retreat to first. Once again, a great play by a Mets outfielder had probably saved the game.

"If I have one chance in 1,000 to catch the ball. I'm going to try to catch it," Swoboda said.

Seaver got the third out and stalked off the mound, angry with himself for allowing the tying run. Now, with the score tied, he began to wonder if he'd miss a second chance to win a World Series game. When the Mets failed to score against Eddie Watt in the bottom of the ninth, the game went to extra innings. Seaver stayed in and retired the Orioles quickly. Now the Mets came up in the bottom of 10th and would be facing right-hander Dick Hall. Jerry Grote led off and hit a short fly to left. Don Buford, however, misjudged the ball, starting back first, then reversing his field. Too late. The ball fell between Buford, center fielder Blair, and shortstop Belanger with Grote winding up on second. Hodges then sent the speedy Rod Gaspar in to run for his catcher. Al Weis was next, and acting manager Billy Hunter ordered him walked to set up a force or double play.

Next Hodges sent J.C. Martin, a left-handed hitter, up to bat for Seaver, and Hunter countered with lefty Pete Richert. Martin promptly bunted. Richert raced in and picked the ball up then threw quickly toward first. But the ball never got there. It hit Martin in the left wrist and bounded away as Gaspar raced home with the winning run. The fans went wild. The Mets had done it again. Great pitching by Seaver, a great catch by Swoboda, a home run by Clendenon, and a little old-fashioned luck when

Richert's throw hit Martin. No matter how you cut the pie, it was beginning to look as if the Mets just couldn't lose.

Now the Mets were a game away. Another win and they would close it out at home. Game 5 took place on October 16. Because of the divisional playoffs, it was the latest date a World Series game had ever been played, and a record crowd of 57,397 jammed into Shea to see if their heroes could wrap it up. It would be the Game 2 pitchers once again, Jerry Koosman facing Dave McNally. Baltimore fans must have been wondering just what could happen next. In the third inning, they had a ray of hope. Mark Belanger opened the inning with an opposite-field single. Next Dave McNally was up.

"With McNally up, we were expecting a bunt," Koosman said. "My job was to throw a high fastball and hope he popped it up. Instead he swung away and hit a two-run homer."

McNally had taken Koosman's first pitch into the left field bullpen, the homer giving the Orioles a 2-0 lead. But the Orioles weren't through. Koosman got the next two hitters, but then Frank Robinson came up. Mets pitchers had held the superstar to just two singles in 16 at-bats. This time, however, Robinson caught one, driving a fastball high and deep and over the center field wall. The second home run of the inning gave the Orioles a rare 3-0 lead. Back in the dugout the Mets weren't about to quit.

"I wasn't happy," Koosman said. "The two-run homer by McNally was a surprise because he swung away. We didn't know how good a hitter he was, but evidently Earl Weaver did. But when I came back to the bench I told the guys to get them back and promised I wouldn't let Baltimore get another run."

Ed Charles, for one, knew how tough the Mets pitchers were, especially the big two. He had seen what Seaver had done the day before and felt Koosman would do the same in Game 5.

"Seaver could win with bad stuff," said Charles. "He was such a competitor with a gift for self-analysis. He always knew just what it would take to win on a given day. Koosman was so strong that he could struggle for the first part of a game then suddenly just start blowing you away."

Would that happen in Game 5? Sure enough, Koosman toughened after giving up the trey in the third inning. The Orioles didn't touch him. McNally, however, was just as good, and it was still a 3-0 game after five. Then in the top of the sixth, Frank Robinson backed off an inside pitch and said the ball had grazed his uniform. Robby and Weaver argued with plate ump Lou DiMuro, who wouldn't budge. He said the pitch didn't hit Robby. Finally, Robinson stepped back in and Koosman struck him out. Now it was the Mets' turn in the bottom of the inning.

Cleon Jones was up first. McNally threw one low and inside. Cleon moved his foot away, but then said the ball had hit his right shoe. Again umpire DiMuro shook his head no. On-deck hitter Clendenon said he saw it hit the foot as well. Then Manager Hodges came out. As usual, he spoke quietly to Jones, then to DiMuro. He shook his head, then retrieved the baseball, looked at it, and showed it to DiMuro. Suddenly, the ump waved Jones to first. Out came the irate Weaver. Apparently, Hodges showed the umpire a smudge of shoe polish on the baseball, proving it had indeed hit Jones's foot. Team of destiny? Things just kept going the Mets' way.

"Gil was always laid back when he was managing the game," Bud Harrelson said. "When Cleon said he was hit, he just came out slowly, took his time, showed the umpire the ball. He didn't get in his face, start screaming, nothing like that. And off to first went Cleon. In the top of the inning Robinson claimed he was hit and didn't go to first."

When McNally got ready to pitch again, he found himself facing Donn Clendenon. The big first baseman worked the count to 2-2, then took McNally's next pitch into the second deck in left field for his third home run of the series. The shot cut the Orioles' lead to 3-2, and the fans at Shea began sensing it. They were rarely quiet for the rest of the game. McNally got out of the inning, then Koosman set the O's down quickly in the seventh. In the bottom of the inning, light-hitting Al Weis led off.

McNally didn't want Weis to start a rally. What he didn't expect was for the thin second baseman to be a one-man rally. Weis took a McNally pitch into the left field bleachers for a game-tying home run. It was his first round-tripper at Shea all season, and it couldn't have come at a better time. Suddenly, the game was knotted, Koosman was cruising, and the Mets' bats were starting to bark. Again, McNally got out of the inning. Koosman returned to the mound and retired the Orioles in one-two-three fashion. Good to his word, he had not only kept the Orioles from scoring after their three-run outburst, but had allowed only one hit since then. As the Mets came to bat in the bottom of the inning, there was a special feeling in the Shea Stadium air. This team, that had come so far so quickly, was on the brink.

Eddie Watt was pitching for the Orioles in the bottom of the eighth, and it didn't take long for the Mets to make noise. Cleon Jones greeted Watt by hitting a long drive over the head of Blair in center. That, in itself, is no small feat. Blair retrieved it off the wall quickly, but Jones steamed into second with a double. The potential World Series-winning run was just 180 feet away. With Clendenon up, Hodges opted for a sacrifice, hoping to get Jones over to third where he might score on a hit, a fly, or even a ground out. But Clendenon bunted too hard and was thrown out at first with Jones holding. Now it was Ron Swoboda's turn.

This was one of the guys who didn't get a single at-bat in the division playoffs because of the manager's platoon system. He had already saved one game with his glove, now he had a chance to be a hero of another kind. Sure enough, Swoboda connected and sent a sinking liner down the left field line. Buford came over and reached down to backhand it. For a second it appeared as if he had made the catch, but he had trapped the ball on the short hop. Jones scored the go-ahead run, and Swoboda wound up on second with a double as Shea Stadium erupted in absolute bedlam. But the Mets still weren't through. After Charles flied out, Grote hit a grounder to first. Powell bobbled the ball, then threw late to the covering Watt, who dropped the toss. Grote was safe, and

Swoboda came around to score the second run of the inning. The Mets now had a 5-3 lead.

Once the ninth inning began, the fans were on their feet and didn't stop screaming. Koosman stood out on the mound, determined to finish what he had started and bring his team home. "I kept pitching my normal game," Koosman said, "Keep the ball down. Fastball, curve, slider, change. Even in the ninth I wasn't about to change."

Sure enough, Koosman still had it. He got the first two hitters as the crowd roar kept getting louder and louder. Now Davey Johnson was up. Koosman went back to work as if it were just the middle of the game. Johnson swung and hit a lazy fly to left. Cleon Jones camped under it, squeezed it in his glove, and then sunk down to one knee as if in prayer. He held the position for a few seconds, and when he arose the wild celebration began. The Mets had done it. They had become the second New York team in nine months to beat a great, heavily favored team from Baltimore. They were World Champions, one of the most unlikely ever. But, boy, were they real. They had done it by playing great baseball, with all 25 players contributing under the guidance of a great manager. Forget the cross-town Yankees. This time it was the Mets who were the toast of New York.

"We were so happy in that clubhouse," Koosman recalls. "It was so noisy you couldn't even talk to the guy next to you. I remembered being tongue-tied and on the verge of tears. There was so much emotion that I didn't even think about the magnitude of our achievement, about the great upset and coming from nowhere. We were just so happy that we had reached that point. None of us had been around that long. Seaver was in his third year, and I was in my second. In fact, most of us were just two or three years into our careers, and we had accomplished this already ... after finishing last and ninth."

The thing that impressed Bud Harrelson the most was the classy way the Orioles accepted defeat. "I never heard anyone on the Baltimore team say we were lucky," the Mets shortstop said. "They took it like men and just said the bastards beat us."

The old adage that good pitching stops good hitting was never more in evidence. For the five games the Orioles had just 23 hits in 157 at bats for a team batting average of .146. This, from the best-hitting team in baseball. Mets pitchers allowed just nine runs. The Mets hit just .220 as a team, but scored 15 and got the clutch hits when they were needed. Mets pitchers had a 1.80 earned-run average for the World Series, as compared with 2.72 for the Orioles staff. Plus there were the great catches, the clutch play, and the shoe polish on the ball. Everything went New York's way. It was just one of the magical moments that can never be duplicated. Donn Clendenon, with his three home runs, was named the World Series Most Valuable Player, but a whole handful of Mets could have easily won that honor. To a man, everyone agreed it had been a team effort.

Needless to say, New York City went wild. There was a second great celebration in nine months, and this one seemed extra special. As one writer put it, "Never before—not for the one-time perennial world champion Yankees, not for the moon men, not for Charles A. Lindbergh, not for anyone. Never before had New Yorkers exploded in quite the way they did yesterday in a spontaneous, unrestrained outpouring of sheer joy when the Mets, their Mets, copped the World Series."

On October 20, the city threw a tickertape parade for their latest heroes. The players rode in open cars, and the fans pressed their way through the barricades, running out into the streets and trying to shake hands with as many of the players as possible. Girls kissed some of the players and fans tried to climb onto the slow-moving vehicles. To their credit, the New York City police showed remarkable restraint, allowing people to celebrate and get close to their heroes as the motorcade moved up Broadway. The fans were wildly ecstatic and demonstrative but didn't get out of hand, and there was very little, if any, vandalism.

At City Hall, Mayor John Lindsay honored the players, presented keys to the city to team owner Mrs. Joan Payson and board chairman M. Donald Grant. Mayor Lindsay also honored Gil Hodges by giving him a replica of a street sign that designated the block on Bedford Avenue, in Brooklyn where Hodges still lived, as Gil Hodges Place for a day.

Hodges also received the city's bronze medallion. It was a joyous occasion in a city that desperately needed some good news in light of the continuing crises, both at home and abroad. Looking back, several members of the team also realized how important their victory was for New York.

"Baseball has always been an escape," Ed Charles said. "It has never been a political thing. We had a large group of fans that came to see the games no matter what was going on. As the season progressed, I think New Yorkers kind of drifted away from some of the problems of the world and the country and began to focus on what was happening with the Mets at Shea. The feeling overflowed from the ballpark into the city. For the moment, people forgot about the war because something good was taking place, and I think the Mets really helped that happen all year."

Ed Kranepool, a native New Yorker, agrees. "The country was in turmoil, and the Mets were an escape," he said. "People were looking to relax and get away from their everyday troubles, so it was a magical year for everyone. As you walked around the city there was a tremendous atmosphere, a good feeling. And when we won, it got even better."

For Jerry Koosman, what happened in 1969 was not a miracle, but more a tribute to the team's talent and the way it was all directed by Gil Hodges.

"Winning the World Series was totally incredible, but it wasn't a miracle," Koosman explained. "It might have seemed like a miracle to those who weren't on the inside and didn't really understand what was happening. What we accomplished wasn't easy. I played on other teams that tried to do the same thing, but couldn't. The more I look back, the more I realize that while we had some outstanding talent, we didn't have as much overall talent as Chicago, Atlanta, or Baltimore. But we had a manager who knew how to utilize everything he had 100 percent of the time. Another manager could not have done it. In my mind, Gil Hodges deserves most of the credit for what happened that year."

Ron Swoboda also echoes the theme of the Mets becoming a unifying force, bringing people together in troubled times. "It was a chance for people to get behind something that was good," Swoboda says, "especially with the protests, the racial strife, and everything else that was swirling around. When the Mets made their run and then won, it allowed everyone to step back from the controversy. There was so much happening then that it was great for the city to be able to enjoy something that seemed so right. I had the sense that it gave people relief. Most fans had followed the team for so long with little expectation, and suddenly that little expectation turned into a world championship."

Perhaps it was Bud Harrelson who summed it up best with just two short sentences. He simply said, "The city embraced the team because what we did was totally unexpected. It was something that can never be duplicated."

# METS
## THROUGH THE YEARS

The 1969 New York Mets did not become a dynasty. They were not about to become the cross-town Yankees and win four or five pennants in a row. Their incredible victory in 1969 was due to a number of factors already mentioned—great pitching, good defense, timely hitting, and some brilliant moves by Manager Gil Hodges. But moves are brilliant only if they work. If the same moves don't work—the pinch hitter strikes out, the relief pitcher gets bombed, the defensive replacement makes a key error—then they aren't so brilliant anymore. Hodges was the same manager in 1970, and the team only finished third in the National League East with an 83-79 record, a game behind Chicago and six games behind division-winning Pittsburgh.

Jerry Koosman feels that the team's amazing win in 1969 might have had an effect on what happened in 1970.

"We all had a very demanding off season," he remembers. "We were called for all kinds of appearances and banquets, and most of us were out there all year long, seeing each other and talking about the year we had. Then when spring training came, it almost seemed as if we never had an off season. The winter had gone so quickly with so many of us hitting the rubber chicken circuit that I don't think we were that hungry to get back in uniform. It wasn't the best thing for us physically, and some of us came in a bit overweight. So we had to lose the pounds before getting in game shape. Some injuries in spring training and then during the year didn't help either, and we were just never able to put it all together again."

No matter what the reason, the comparison is interesting. In 1970, the Mets as a team led the National League in pitching with a 3.46 earned-run average. A year earlier they were at 2.99, but second to the Cards. Some of the hitters also did very well. Donn Clendenon, with the team all year, hit .288 with 22 homers and 97 RBIs in 1970. Agee had another fine year, batting .286 with 24 homers and 75 RBIs. Others had seasons comparable to the year before. In fact, the team scored 695 runs as opposed to 632 in their World Series year. They even hit 11 more homers as a team. But look at the pitching records. Seaver was 18-12 and led the National League with a 2.81 ERA. Koosman missed some more time and was just 12-7. Gentry was at 9-9, McAndrew 10-14, Ryan 7-11, McGraw 4-6. What was different? Things just didn't always turn out as well as the year before. Whatever that magic was that enabled the Mets to go on that late-season tear that carried right over to the World Series was gone.

By contrast, the Baltimore Orioles won 108 games in 1970, only one fewer than they had won the year before. Once again they progressed to the World Series and this time beat the Cincinnati Reds in five games. The Orioles were a great team, and their consistency showed it when they won 101 more in 1971. The Mets, by contrast, had another 83-79 season under Hodges in 1971, tying the Cubs for third. Seaver was brilliant, finishing at 20-10 with just a 1.76 earned run average, but the supporting cast just didn't get the job done, and the team failed to hit despite its pitchers leading the league with a 3.00 ERA. They obviously needed an infusion of talent.

The one consistent in those years was Hodges. Though 1969 was obviously a one-of-a-kind magical year, he was still considered an outstanding skipper and the both the spiritual and physical leader of the Mets. Since his mild heart attack in 1968, the manager was given a clean bill of health, and to everyone's knowledge, had been fine ever since. In late March there was a player's strike and spring training was suspended just as the team was preparing for the opening of the 1972 season. That's when the team suffered what is still called the deepest tragedy in franchise history. Jerry Koosman was in Florida when it happened.

"We had been playing in West Palm Beach when the players went on strike. Just about everyone went home except me. I figured I'd wait a couple of more days to see if the strike ended and then go to New York. I was at the hotel with the coaches and some of the beat writers, Red Foley and Jack Lang. Gil was out playing golf with Rube Walker, Eddie Yost, and Joe Pignatano. They were talking to Jack Sanford, the old Giants pitcher, who was the golf pro there. It was my day to throw, so I went up to them and asked Rube to catch me. But management wasn't supposed to talk to us, and Rube told me he couldn't catch me because we were on strike. He suggested I go get a bag of baseballs and just throw them against the wall of the hotel.

"I got the baseballs and was walking through the pool area when I ran into Mick Tingelhoff, who was the center for the Minnesota Vikings. I told Mick what I was doing and he volunteered to catch me. Well, I'm throwing harder and harder, and soon I'm hitting Mick on the knees and shoulder. Then Jack Sanford came over and he caught me for a while. After that we talked a bit and then I went up to shower. When I came out I heard sirens from an ambulance but didn't think anything of it. You hear them all the time. But when I came down to eat, Red Foley came up and said the ambulance took Gil to the hospital.

"Red and I went to the hospital together and we were directed to a room where the coaches were, along with Artie Friedman, our statistician. They were all very somber, and when I asked Artie how Gil was he wouldn't answer me. Then Rube came over and quietly told me that Gil had died. He said they had finished golfing and were walking back to the hotel. Gil was going one way and Piggy hollered to him, asking what time he wanted to meet for supper. As he started to turn, Gil just fell backwards and hit his head on the pavement."

Gil Hodges had suffered a massive and fatal heart attack. The news spread quickly. The suddenness of his death left everyone in shock. The Mets had lost their leader, their strength, the man who had orchestrated the miracle of 1969, held it all together throughout the season, and led them right down to the final out. His death was really the final separation of that team and everything that followed. Yogi Berra took over the ball club, and in 1973, the Mets pulled off another near-miracle, coming from last place at the end of August to a division title. But it was a weak National League East that year, and the team won with just an 82-79 record. Yet once again pitching keyed their victory over Cincinnati in the playoffs and brought them within one game of another World Series victory. That October they were beaten in seven games by the Oakland A's. They wouldn't return to the fall classic again until 1986.

But it is still 1969 that is most remembered. Ironically, only two members of that team are in the Baseball Hall of Fame, but one of them spent the bulk of his career elsewhere. The first is Tom Seaver, who finished his 20-year tenure in 1986, having won 311 games while striking out 3,640 hitters. But not even Seaver did it all with the Mets. After a salary dispute with team management, he was traded to Cincinnati on June 15, 1977, for several players, none of whom made much of a mark with the club. He returned to the Mets for one season in 1983, then finished his career in the American League with Chicago and Boston, ironically winning his 300th game while pitching for the White Sox against the New York Yankees at Yankee Stadium.

The other Hall of Famer is Nolan Ryan, who pitched so well at the tail end of the 1969 season. Ryan was a raw talent, but the Mets apparently ran out of patience. On December 10, 1971, Ryan was traded to the California Angels for veteran infielder Jim Fregosi. Fregosi never played well for the Mets, while Ryan took off as soon as he was put into the regular starting rotation with the Angels. It's remembered today as the worst trade the Mets ever made. Playing for several teams in an incredible 26-year career, Ryan won 324 games, threw a record seven no-hitters, and is the all-time strikeout leader by a country mile with 5,714 whiffs. When Ryan's name is mentioned to Mets fans, they immediately begin to think of what could have been.

Gil Hodges didn't manage long enough to be considered for the Hall of Fame as a manager. Many feel he belongs as a player. A great defensive first baseman, Gil was also a power hitter on the great Brooklyn Dodger teams of the late 1940s and 1950s. He played for 18 years and was a .273 career hitter with 370 home runs and 1,274 RBIs. Though he hasn't made the Hall, he is still fondly remembered in New York and especially by the dwindling numbers of fans of the old Brooklyn Dodgers.

As for the other members of the 1969 Mets, they had varied careers. Koosman came the closest to greatness, though his career was somewhat sabotaged by repeated arm problems. He left the Mets after the 1978 season and pitched for Minnesota, the White Sox and finally the Phillies in a 19-year career. He wound up winning 222 games and striking out 2,556 hitters. He was a 20-game winner on two occasions but was probably never as dominating as he was his first two Mets seasons of 1968 and 1969.

Ron Swoboda was traded to Montreal after the 1970 season, was shipped to the Yankees midway through 1971 and played a part-time role with the Bronx Bombers until retiring after the 1973 season. Tommie Agee left the Mets after the 1972 season and played just one more year, splitting time with Houston and St. Louis in 1973 before retiring with a .255 lifetime batting average. Tommie died in January of 2001. Cleon Jones remained with the Mets through 1975, played one year with the Chicago White Sox and retired with a .281 lifetime mark. For Ed Charles, the World Series triumph of 1969 was the crowning achievement of his career. The oldest of the Mets players that year, the clinching victory over the Orioles would be his last game in the major leagues.

Jerry Grote, the fine catcher, stayed with the Mets through part of the 1977 season, was traded to the Dodgers and retired after the 1981 season. He had a solid, 16-year career. Shortstop Bud Harrelson remained with the Mets through 1977. He played three more years with the Phils and finally the Texas Rangers before retiring after 1980. He later became a coach and returned to manage the Mets for parts of the 1990 and 1991 seasons. Big Donn Clendenon remained with the Mets through 1971 and finished his career with St. Louis in 1972. He retired with 159 homer runs, but is best remembered in New York for the three he hit in the World Series. Ed Kranepool, the native New Yorker, had the longest Mets career of all. He spent his entire 18-year big-league life with the Mets, getting a cup of coffee as a 17-year-old in the team's first season of 1962, and finally retiring after 1979. He wound up with a .261 lifetime batting average, was always a fine defensive first baseman, and later in his career became an outstanding pinch hitter.

Tug McGraw went on to become a great short reliever, pitching for 19 years, the first nine with the Mets, and the final 10 with the Phillies. His "You Gotta Believe" slogan spearheaded the Mets' 1973 pennant drive, and he helped the Phils win a world championship in 1980. Always one of baseball's zany characters, McGraw died in February of 2004. Gary Gentry, the rookie who was 13-12 in 1969 and seemed to have such a bright future, was also short circuited by arm problems. He remained essentially a .500 pitcher with the Mets, went to Atlanta in 1973 and retired after the 1975 season at the age of 29 with just a 46-49 lifetime mark.

So the baseball life of many of the Mets after 1969 was something less than outstanding. Seaver and Ryan had A-plus careers; Koosman and McGraw were a notch or so below, and everyone else was somewhere below that. Many of their careers ended prematurely, and quite a number of them were gone from the team within five years of the miracle championship. Yet that amazing season remains the link even today, the closeness of that team with the players brought together under the guiding hand of

their manager, Gil Hodges. Ed Charles still looks back with fond-
ness and feels for one year that Mets team was special.

"We did so many things together," Charles said. "We went out
as a group a lot after games. One time Swoboda's parents came
up from Baltimore and brought soft shell crabs for all of us.
Sometimes we'd go to Kranepool's and they would cook steaks
for everyone. We always felt like we were a team, and we still get
together today as much as we can. I always think of that season
as a one-time thing that can never happen again. And I think
when we all get together now, the lies just get a little bigger."

Bud Harrelson is another who feels a special bond with his
teammates from long ago. "I had a genuine love for all of the
guys on the ball club," he says, "and we all have a common bond
for life. When we see each other we usually hug, especially with
the years going by now. We're all getting into our 60s and we've
already lost Tug and Tommie, so you never know. I'm not sure the
city ever embraced another team the way it did us, and we still
realize that we all did something together that's still pretty special."

Jerry Koosman still remembers something special that happened just before the start of the fifth game of the Series when
he was in the bullpen waiting to take the mound in what would
be the biggest game of his life.

"Pearl Bailey, the singer and entertainer, was set to sing the
National Anthem that day. She was a huge Mets fan, always sitting next to the dugout. She saw me pacing around the bullpen,
came over to me and said, 'Relax, Koos. I know you're gonna
win the game today. I can see the number eight in my mind.'
Well, we won the game, 5-3. It was almost as if she had ESP,
because she did that several times. I remember she came in the
clubhouse after the game and I gave her a big hug."

But perhaps it is Ed Kranepool, a New Yorker all his life and
a kid who came out of James Monroe High School, the same
school that the great Hank Greenberg graduated from years earlier, who best summed up the essence and meaning of that
incredible season.

Said Kranepool, "That season, that victory will keep the Mets within the hearts of their fans forever. It has been 35 years now, but the fans never let you forget about 1969. People still talk about it, still relate to it. Everyone I speak with says they were there. I still can't walk down the street all these years later without having a middle-aged guy come up to me and want to talk about 1969. Oddly enough, no one reminds me of 1973, but 1969 is entrenched in New York forever. It's something I really appreciate, because I'm a New Yorker and speak to people about it all the time. To me, it will never get old."